The Wal-Mart Revolution

3/08

The Wal-Mart Revolution

How Big-Box Stores Benefit Consumers, Workers, and the Economy

Richard Vedder
and
Wendell Cox

te

Distributed to the Trade by National Book Network, 15200 NBN Way, Blue Ridge Summit, PA 17214. To order call toll free 1-800-462-6420 or 1-717-794-3800. For all other inquiries please contact the AEI Press, 1150 Seventeenth Street, N.W., Washington, D.C. 20036 or call 1-800-862-5801.

NRI NATIONAL RESEARCH INITIATIVE

This publication is a project of the National Research Initiative, a program of the American Enterprise Institute that is designed to support, publish, and disseminate research by university-based scholars and other independent researchers who are engaged in the exploration of important public policy issues.

Library of Congress Cataloging-in-Publication Data
Vedder, Richard K.
     The Wal-Mart revolution : how big-box stores benefit consumers, workers, and the economy / Richard Vedder and Wendell Cox.
          p. cm.
     Includes bibliographical references and index.
     ISBN-13: 978-0-8447-4244-1
     ISBN-10: 0-8447-4244-9
     1. Wal-Mart (Firm) 2. Discount houses (Retail trade)—United States—Management. I. Cox, Wendell. II. Title.

     HF5429.215.U6V43 2006
     381'.1490973—dc22

                                                                    2006036035

11 10 09 08 07 06   1 2 3 4 5 6

Printed in the United States of America

Richard Vedder dedicates this book
to his wife, Karen Vedder

Wendell Cox dedicates this book
to his wife, Jean Love

Contents

List of Illustrations

TABLES

Preface

Sometime in 2004, Jeff Judson, the former president of the Texas Public Policy Foundation and a friend of ours, contacted each of us to suggest we delve into the growing controversy about Wal-Mart stores. We both had mixed, but mostly positive, reactions to the idea. While neither of us had spent much time researching or writing about retail trade issues, we both were intrigued by the idea, for somewhat different reasons.

One of us (Richard Vedder) is an economic historian who has spent a lifetime telling students about how the seemingly mundane process of engaging in what Adam Smith called "truck and barter" has changed so radically over time, and how changes in retailing dovetail well with broader changes in the American economy. He knew that corporate critics emerged whenever a business became rich and powerful—witness the attacks on the Standard Oil Trust a century ago. And he knew that usually the concerns raised by the critics were at least excessive, and sometimes even totally misguided. Moreover, he found the changes happening in retail trade a beautiful example of what Joseph Schumpeter incisively called "creative destruction"—change for the sake of progress.

The other of us (Wendell Cox) had spent a lifetime dealing with issues of transportation and urban sprawl. The "Wal-Mart Revolution" seemed to be closely tied to these issues. The automobile was critical in defining the type of operation that Sam Walton and other entrepreneurs developed in the last half of the twentieth century, and the decline in mass transit (never very popular with Americans) is closely tied with suburbanization—the development of shopping centers and malls, and so forth.

At the same time, being unfamiliar with much of the literature on Wal-Mart, we were uncomfortable taking any position on the Wal-Mart question until we reviewed the evidence. One of us had already completed a book for the National Research Initiative at the American Enterprise Institute, and thought that the NRI might be a good outlet for a broader examination of this issue. We also both felt that, although we wanted to give special emphasis to Wal-Mart, some examination of the entire "big-box" retail industry was appropriate. Fortunately, the folks at AEI agreed with us, and this project was born.

We have been extremely careful in trying not to become overly biased by propaganda from either side in the Wal-Mart debate, and we rather carefully avoided any contact with Wal-Mart at all until fairly late in the process of writing this book. Neither of us owns stock in the company, nor have we received a penny of remuneration from it, nor have we met with high level company officials, or been to their headquarters in Arkansas. At one point, we felt we needed to contact the company in order to get some needed information. Interestingly, the company largely ignored our request, modestly limiting our ability to analyze some issues in greater depth, and suggesting that Wal-Mart is smarter at selling goods than in conducting public relations. By keeping our distance from the company (to an even greater extent than we wished), we certainly assured that no one can complain we were unduly influenced by Wal-Mart-induced propaganda.

Actually, a New York Times reporter, Michael Barbaro, did raise the issue of inappropriate Wal-Mart influence with Richard Vedder in an early September 2006 phone conversation. Barbaro informed him, after this manuscript was at the publisher, that the American Enterprise Institute had received some contributions from the Walton Family Foundation. Since this book was essentially completed at that point, these contributions (which in any case were trivial in relation to AEI's budget) obviously had no impact on this work. AEI goes to great lengths to separate its fundraising efforts from its scholarly and editorial mission, and any suggestion that this book has been influenced in any way by Wal-Mart's support for AEI is entirely false. Indeed, the authors would never have known of the Walton Family Foundation's support for AEI had the New York Times not made them aware of it, so great is the separation between AEI's fundraising and scholarship.

While we had little contact with Wal-Mart, we did, however, both get some help from others. Of dominant importance in this regard was Bryan O'Keefe, an AEI staffer at the beginning of the project who has since gone on to a new position. He had a strong interest in the topic and did yeoman's service ferreting out information, producing graphs, and even helping with some editing chores on an early draft of the manuscript. Bryan's contribution was so great that it almost merits his being named a coauthor on this work. We appreciate his help immensely, and are pleased that we have made a new and valued friend.

Other members of the AEI and National Research Initiative staffs helped us, including Ryan Stowers, Courtney Myers, and Kim Dennis. The publication people at AEI, led by the estimable Sam Thernstrom and Karlyn Bowman, were great colleagues, friends, and helpers, rather than adversaries, as is sometimes the case in book publishing. Véronique Rodman has been helpful in getting the word out about this book. A former student of Richard Vedder's, Bob Moran, helped get some data from Wal-Mart that proved useful. Our families put up with us as we burned, in some figurative sense, the midnight oil (purchased, no doubt, at Wal-Mart) in our desire to finish the project. To all of them, we express our deep gratitude.

Introduction: Wal-Mart and the Big-Box Discount Store Revolution

Imagine that you are an American senior citizen who has just reached the biblical lifespan of "three score and ten" (seventy years), and that you are reflecting on a shopping trip you took with your parents as a teenager in 1950 to purchase the family's first television set and some back-to-school clothes. If you lived in a city, you might have taken a bus or subway to go downtown to the local department store, since parking was both scarce and expensive. If you lived in a smaller town, you might have gone to the local Sears, Roebuck or J. C. Penney for the clothes, and then on to an appliance store to look at television sets. At any of these stores, a clerk would have waited on you, and you would have paid for the merchandise at cash registers dispersed throughout the store. If your mom also needed some yarn, a window fan, or cheap gardening gloves, she might have gone to a local variety store such as Woolworth's, or perhaps consulted her Sears, Roebuck or Montgomery Ward catalogue. For groceries, she would probably have gone to one of the chain stores such as A&P or Safeway— possibly a "supermarket"—instead of patronizing the old, small grocery store downtown.

The grandchild of that senior citizen today shops in an altogether different way. Though driving with parents to the local mall department store for the clothes is not too different from what the grandparents did in 1950, he or she almost certainly will also head to a big-box discount store—for both the TV and the clothes, and countless other staples of life. There are no clerks to wait on you; you simply haul the merchandise to the front of the store to a common checkout area. The atmosphere may be "no frills"— but choices are greater, parking is better, and prices are lower. We shop a lot differently than our grandparents did, in large part due to the advent of big-box discount stores. Wal-Mart has been a leader in this retail revolution but it includes also many imitators, specialty stores, and variants on the big-box concept such as warehouse clubs.

How has the Wal-Mart revolution affected our lives? Has it been good or bad? Should we be doing things as a society to control, downsize, upsize, encourage, discourage, subsidize, or tax the retail changes that are occurring? Are we a richer society because of these changes? Have all groups, rich and poor alike, benefited from the Wal-Mart revolution? These questions and more are addressed in this book.

Wal-Mart and Its Imitators: Saints or Sinners?

Getting goods from producers to their ultimate consumer is the job of wholesale and retail trade, the latter of which is the focus of this book. Performed inefficiently, this trading function raises costs to consumers and lowers productivity and income. It compromises exchanges and prevents some of the gains from specialization and the division of labor from occurring. Conversely, major innovations in retailing potentially can save consumers large sums of money (by reducing the margin between the producer's price and the final retail price) and free up resources for other purposes. Economists say that retail innovations enhance "consumer surplus"—the gap between what people actually pay for goods and the amount they would have been willing to pay. Some estimates regarding Wal-Mart value those welfare gains in the tens of billions of dollars annually.

Despite the theoretical advantages of more efficient retail trade, criticisms are mounting against the great retail innovators, especially Wal-Mart. We are told that Wal-Mart pays its workers poorly, or offers them little or nothing in the way of health care benefits. The critics claim that when Wal-Mart comes to town, jobs are lost, cohesive downtown business communities are destroyed or severely damaged, urban sprawl intensifies, and a myriad of other secondary effects occur, ranging from deterioration of the local community to loss of jobs due to globalization and the sale of imported goods. Forced to compete with Chinese and Indian workers producing goods for Wal-Mart, American firms have laid off workers and cut wages and benefits.

So some portray Wal-Mart as having made positive contributions to American life by making goods more affordable, giving consumers more choices, providing job opportunities, raising our standard of living, and especially helping the poor. Others say big-box retailers are destroyers of much of what is good in America and a threat to our economic vitality. Which is right? Is Wal-Mart a saint, or a sinner? Are its contributions mostly positive or mostly negative?

The Genesis of the Big-Box Revolution

Retail trade has been in a state of constant change for centuries. Beginning with small general and specialty stores located in the towns of colonial America and itinerant peddlers on the American frontier, retail trade was both a cause and a consequence of more general rapid economic growth in the nineteenth and twentieth centuries. General stores morphed into specialty shops or, ultimately, became department stores. With territorial expansion and the evolution of a postal system came mail-order catalogues. The chain variety and grocery stores of the early twentieth century were still important in 1950—names like Woolworth's, Sears, Roebuck, and A&P. Then came the discount houses—large stores with parking and self-service, relatively low prices, and a great many choices. Kmart emerged as the industry leader in the mid-1960s, although other regional chains emerged as well, including, in Arkansas, Sam Walton's Wal-Mart.

Sam Walton was the most important retail entrepreneur of the twentieth century. He transformed general merchandise retailing and had an impact on other forms of retailing as well. Uncannily similar in personal attributes to the leading entrepreneur of the beginning of the twentieth century, John D. Rockefeller, Walton was the quintessential American entrepreneur—bold, risk-taking, God-fearing, innovative, and visionary. The company he founded was obsessed with cutting costs and bringing low prices to its customers, and it found new ways to do so, most importantly through its widely praised computerized inventory control system. A classic middle-class American, Sam Walton became America's richest man before his death in 1992.

Yet Sam Walton did not operate in a vacuum. He took (some say stole) some of his good ideas from competitors, whose stores he regularly visited.

And these stores started to imitate him, as well. Some strong competitors, like Kmart, weakened over time, while others, like Target, evolved from traditional department store retailing. The big-box discount retail concept perfected by Wal-Mart spread to home improvements (Home Depot and Lowe's), office supplies (Staples, Office Depot, and OfficeMax), electronics (Best Buy and Circuit City), and other specialty areas. As Wal-Mart became huge, it started to lose some of its growth momentum to these nimble upstarts, so that by 2006 Wal-Mart is less well-regarded on Wall Street than some of its much smaller and generally less profitable competitors.

The Economic Impact of Wal-Mart and Other Big-Box Stores

Did Wal-Mart and its imitators have generally positive or negative economic effects on the population? Our answer is unambiguous: Wal-Mart has been good for America, and, increasingly, for the rest of the world as well.

As we will show, studies have found that on average Wal-Mart has lowered prices by several percentage points, providing billions of dollars of benefits to its customers. Wal-Mart has also provided job opportunities for thousands of workers. The preponderance of the evidence supports the view that the company creates more jobs than it destroys. Most communities with a new Wal-Mart have a more favorable labor market environment after the store opens than before—and better than in comparable non-Wal-Mart communities. The era of Wal-Mart dominance has had lower average unemployment rates than in, say, the 1970s, the last decade before the company ascended to major national importance.

The notion that Wal-Mart treats its employees badly seems without foundation as well. Average pay levels, while not high (around $10 an hour for hourly workers) are not sharply out of line with standards for the retail trade industry. Large numbers of employees are shareowners in the firm, which may explain, in part, the fairly high level of employee loyalty and the unwillingness of workers to support collective bargaining. While it is true that less than one-half of employees have Wal-Mart-subsidized health insurance, a large portion do not need or want such benefits, as they have other options (for example, a spouse's insurance or Medicare). While it is indeed true that some Wal-Mart workers are on Medicaid, the use of public assistance to provide health care benefits is common for workers in relatively unskilled occupations in industries such as retail trade or the hotel and restaurant industry.

We reject the idea that Wal-Mart destroys communities and adds to urban sprawl. Downtowns were declining long before Wal-Mart became an important retailing force, and the big-box retail revolution is but one additional factor in the demise of retailing in central business districts where parking is typically relatively scarce. While it is true that some stores go out of business when Wal-Mart enters a community, the opening and closing of stores in response to changing tastes and technology has been part of the retail landscape literally for centuries. Wal-Mart does not force stores out of business—customers do, by voting with their feet and going to Wal-Mart with its lower prices and greater choices than the local alternatives. People prefer Wal-Mart, and, in exercising their preferences, they are enhancing their own welfare, and thus that of the communities the stores serve.

Wal-Mart serves customers at all income levels and walks of life, as do Target, Home Depot, Best Buy, and other big-box stores. They appeal to consumers at all income levels—but Wal-Mart disproportionately serves the poor. Wal-Mart stores are more often located in areas with below-average incomes, and surveys show that a larger proportion of lower-income people shop at Wal-Mart than people from affluent families. So the store's consumer welfare benefits particularly aid the poor—and consequently, attempts to keep it out of communities hurt the poor far more than the rich.

Sam Walton and his disciples were and are tough bargainers. They want the lowest possible prices from their suppliers—that is a key to offering true "everyday low prices." Are suppliers being squeezed and exploited? It appears not to be the case. No one is forced to sell goods to Wal-Mart. Suppliers unhappy with the terms of agreements with Wal-Mart can simply stop dealing with them. And anecdotal evidence (as well as economic logic) suggests that other large retailers, notably Home Depot, are every bit as tough at negotiating as Wal-Mart.

What is the bottom line in terms of Wal-Mart's impact on the broader economy? Convincing government data show that productivity has risen sharply in the Wal-Mart-dominated component of retail trade. Using reasonable, plausible assumptions, it is easy to conclude that the Wal-Mart revolution has created tens of billions of dollars of new income and output annually in America, and has contributed to a quickening in the rate of economic growth. Sales and resources are shifting from the sectors of retailing with low productivity growth (like traditional grocery stores) to the sectors, including stores like Wal-Mart, where productivity is rising sharply as a consequence of better inventory controls, economies of scale in purchasing, and lower transportation costs.

Trite and mundane as it is to say, it is nonetheless true that we live in an ever-shrinking world where economies are increasingly integrated, partly for technological reasons (lower transportation and communications costs), and partly because of public policies that have, on balance, reduced protectionism and promoted international trade. This has had two major effects on American retailing. First, retail operators like Wal-Mart, Target, and Best Buy look all over the world, not just in the United States, for goods and services to sell at low prices. It is hard to believe an electronics store like Best Buy could even stay in business if sales were confined to domestically made goods—how many televisions and DVD players are made in the United States?

A second dimension of even greater importance is the spread of the big-box revolution to other nations. Companies like Wal-Mart and Home Depot are investing vast amounts in rapidly growing overseas economies, especially in China. And there are international imitators of Wal-Mart as well. Carrefour, a French company, is the second-largest retailer in the world, for example, and it faces stiff competition from other smaller, but perhaps more nimble, European upstarts.

What Should We Do About Wal-Mart?

Wal-Mart's critics, by and large, are simply wrong. Wal-Mart treats its employees decently, generally helps rather than hurts communities, and improves the lives and the standards of living of its customers. It has probably helped reduce poverty. Like many other large firms, Wal-Mart has had some rogue employees who have done illegal and unethical things, but that is not a reasonable basis for evaluating the entire company. And Wal-Mart's critics are hardly disinterested observers; many are political activists with their own ideological agendas. Wal-Mart may be no saint, but it is certainly not a particularly egregious sinner either—and its critics are not beyond reproach either.

What should we "do" about Wal-Mart? Subsidize it because it is a force for good in our society? Tax and regulate it, given its alleged excesses? We prefer neither option; we should simply treat it as just another business enterprise—no better, no worse. Pro-Wal-Mart policies, such as giving the company especially favorable tax abatements, lead to a distortion of resources and create an uneven playing field among competitors, but so do policies specifically requiring Wal-Mart to pay employees health benefits, or designing zoning laws to prevent Wal-Mart (or other big-box retailers) from locating in a community.

Wal-Mart has not been particularly adroit in handling criticism. It has mounted a campaign to appease organized labor and environmental groups, tinkering with health care plans and entering the organic fish business, among other things. It strikes us that it may be abandoning its principles of everyday low prices to pander to its opponents, many of whom probably do not represent mainstream American thinking. We wonder whether Wal-Mart is trying to "appease the unappeasable."

Wall Street has been down on Wal-Mart in recent years, just as it has been enthusiastic about other competitors such as Best Buy and Lowe's. The perception is that Wal-Mart has saturated the market, and the market itself is changing. To deal with that, the company has tried to push more upscale goods (capitalizing on rising American family incomes), but in doing so it risks alienating its strong base of value-oriented customers. It is also—understandably, in our view—expanding aggressively into markets like China and even Central America. Another promising venture is to enter the banking business, from which it has been thwarted by competitors afraid of the competition. Perhaps the company should also consider doing what Sam Walton speculated about more than a decade ago—spin off an upscale version of Wal-Mart, and maybe divest itself of Sam's Club, its warehouse operation, as well.

Retailing is constantly in flux. The discount-house revolution of the 1960s that morphed into the big-box revolution of the '80s and '90s may be in the process of being supplanted by another retail innovation—Internet shopping. Firms like Amazon.com and eBay are booming, with rapid sales growth, big and growing profits, and a perception by financial markets of a bright future. Just as Sears and Roebuck and Woolworth's lost their retail supremacy in earlier decades, so may Wal-Mart lose its leadership role in the future. But if it does, it should be on the basis of marketplace decisions by consumers, not government policies that distort the allocation of resources and subvert the tastes and preferences of a vast consuming public.

PART I

Why Wal-Mart Matters

1

The Importance of Retail Innovations

In their limited time on earth, human beings try to be happy and satisfied—or, to use the jargon of economists, they try to "maximize their utility." Some utility (happiness or satisfaction) derives from things that are not materialistic in nature—people obtain enormous pleasures from falling in love, from winning athletic events, or from experiencing religious revelations—and none of these involves much in the way of financial outlay or uses many resources. Yet much of our utility is derived from consuming goods and services. It is a basic proposition in economics that utility-maximizing individuals prefer consuming more to consuming less, as additional consumption provides added satisfaction ("marginal utility"). Anything or anyone that allows people to buy more DVD players or some other gadget is contributing to human welfare or well-being by increasing individual satisfaction.

The rise of the discount retail chains like Wal-Mart served to increase the number of goods and services the typical family could afford, and thus promoted consumer welfare or satisfaction. Suppose, in the era shortly after Wal-Mart and Kmart were created in the 1960s, a person could go to a local variety store or use a Sears, Roebuck catalogue to buy two pairs of slacks for $30 ($15 each). Suppose Wal-Mart now opened a store and offered the same slacks for $10, and the individual bought the two pairs for $20 instead of $30, and spent another $5 buying a shirt, and $5 buying two movie tickets. By shopping at Wal-Mart, the customer derived the same utility from purchasing slacks as before—but added satisfaction from also buying a shirt and going to a movie with a friend. Discount stores allow people to buy more goods and services and derive greater happiness. Thus, the development of the discount store in the 1960s contributed to a higher standard of living and greater satisfaction for the American people.

To be sure, we cannot say with precision how much happier the person is because of the opening of a new Wal-Mart or Target or a Home Depot. Economists say that "cardinal utility cannot be measured," meaning we cannot put exact quantitative measures on the satisfaction derived from the fact that the customer now has a shirt and attended a movie that was unaffordable before the Wal-Mart opened. But we can say the customer is at least somewhat happier, since by going to Wal-Mart instead of older, traditional stores, he or she revealed a preference for Wal-Mart, finding it provided more satisfaction (through lower prices and also probably better choices of goods). Presumably people try to make themselves happier, and by choosing Wal-Mart (or Target or Home Depot) to shop at instead of a more expensive store, individuals are making their lives better.

All of this does not demonstrate conclusively that Wal-Mart and other discount stores have been, on aggregate, a force for the public good. Critics argue that Wal-Mart has some undesirable "spillover effects," or what economists call "negative externalities," that make continued expansion undesirable. We will deal with those arguments later. But the fact that people are voting with their feet to shop in huge numbers at Wal-Mart (and similar stores such as Target and Costco) indicates that there is a lot of positive utility and value derived from them, and the arguments to constrain their growth must deal with that.

The Economic Importance of Retail Trade

In a world without any trading, each individual economic unit (usually the family) produces goods and services for its own use. Since each unit is not very good at producing some things, and perhaps totally incapable of producing others (due, for instance, to a lack of raw materials), in a world without trade, it is typically able to produce barely enough to live; no non-trading geographic area has ever been very affluent. Trade allows each manufacturer to specialize in producing a few products or services very efficiently, selling its output to others in exchange for goods that cannot be produced cheaply, if at all. The importance of trade and exchange in the creation of wealth and prosperity was emphasized by Adam Smith in the first classic work of modern economics literature.[1]

Aside from trading among producers, a critically important matter is the conveyance of goods from producers to consumers. Retail trade evolved as a means of lowering the costs of getting goods from producers to consumers through the use of intermediate agents—middlemen. The evolution of modern retailing, discussed at length in chapters 3 and 4, has involved moving from fairs and local markets to peddlers and small general stores to larger department stores and specialty shops, and finally to chain stores and modern discount stores. The evolution continues, as the rapid rise in Internet shopping attests.

To an economist, the evolution of retail trade has been a long story of continually falling transactions costs—the costs of getting goods from the seller (producer) to the buyer (consumer). As these costs have fallen, some trade that was previously prohibitively expensive has become possible and has grown. In 1850, it was unusual to buy goods made in China, something that Americans now do in massive quantities, helped by innovative discount retailers like Costco and Wal-Mart. The increasing efficiency in retail trade has reduced the markup in price between the producer and the consumer levels, and this has made consumers better off. With falling prices have come increases in the quantity of goods produced, often leading to economies of scale that have lowered production costs and, ultimately, consumer prices still further.

As the costs of goods to consumers fall because of declining distribution costs, pioneered by merchant entrepreneurs like Harry Cunningham of Kmart and Sam Walton of Wal-Mart, people see a rise in their real income—the purchasing power of their wages and other income. This, in turn, has all sorts of secondary effects—for example, people may increase their saving, expanding the pool of funds available for investment. The result is lower interest rates, leading to more capital formation and productivity growth. Consumers may use some of the savings on purchases of goods to buy more services, such as transportation or vacations that previously would not have been taken. Thus, in an indirect way, the development of discount stores has stimulated the development of discount airlines like Southwest, Jet Blue, and Air Tran. In addition, the fact that the big discount stores carry a larger variety of goods gives consumers more choices—and leads to consumption of products previously not purchased because of a lack of ready availability.

Innovations like Wal-Mart, then, potentially have far-reaching economic effects that are not readily apparent as one is standing in the checkout lane to buy a good a little cheaper than at a traditional retail outlet.

The Discount Revolution and Consumer Surplus

Writing more than 170 years ago, the rather obscure French railway engineer Jules Dupuit advanced the notion that is now known as consumer (or consumer's or even consumers') surplus.[2] The term was largely ignored for decades, until Alfred Marshall brought it into greater use with his better description of the concept in a popular textbook published in 1890.[3] According to Dupuit and Marshall, if a consumer is willing to pay $15 for something but is able to buy it for $12, the consumer is deriving $3's worth of surplus utility—a welfare gain conferred by the ability to obtain the good for less than the maximum price the consumer was willing to pay. The sum of consumer surplus to all consumers is a measure of the positive welfare effects of trade in a given commodity or service on the purchasers. It is a measure derived from people's tastes or utility for goods.

If the price of a good falls further, say from $12 in the example above to $10, the amount of consumer surplus rises, for two reasons. First, customers who would have purchased the product at the old price of $12 now derive $2 more of consumer surplus for each item purchased. Second, some new customers will be induced to buy the product as the price falls below $12. The customer who was willing to pay $11 for the good previously would not have purchased it, but now does so at $10 and derives a dollar of consumer surplus as well.

When innovations in the distribution of goods occur that lower the cost of the middleman services provided, prices to consumers fall, and consumer surplus is increased. That is precisely what Wal-Mart and its imitators and competitors have done—created consumer surplus for American shoppers and, increasingly, for those in other countries as well.

For those readers wanting a slightly more rigorous technical description, the points above can be presented graphically using the economist's favorite tools, demand and supply curves.[4]

FIGURE 1-1
DEMAND AND SUPPLY OF ORANGES

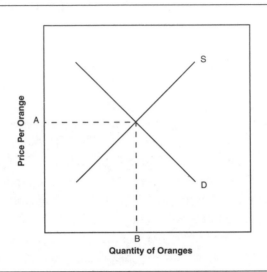

SOURCE: Authors' representation.

FIGURE 1-2
THE EFFECT OF RETAIL INNOVATIONS

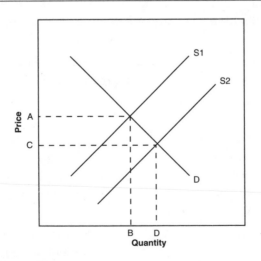

SOURCE: Authors' representation.

FIGURE 1-3

RETAIL INNOVATIONS AND CONSUMER SURPLUS

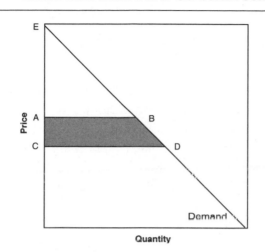

SOURCE: Authors' representation.

In figure 1-1, the price of oranges is determined by the intersection of demand (denoted D) and supply (denoted S) curves, at price A and quantity B. The demand curve represents the quantity of oranges that people will buy at different prices, and it slopes downward because of the law of demand, a basic proposition of human behavior: At lower prices, people will buy more goods. The supply (or S) curve slopes upward, typically, denoting that producers or distributors of goods will be willing to supply more the higher the price; higher prices increase potential profits and incentives to produce goods. The point where the two curves cross is what economists call an equilibrium point—a state of balance, where the wishes of demanders (consumers) are exactly provided for by the suppliers, and there are neither shortages nor surpluses of the good or service. This intersection point determines the actual market price of the good and the quantity sold.

What the retail trade revolution has done is increase the quantity of goods supplied to consumers at any given price—or, to put it differently, at any given quantity of goods provided, they are offered at lower prices. There is an increase in supply, denoted graphically in figure 1-2 by a downward shift in the supply curve, to curve S2 from the initial curve, now called

S1. This leads to a lower price than before (price C instead of A) and also to larger quantities sold (D instead of B).

The analysis in figures 1-1 and 1-2 leads us to showing how discount stores have increased consumer surplus—our measure of the welfare effects of trade. In figure 1-2, the introduction of retail innovations by entrepreneurs like Sam Walton led to increased supplies of goods being offered for sale at any price (a shift downward in the supply curve) and a decline in price of the product from A to C. In figure 1-3, for simplicity, we look at only the market price (excluding the supply curve that helps determine the price).

The introduction of discount retailing led prices to fall from A to C. The shaded area represents consumer surplus—the dollar value on the excess utility derived from the fact that people are able to get goods for less than they are willing to pay. Originally, before discount stores, that area was the triangle EAB. The decline in prices brought about by Wal-Mart and other discount stores increased consumer surplus, to the larger triangle ECD. The area ABCD represents increased consumer surplus arising from the arrival of Wal-Mart and similar lower-cost retailers on the scene.

In a practical sense, is the increase in consumer welfare as indicated in figure 1-3 large or small? That is not an easy question to answer, as the measurement of consumer surplus is fraught with some technical difficulties, despite advances by mid- and late-twentieth-century economists such as J. R. Hicks, Arnold Harberger, and Jerry Hausman.[5] To cite just one difficulty, the consumer surplus varies with each good sold, in part because the sensitivity of customers to price (what economists call elasticity) varies from product to product, and, indeed, from customer to customer. A fall in price will lead to more new consumer surplus when customers are price-sensitive (the demand is elastic) than when they are insensitive to price (the demand is inelastic).Thus, the total consumer surplus of a store like Wal-Mart is the sum of many different estimates of consumer surplus. Since the mere estimation of price elasticity, which determines the slope of the demand curve in figures 1-1 and 1-2, is in itself somewhat difficult, the task of estimating aggregate consumer surplus is therefore somewhat formidable.[6]

Nonetheless, some economists have made estimates of consumer surplus in various situations. Recently, three scholars from the Massachusetts Institute of Technology and Carnegie Mellon University estimated consumer surplus arising from another retail innovation: the introduction of

online book purchasing.[7] Using data for 2000, online book sales were estimated at about $1.475 billion, and the consumer surplus associated with
lower prices from those sales at slightly over $100 million, or slightly less
than 7 percent of sales. If we assume that the consumer surplus of Wal-Mart
sales was about the same proportion of sales as that of online booksellers
such as Amazon.com, the total consumer surplus of Wal-Mart sales in
fiscal year 2005 (which fell mostly in calendar year 2004) would have
approached $20 billion (when sales were slightly over $285 billion). Since
about 20 percent of sales were overseas, the actual surplus was more like
$16 billion, or about $55 per person.

The $20 billion estimate above, though, probably grossly understates
total consumer surplus and welfare enhancement arising from the development of large-volume discount retailing, for two reasons. First, Wal-Mart
comprises only about one-half of the total modern "big-box" discount retail
industry. Aside from direct competitors like Target and Costco, there are
specialized providers like Home Depot and Lowe's in the home improvement sector, Best Buy in electronics, and Staples, OfficeMax, and Office
Depot in office supplies. Looking at the aggregate big-box discount retail
sector, and using the same assumption as above, consumer surplus in the
aggregate might nearly double, to perhaps $40 billion.

Second, another form of consumer welfare derived from discount retailing may well dwarf the welfare enhancement from lower prices reflected in
consumer surplus. In the study on bookselling, the authors estimated welfare
gains of somewhere between $733 million and $1.03 billion resulting from
customers' ability to obtain goods (books, in this case) that were simply
unavailable (at any reasonable cost) otherwise. This amount represents seven
to ten times the gains from consumer surplus as conventionally measured.

Since Amazon.com carries more than twenty times the number of titles
than are on the shelves of even the biggest bookstores, a customer can find
that relatively obscure book he or she has been salivating over for years—
and can buy it for, say, $25, though willing to pay $100 or more for it. Wal-
Mart (and Home Depot, Target, and others) have the same impact. The
typical Wal-Mart Supercenter in a small town has several times the quantity
of goods available at the local variety or small department store; similarly,
Home Depot or Lowe's will have lots of items that are unavailable at the
local hardware stores.

It seems plausible to us that the gains from offering consumers more choices might easily equal or exceed those associated with lower prices and more competition on goods that are readily available. If so, the $40 billion consumer surplus is augmented by at least $40 billion more in welfare-enhancing choice, giving aggregate gains in welfare valued, conservatively, at $80 billion. Even after eliminating a moderate amount in foreign sales (companies like Home Depot do not yet have a large foreign presence), the annual American-derived welfare gains are probably still in excess of $65 billion, or about $225 for every American, or $900 for a typical family of four. This is a sizable welfare gain from one innovation—the modern retail discount store.

A number of caveats are in order. Consumer surplus depends in part on the elasticity of demand, and the elasticity of the demand, on average, for Wal-Mart products may be more or less than that for books purchased online. Also, our assumption that the increased consumer choice argument is relatively far less important at Wal-Mart than with online booksellers, but is still quantitatively just as important as measured consumer surplus, is just that—an assumption. We would argue, however, that it is a plausible, even conservative assumption, and that the resulting welfare gains are very large indeed and an important factor in the rising quality of life of the American people in modern times. Even varying the assumptions about consumer surplus and the welfare gains from increased choice fairly considerably would still yield gains in the tens of billions of dollars. If we add in the global effects—the spread of the mass discount house to other countries through such imitators as Carrefour—the global numbers become still larger.

Recently, a number of studies published by prominent economists or in top-tier academic journals have shown that Wal-Mart's presence has had a significant impact on consumer prices and hence on consumer surplus and welfare. Emek Basker shows through exhaustive analysis of ten specific products that Wal-Mart's presence tends to lower prices by varying amounts, but perhaps approaching 10 percent in the long run.[8] This is consistent with national consumer savings of well over $20 billion annually, excluding the impact of Wal-Mart overseas or any spillover effects due to lower prices at other stores driven by Wal-Mart's competition.[9]

Similarly, the distinguished MIT economist and leader in consumer surplus research, Jerry Hausman, along with Ephraim Leibtag, argues that the

impact of Wal-Mart is quite considerable. According to Hausman and Leibtag, consumer welfare gains are even larger than those estimated by Basker,
probably in excess of 20 percent of sales. This analysis is confined to grocery sales, but if it holds for nongrocery categories as well, estimates of $50
billion or more in annual consumer welfare gains from Wal-Mart in the
United States alone seem quite reasonable. It is interesting, and somewhat
reassuring, that all of these estimates show considerable welfare gains, of
roughly equal magnitude.

The Supply Side

Up to this point, we have looked at the effect of mass discount retailing on
consumers— the demand side of the retail goods market. But there is also a
supply side, and it can be argued that the gains received by consumers in
the form of consumer surplus and greater choice are offset by losses suffered by suppliers other than the big-box discount stores—traditional retail
outlets, manufacturers, and wholesalers who face smaller price margins.

Just as consumers derive satisfaction from consumer surplus—getting
goods for less than they were willing to pay—so producers derive satisfaction (in the form of added revenues) by selling goods for more than the
rock-bottom minimum price that they will accept. This is called producer
(or producer's or even producers') surplus. When Wal-Mart (or Target or
Costco or Home Depot) enters a community, existing retailers often find
they have to reduce prices somewhat to stay in business. Similarly, manufacturers wanting a huge account (with a store the size of Wal-Mart, for
example) may have to accept smaller margins as well. These suppliers find
their producer surplus is reduced—which is a loss to human welfare, as
suppliers are owned and run by human beings.

It can be shown graphically that the gains in consumer surplus by buyers are partially—but only partially—offset by a loss of producer surplus by
sellers. The graphics get quite complicated and technical for the lay reader,
and thus are excluded here, but they are available in many principles of
economics textbooks.[10] As the study on online book retailing indicates,
however, much (sometimes most) of the gain in welfare from any retail
innovation comes from the increases in choice—and that is not offset by

any loss of producer welfare. The small-town resident who wanted a certain type of product before the building of the local Wal-Mart may have simply been frustrated, or may have had to drive dozens of miles to buy the product, imposing significant transportation costs and a loss of leisure time.

Suppose that we accept the above estimate of $40 billion in consumer welfare gains (consumer surplus) and another $40 billion in gains from enhanced consumer choice, and that the loss of producer surplus is 75 percent as large as the gains from consumer surplus, or $30 billion. Then the $80 billion in welfare gains on the consumer side will be partially offset by $30 billion in losses on the supply side—still leaving a sizable $50 billion in net welfare gains. Remember, if the study on bookselling is at all relevant, our estimates of the gains from enhanced consumer choice are very conservative.

The gains from the mass discount retail revolution are similar in many regards to those that have resulted over time from increased international trade. Globalization has brought more foreign goods to our shores, many sold in stores like Wal-Mart, at somewhat lower prices than previously offered domestic goods. This has provided consumer surplus to buyers, but imposed losses in the form of reduced producer surplus to suppliers. On balance, though, economists are almost unanimous in their belief that the gains from trade outweigh the losses. This is merely an extension of that argument domestically: More trade is better than less, and more choices are better than fewer.

Spillover Effects, or "Externalities"

Sometimes economic activities or transactions affect third parties— individuals not involved in the activity or party to the transaction. A chemical plant discharges pollutants into a stream, and it kills fish. People who enjoyed recreational fishing in the stream find their utility reduced. This "spillover" effect is formally termed a "negative externality." My neighbor has a gorgeous outdoor Christmas display that I enjoy. His display raises my utility, and this is a "positive externality."

Critics of Wal-Mart and other mass discount retailers often use negative externality arguments to suggest that these stores are, on balance, harmful to our society. For example, the building of a new Wal-Mart may add to traffic congestion on the road on which the store is located, lengthening the time it takes some drivers to get to work. Or perhaps the Wal-Mart is constructed on a pristine open meadow that was aesthetically pleasing to local residents, and the destruction of the meadow lowers utility to many in town. Or perhaps Wal-Mart aggressively imports cheap goods from China, which has the impact of lowering sales of American-made goods, putting some American workers not involved in transactions at Wal-Mart out of work.

In theory, it is possible that negative spillover effects such as these could have a dollar value greater than that on the gains associated with consumer surplus and greater customer choice. Yet Wal-Mart (and Target and Home Depot) can have positive externalities as well. For every Wal-Mart built on a pristine meadow, we suspect there is at least one built on land that formerly held an old dilapidated strip mall, junkyard, or other unsightly thing. The new discount store actually improves neighborhood aesthetics. The added dollars Chinese businessmen receive from the sale of goods to Wal-Mart may be used to finance tourist travel to the United States or the purchase of U.S. goods, both in a stealth fashion creating jobs for Americans working in, say, the tourist industry. In a world like ours with flexible exchange rates, Wal-Mart's demand for foreign goods, all else being equal, lowers the value of the dollar relative to other currencies, effectively lowering the price of American exports and thus increasing their sales and creating income for others. The success of Wal-Mart in towns sometimes leads to the construction of additional retail outlets, such as Home Depot or Lowe's, creating still more jobs and consumer choices—almost certainly a positive externality.

A very real positive welfare effect comes from Wal-Mart's charitable giving. In calendar year 2004, Wal-Mart gave over $170 million to various worthy causes, most of them in local communities where Wal-Mart exists.[11] Wal-Mart was a godsend to thousands of homeless persons in the aftermath of the worst storm to hit America in recent decades, Hurricane Katrina. One *New York Times* columnist half-seriously suggested turning the Federal Emergency Management Agency (FEMA) over to Wal-Mart and renaming it WEMA—Wal-Mart Emergency Management Agency.[12] While FEMA took days to get into the ravaged region, Wal-Mart was moving goods, emergency generators, water, and other vitally needed supplies to its stores even before the storm hit—and later donated $17 million to help victims of the storm.

In short, the mass discount retailing industry has created both some negative and some positive externalities, and it is extremely difficult to say which are greater, mainly because externalities are very difficult to measure or even identify. Indeed, a negative externality for one person could be a positive externality for another. Some with a strong sense of tradition may be offended by the replacement of an aging shopping center with a Home Depot, while others will be pleased at the destruction of an eyesore to make way for an attractive new retail facility. Those citing specific examples of clear negative externalities to make an anti–Wal-Mart case very often ignore the very real offsetting positive externalities, not to mention the real benefits to consumers discussed above.

Public Attitudes Concerning Retail Trade in America

If discount houses and other large retail institutions had very real and substantial negative impacts, either directly or through adverse spillover effects, one would expect Americans to be rather critical of the industry as a whole. The Gallup Organization occasionally polls people about their attitudes toward various sectors of American society.[13] Consistently, attitudes toward retail trade have been on balance quite favorable. In their August 2005 poll, for example, 52 percent of Americans ranked the industry in a "very positive" or "somewhat positive" manner, compared with only 15 percent who had "somewhat" or "very negative" attitudes. These proportions have remained rather steady over the last several surveys, despite rising criticism of parts of the industry—notably Wal-Mart—by various groups.

It is interesting to note that of the twenty-five industries or sectors included in the Gallup Poll, the retail trade industry ranked fifth in terms of net positive attitudes, behind only the restaurant, computer, and grocery industries—and some mass discounters, including Wal-Mart, are major players in the grocery industry as well—and farming. It ranked dramatically above such important industries as autos, banking, the Internet, airlines, pharmaceuticals, and movies, as well as the federal government. For example, while 52 percent viewed retailing positively and 15 percent negatively (for a net positive figure of 37), the federal government received only 33 percent positive evaluations and 45 percent negative rankings, for a net negative statistic of 12. The negatives for the federal government were triple those for retailing. The consumer surplus and high level of choice from retailing seem to outweigh by far any alleged negative externalities in the minds of the American public.

Conclusions

The innovations in the retail industry since the 1960s have had significant effects on the lives of Americans. For most people, namely the vast majority of the population who shop at least occasionally at the new discount mass retailers, the revolution brought about by Wal-Mart and others has meant lower prices and more consumer choices. Both of these factors bring sizable amounts of satisfaction, probably worth at least tens of billions of dollars a year. By increasing what economists call consumer surplus and by giving consumers more options, Wal-Mart and other mass retailers have improved the quality of their lives.

To be sure, whenever innovations come into being, there are losers as well as winners. Stables, horse breeders, buggy manufacturers, and others lost income and jobs when the automobile became the premier means of personal transportation, but it is virtually universally acknowledged that the automobile on balance improved people's lives—consumer gains outweighed losses among some producers. So it is with Wal-Mart and other retail innovators like Home Depot. No doubt there are some negative spillover effects with some of these retail innovations, but some positive ones as well. It seems implausible that the spillover effects are, on net, so negative that they offset the tens of billions of dollars of welfare gains arising from offering consumers more goods, at lower prices. Positive public attitudes toward retailing tend to reinforce the general impression that innovations in this sector have improved the public welfare.

2

Wal-Mart and Its Critics

Big-box stores have generated strong opposition from a variety of interests. As the largest American big-box chain by far, it is not surprising that Wal-Mart receives most of the criticism. But similar critiques could as readily be directed toward virtually all of the big-box stores.

The battle against Wal-Mart and sometimes other big-box stores is being waged on many fronts. One is the legislative arena, where at the local, state, and national level the critics have tried to prohibit certain allegedly inappropriate practices—for example, by requiring health insurance for employees, or by using zoning laws to restrict the building of new stores. They have also used the judicial system to try to have courts fine the companies for allegedly illegal conduct. But much of the war is being waged in the court of public opinion—trying to disseminate information designed to turn public sentiments against the big-box operators in order to have a more favorable environment to attack on legislative, judicial, or regulatory fronts.

The criticism of Wal-Mart and its competitors has been disseminated in many ways—via demonstrations and pickets, through movies such as Robert Greenwald's 2005 *Wal-Mart: The High Cost of Low Price* or Micha X. Peled's *Store Wars: When Wal-Mart Comes to Town*, and through books, newspaper stories, and advertisements. For example, some internal Wal-Mart memos have been leaked to sympathetic members of the press in an attempt to show that the company is following dubious policies, such as trying to prevent employees from getting insurance or not paying overtime pay.

To a considerable extent, the war against Wal-Mart is being waged on the Internet. Critics of big-box stores operate a number of Internet websites, the most influential of which is probably the largely union-funded Wal-Mart Watch (www.Wal-Martwatch.com).[1] Wal-Mart Watch is decidedly anti–Wal-Mart, offering a daily email newsletter that allows subscribers to "receive updates and local alerts on how you can take action against Wal-Mart." Similarly, authors like Al Norman (*Slam-Dunking Wal-Mart!; The Case Against Wal-Mart*), John Dicker (*The United States of Wal-Mart*), Bill Quinn (*How Wal-Mart Is Destroying America*), and Anthony Bianco (*The Bully of Bentonville: How the High Cost of Wal-Mart's Everyday Low Prices Is Hurting America*) are peddling books that take Wal-Mart to task.[2]

To be sure, there are books that are less one-sided in their assessments of Wal-Mart, and others that are unabashedly admiring of the company, beginning, of course, with Sam Walton's own autobiography.[3] Yet the literature receiving the most press coverage seems to be the anti–Wal-Mart criticism.

The anti–Wal-Mart campaign is composed of various interests that are generally to the left of the political spectrum. The most important appear to be aligned with organized labor, particularly the United Food and Commercial Workers International Union (UFCW), which represents retail clerks. There are also organizations that advocate for low-income households, and so-called "antisprawl" interests.

Many of the Wal-Mart critics are on the political left, and 2008 presidential aspirants in the Democratic Party have been generally critical of Wal-Mart, probably in large part because unions are an important part of their financial and electoral base. However, generalizations about this are dangerous: some on the left have adopted a position very similar to that found in this book, namely that progressives should be supportive of Wal-Mart, since it caters to the poor and provides them with goods at lower cost than previously available. Particularly notable in that regard is Jason Furman.[4]

As with any other issue, a case could be made that at least some of the opposition is driven by selfish interests that believe they are threatened by big-box stores. But regardless of their motives, the critics raise issues that, if valid, might provide a case for public policies designed to thwart expansion.

The Criticisms

Wal-Mart can be attacked on several different fronts. One is on grounds of illegality and dubious ethical conduct. If Wal-Mart is systematically and intentionally breaking the law, for example, it is a criminal menace that needs to be eradicated and brought to justice in order to maintain the rule of law. A second area of potential criticism is reduced social welfare and satisfaction. For example, if Wal-Mart has negative effects on people—robbing consumers of shopping opportunities or gouging them on prices, hurting workers through loss of jobs or diminished paychecks, or destroying the environment (one of the "negative externalities" discussed in the previous chapter), there is a legitimate basis for some constraining of the Wal-Mart revolution.

Some of the specific principal criticisms of big-box stores involve the following:

- *Labor compensation.* Big-box stores are charged with paying substandard wages and benefits to their workers. It is claimed that, as a result, big-box employees are forced to rely on public assistance programs. This, it is further claimed, equates to government subsidizing big-box stores as, led by Wal-Mart, they shirk their financial responsibility. Further, it is charged that the influence of big-box stores drives down wage and benefit levels in retailing and related industries, leading to adverse spillover effects on workers outside the industry.

- *Loss of jobs.* When Wal-Mart (or Home Depot or other big-box retailer) comes to town, it eliminates many jobs in local businesses, usually positions filled by loyal employees of many years of service. Local businesses who loyally support community charitable causes are punished by selfish out-of-town interests.

- *Impact on competitors and communities.* It is claimed that big-box stores drive out of business smaller enterprises that are pivotal to the cohesiveness and economic vibrancy of local communities. Further, it is claimed that big-box stores can take advantage of their positions to exert monopoly power that will raise consumer prices. They also bring about traffic congestion and lower the quality of life.

- *Burden on government and taxpayers.* It is alleged that by not providing health insurance benefits, Wal-Mart is burdening public assistance programs like Medicaid. Also, local governments are required to pay for infrastructure related to Wal-Mart's arrival, such as widened streets. Tax abatements for Wal-Mart force up tax rates for other taxpayers, including Wal-Mart's competitors.

- *Impact on suppliers.* It is claimed that big-box retailers place undue pressure on their suppliers to lower costs, potentially reducing quality, destroying the value of brand names, driving companies out of business, or even encouraging suppliers to move their manufacturing facilities outside the United States.

- *Globalization.* It is claimed that big-box stores work to weaken the American economy by purchasing goods from overseas, particularly from China. The importation of foreign goods allegedly creates a trade deficit that effectively mortgages our nation's future to foreigners, and has contributed to a massive loss of high-paying manufacturing jobs in this country.

- *Insensitivity to the environment.* The construction of stores often leads to the destruction of pastures or woodland areas, causing environmental damage and adding to traffic congestion and urban sprawl. Big-box retailers also sell products that use production processes harmful to the earth, air, and water.

Most of the remainder of this book examines these and other criticisms. For example, chapter 6 evaluates the claims that big-box discounters have adverse wage and employment effects and chapter 7 the arguments that they adversely affect communities. Chapter 10 discusses globalization effects, and chapter 11 offers a general assessment of the criticisms mentioned in this chapter.

The Intensity of the Rhetoric

Many Wal-Mart critics are not objective observers who use evenhanded analysis to show shortcomings of the company. They are a passionate group of activists who often have developed genuine hatred toward America's largest company (measured by sales), displaying their hatred in strong, arguably intemperate language. A few quotes taken from the leading anti–Wal-Mart website, Wal-Martwatch.com, illustrate the point.

The website urges readers to send emails to friends, with the following canned introductory message:

> I thought you might enjoy this story from Wal-Mart Watch, a group who is committed to exposing Wal-Mart for their bad labor standards, political corruptness and overall bad citizenship. . . . Have you heard about Wal-Mart's systematic assault on women in America? They are subject to the largest class action lawsuit in American history.[5]

A press release on the site concerns the appointment of Wal-Mart CEO Lee Scott to an advisory panel to assist the British Treasury on globalization issues:

> The charity War on Want said it was "amazing" that Mr. Brown was "willing to trumpet the fact that he is taking advice from Lee Scott, a chief executive who pays staff low wages yet earned $17.5 m in 2004" . . . Matthew McGregor, War On Want's senior campaigns officer said: " . . . The government should take the lead on making its businesses the most socially responsible in the world, not taking advice from a man whose company is an international byword for exploitation."[6]

Another press release attacks the Walton family as selfish, evil persons who are contemptuous of the public interest:

> Forbes last night released its annual list of "The World's Richest People." . . . Five of the top eleven U.S. billionaires are Waltons . . . Alice Walton spent $35 million to purchase "Kindred Spirits" by Asher B. Durand; it was the most ever paid for an American painting. As a point of comparison, Walton paid over $7 million more for the single painting than the $27.7 million the state of Ohio spends on public health aid for Wal-Mart employees and their children . . . (*Columbus Dispatch*, 2/25/06). The Waltons have joined a coterie of wealthy families trying to save fortunes through permanent repeal of the estate tax.[7]

A reader of Wal-Martwatch.com is led to believe that Wal-Mart is owned by rich persons who rob the taxpayers to support their own conspicuous consumption, is run by a CEO who administers a company that revels in and profits from exploitation, and is engaging in a massive assault on the women of America.

Another website, ilcaonline.org, represents mostly union writers on labor issues, and it lists the motives some cite for their participation in anti–Wal-Mart campaigns:

> For Adam Eidinger, Wal-Mart represents a mass retailer that exploits workers and is now trying to horn in on the organic foods markets with phony organic foods. For Brendan Hoffman, it's the waste of gas as people drive miles through suburban sprawl to Wal-Mart's "big-box" stores, passing up union retailers and mom-and-pop establishments to buy from a firm that imports 60 percent of its goods from China—wasting even more energy. . . . For Nikolas Schiller, it's Wal-Mart's attempt to open a bank in Utah— a bank that, of course, would not help local people and would run other banks out of business. And for Marco Del Fuego, it's Wal-Mart's exploitation of Latino workers, and shoppers.[8]

Again, the word "exploit" or "exploitation" arises. Wal-Mart treats workers badly, these critics say. The allegation that Wal-Mart will run other banks out of business (in a business the company has not even entered as yet!) is a continuation of a theme that Wal-Mart mows down competitors. The reference to "suburban sprawl" picks up on another common theme among the critics, as does the complaint that Wal-Mart buys lots of goods from overseas (although, factually, a majority of its sales comes from non-Chinese goods). The comment that customers are passing up unionized stores to go to nonunionized Wal-Mart reflects the fact that a substantial element of the anti–Wal-Mart opposition is coming from unions.

The intensity of dislike of Wal-Mart sometimes reaches a fever pitch, as one author of an anti–Wal-Mart book candidly admits:

> It's no secret that we hate Wal-Mart. Those Bentonvillains have been under this author's skin for more than twenty-one years

now, and we don't love those blankety-blanks any more now than we ever have—which is not at all. Want to know another of the many things we hate about Wal-Mart? You can't trust it any more than you could trust Satan with a snow cone.[9]

The author goes on to cite examples of allegedly unethical, untrustworthy behavior on Wal-Mart's part. He starts with the fact that around 1990, in response to a new company policy and after nine years of not doing so, Wal-Mart began opening its Pella, Iowa, store on Sundays, despite Sam Walton having allegedly once said that Wal-Mart would not be open on Sundays.

Thus, many of the objections to Wal-Mart are highly emotional and based on some perceived facts, rather than on a full scholarly review of the evidence. For example, any analysis of whether Wal-Mart "exploits" workers would carefully look at what Wal-Mart pays relative to other employers whose workers have similar jobs and skills. Any evaluation of citizens passing up unionized stores to shop at Wal-Mart would have to ask: Why are they doing this? Why do the consumers prefer Wal-Mart to the unionized competitor? If Wal-Mart buys a lot of goods in China, why does it do so? What are the arguments for doing so, aside from the oft-cited arguments against the practices?

One form of reasoning that seems to pervade almost all of the criticism of Wal-Mart is very narrowly based, without much thought of broader implications. For example, Wal-Mart, and by extension other big-box discounters, allegedly cost workers jobs in supermarkets, hardware stores, and so forth. The critics see the very visible individuals who worked for the small hardware store that went out of business, but are more myopic when it comes to the other employment effects of the new big-box stores—the hires at the new store, the new teacher hired at the local high school from incremental property tax revenues received when the store was built, and the effect that increased disposable income of customers (arising from lower prices) has had on their spending in other businesses—say, local restaurants.

Much of the debate about Wal-Mart and other big-box retailers suffers, in our judgment, from the same sort of intellectual myopia that pervades efforts to impose protectionist economic policies. The distinguished economist Murray Weidenbaum once said, "Protectionism is a politician's delight because it delivers visible benefits to the protected parties while imposing the costs as a hidden tax on the public."[10] One might apply the same logic to this issue: Imposing restrictions on Wal-Mart to suit its critics is a delight of politicians and union leaders because it promises to deliver visible benefits to certain protected parties while imposing the costs as a hidden tax on the public.

Having made that point, this chapter is not a comprehensive evaluation of the arguments made by critics of Wal-Mart and other big-box stores. That comes after several chapters of analysis of the economic impact of Wal-Mart and its big-box competitors, especially in chapter 11. At this point, we largely present the arguments of the Wal-Mart critics in a relatively unvarnished fashion, leaving a more detailed critique to follow some background information on the growth of Wal-Mart and other big-box stores, as well as an analysis of their economic effects.

Who Are the Critics?

Are the critics of Wal-Mart and other big-box retailers a more or less random sampling of the American population? While it is true that informal, ad hoc groups of ordinary citizens form coalitions within communities to oppose the latest Wal-Mart (or Home Depot) entry into their towns, the national anti–Wal-Mart movement is led by a disparate group of organizations, most of which have a pronounced left-of-center political orientation. A look at the supporters of Wal-Martwatch.com is instructive.[11] Several of the sponsors are labor unions, led by the Service Employees International Union (SEIU), United Food and Commercial Workers (UFCW), and the Teamsters. A second group of supporters comprises activist left-wing Christian groups, such as Sojourners ("Christians for Justice and Peace"), and the Chicago-based Interfaith Worker Justice.

Other participation comes from environmental groups (notably, the Sierra Club), women's organizations (the National Council of Women's Organizations, an alliance of dozens of different groups), and student groups (Campus Progress). Finally, there are those who might be called the professional Wal-Mart-bashers, persons or groups who have made some money attacking Wal-Mart. Leading them is Al Norman (Sprawl-Busters) and Brave New Films (Robert Greenwald's film company).

Many of these groups are made up of well-meaning persons of the left who genuinely see damages to society from Wal-Mart (the Sierra Club and the religious groups generally fit into this category). A number of the groups, however, have a direct pecuniary interest in the demise or containment of Wal-Mart, notably the unions who have failed to organize Wal-Mart workers (such as the UFCW, SEIU, and the Teamsters), and people like Greenwald and Norman who push their movies and books. As stated above, however, that does not mean their arguments are wrong.

Tactics of Wal-Mart's Critics: Litigation and Legislative Changes

The critics of Wal-Mart fight their battle for public opinion through articles, books, Internet blogs, and the like. But an important strategy is to seek legislative remedies for perceived problems, and to engage in litigation. The critics are no doubt correct that the big-box stores are involved in an inordinate amount of litigation, although much of it has been induced by the critics themselves. One report of the Democratic staff of the House of Representatives Committee on Education and the Workforce, published as *Everyday Low Wages: The Hidden Price We All Pay for Wal-Mart* (referred to as the "Miller Report") cites suits claiming underpayment of wages or unpaid overtime.[12] There are also filings on other labor relations subjects, such as discrimination against women. But these legal actions are not limited to Wal-Mart. For example, Costco, like Wal-Mart, lists employee legal actions over failure to pay overtime and gender discrimination in its 2004 annual report. This is the same Costco that Wal-Mart Watch praises for being unionized and paying higher wages.

Wal-Mart is charged by critics with being the most-sued entity in the United States, outside of the federal government. This should not be surprising. Retailing is one of the largest industries, and Wal-Mart has more employees than any other private business enterprise in the United States. It is a labor-intensive business, and retailers have more daily physical contact with people than occurs in most other sectors. If Wal-Mart is the most sued, it might be because its exposure to legal action is greater than that of other entities—and it has an organized opposition that generates lawsuits in the hope of reversing policies of the company perceived to be wrong.

On the legislative front, Wal-Mart critics have been successful in some areas in persuading city councils, planning commissions, zoning boards, and other agencies with governmental powers to prohibit big-box stores, usually by prohibiting stores larger than a certain size, say, one hundred thousand square feet. At the state level, the most successful effort at this writing has been the passage in Maryland, over the veto of Governor Robert Ehrlich, of a bill requiring Wal-Mart to provide health care benefits for most of its employees (although it was later negated by federal court action). Attempts at passing similar laws have been mounted in a majority of the states, to date largely without success. At the national level, a bevy of anti–Wal-Mart organizations, along with some potential competitors from the financial services industry, has been successful so far in keeping the company out of the banking business.

Big-box stores are criticized for their political activities. The Miller Report is critical of Wal-Mart for contributing to efforts to defeat a California referendum requiring large employers to pay health insurance for all of their employees. The Miller Report also complains that Wal-Mart has recently increased its political donations substantially to both parties, becoming in 2003 the second-largest contributor to federal campaigns. For the nation's largest company to be the second-largest contributor to political campaigns is not remarkable. In fact, Wal-Mart has historically been relatively inactive in political affairs and appears to have become more active only as it has become the object of focused political attack.

One area where we have some sympathy for the position of critics relates to subsidies. The use of the political process to achieve economic ends is not confined to the critics of Wal-Mart, such as labor unions. The company itself has received numerous subsidies for locating in certain areas. In "Shopping for Subsidies: How Wal-Mart Uses Taxpayer Subsidies to Finance its Never Ending Growth," an organization called "Good Jobs First" provides a list of typical subsidies. This includes free or reduced-price land, infrastructure assistance, tax increment financing, property tax breaks, state corporate income tax credits, sales tax rebates, enterprise zone (and other) status, job training and worker recruitment funds, tax-exempt bond financing, and general grants as examples of such subsidies. Good Jobs First claims that Wal-Mart has received more than $1 billion in subsidies, and that 90 percent of its distribution centers have been subsidized.[13]

We cannot vouch for the accuracy of that claim, and will return to the issue of subsidies in chapter 12.

Conclusions

The critics of Wal-Mart are numerous, vocal, and influential. They argue that Wal-Mart (and, often, other big-box stores) have paid substandard wages, given inadequate benefits, cost jobs, destroyed the heart of communities, hurt American manufacturing, promoted urban sprawl, caused environmental problems, engaged in anti-women, anti-minority labor policies, and so on. Their criticisms have been forthcoming in traditional ways, such as labor union picketing and accusatory books, as well as such nontraditional methods as Internet campaigns, documentary movies, and heavy political lobbying (including campaign donations to sympathetic politicians). The accusations against Wal-Mart and other big-box discounters are notable for the sheer number and intensity of complaints. Are these complaints valid? After pausing to examine the evolution of modern retailing, we will return to this question by reviewing the economic impact of big-box stores on the American economy.

PART II

The Wal-Mart Revolution

3

A History of Retail Innovation in America before Wal-Mart

A criticism of Wal-Mart and other big-box discount stores is that they are disturbing the way of life in American towns and cities and destroying traditional retailing. Students of the history of retailing know that very few of these complaints have not already been heard in an earlier era in a slightly different context, directed against the dominant retailers of those times. Yet as innovative, often radically different, approaches to getting goods from manufacturers to customers have emerged in the past, the nation not only has survived them economically and culturally, but it has become a better and more prosperous place because of them.

As indicated earlier, retail innovation creates consumer welfare by reducing the spread between what the manufacturer charges for a product and what the consumer pays for it. Because these spreads were huge in early American history, retail trade was modest in scope. There was less specialization in the production of goods, and thus fewer economies from large-scale production. Reduced specialization also lowered the qualitative advances associated with having experts skilled in making specialized products. The innovations in retail trade have thus not only promoted efficiencies by lowering the cost of the middlemen operating between manufacturer and consumer, but they have also even helped enhance the efficiency of manufacturing itself.

Retailing in America before Wal-Mart

In early America, as in most countries before major industrialization, the population was heavily concentrated in rural areas.[1] Population densities in general were low—fewer than five persons per square mile during the colonial era, for example. In the eighteenth century, less than 5 percent of the population lived in cities, none of which had as many as fifty thousand persons. Additionally, per-capita income levels were low—surely no higher than $2,000 in today's dollars—even as late as 1820. Angus Maddison, perhaps the world's foremost scholar of national income accounting, estimates the U.S. gross domestic product (GDP) in 1820 at $1,257 in 1990 dollars, or about $1,800 today.[2] That contrasts with a current GDP per capita of over $40,000. Thus, the typical American in 1820 took a year to produce what it takes about sixteen days for his counterpart to produce today. Finally, transportation costs were high in nineteenth-century America, and cheap methods of land transportation were nonexistent.

For all these reasons, retail trade was in its embryonic stages before 1800 The most important form of urban retailing was the public market, held as little as once a week or as often as every weekday, where customers purchased food items from farmers. As towns grew, along with the distance between farmers and customers, regular grocery stores sometimes operated. For the vast majority of the population living in rural areas, peddlers sold items carried with them on horseback or, later, on wagons. Farmers would buy from them things that were hard to make on the farm, such as needles and thread, spices, or clocks. In time, there were actually chains of peddlers (a forerunner of things to come), each traveling salesperson having his own territory.[3]

After communities reached a certain size (often fewer than 1,000 persons), general stores opened, selling a variety of items. Western storekeepers made trips perhaps twice a year to the East to buy goods from wholesalers or manufacturers.[4] With the growth of towns beyond some threshold— perhaps 2,500 persons—it became possible to open specialty stores selling only dry goods, such as yarn and cloth and early factory-made clothes, hardware, and farm implements. As towns grew larger still, even more specialty shops opened, such as drugstores, men's clothing stores, and jewelers.

With the passage of time, several factors worked in favor of more extensive retailing, as well as retail innovations. The nation's population grew rapidly—3 percent annually until 1860, and above 2 percent a year into the twentieth century. While the country was expanding west, population densities were rising, as was urbanization. After the Civil War, cities with more than a hundred thousand residents were common, and by the early twentieth century, the urban population exceeded the rural one. Incomes were rising as well, and by the time World War I broke out in 1914, the United States had per-capita output of over $7,000 in current dollars, quadruple the levels of 1820, and the highest in the world.[5]

Meanwhile, the Industrial Revolution had spread to America, and the rising availability of cheap manufactured goods plus increased family income opened the door for expanded retailing. Important also was the Transportation Revolution. The development of improved roads, canals, steamboats, and, above all, the railroad, dramatically lowered the costs of moving goods, reducing the markup needed to provide goods at affordable prices to an increasingly affluent public.

With these changes came new forms of retailing. Beginning about the time of the Civil War, department stores began to emerge in the growing large cities. Some of the names are familiar today—Macy's in New York, Marshall Field in Chicago (recently converted to the Macy name, to the irritation of many Chicagoans), and Wanamaker's in Philadelphia are three examples.[6] The department store combined the choices available in specialty shops with the convenience of the one-stop shopping found in general stores (which generally declined in importance after towns grew beyond about 2,500 in population). Other innovations, such as the development of elevators and advances in architectural techniques that allowed for larger, taller buildings, along with improvements in ventilation and the advent of electricity, were also important in the evolution of the modern, big department store.

In the rural areas following the Civil War, peddlers were increasingly supplanted by mail-order houses. They were led by Montgomery Ward and followed by Sears, Roebuck and Company, a firm that ultimately became the nation's leading retailer until dethroned by Wal-Mart in just the past generation. In the early days, Ward's and Sears operated exclusively by catalogue and serviced orders from massive warehouses in Chicago or other locations. This was a precursor to both the Wal-Mart distribution system and the even more recent Internet sales operations of such companies as Amazon—not to mention Sears itself. The mail-order houses allowed rural Americans to obtain a wide variety of good-quality wares at reasonable prices without leaving home. They had a reputation for integrity, and dissatisfied customers could get their money back for faulty products. While Montgomery Ward was the originator, Sears, Roebuck was more aggressive, and became the largest mail-order firm early in the twentieth century.

A very important development in the post–Civil War period was the emergence of chain stores. In groceries, the pioneer was the Great Atlantic and Pacific Tea Company, better known as the A&P. Shortly before World War I, A&P had over four hundred stores in operation. By buying in large quantities, chains could get goods at lower prices from manufacturers, offering customers somewhat lower prices in the process. Perhaps the greatest retailer of the era, however, was Frank Woolworth, who organized the nation's leading variety-store chain, beginning in 1879. Woolworth had several failures before opening his first successful store in Lancaster, Pennsylvania.

Woolworth's, its leading competitor, S. S. Kresge (which later morphed into the Kmart Corporation), and others (such as W. T. Grant and Ben Franklin stores) were the progenitors of the variety-store concept that was an important feature of small town America as late as 1970, and which helped spawn the modern discount store that is the focus of this book. Woolworth's offered a wide variety of small goods that people needed at very low prices. Until the day he died in 1919, F. W. Woolworth never charged more than a dime for any item in his stores (to be sure, with inflation, that is the equivalent of about $1.10 today).[7] Several factors contributed to his success: he bought goods in large quantities, used open display cases to sell them, and had a reputation for reliability. His wealth grew so much that before World War I he was able to build the tallest building in the world (792 feet) in New York City (a feat replicated two generations later in Chicago by another retailer, Sears, Roebuck).[8]

While the chain stores evolved in the late nineteenth and early twentieth centuries, their period of most aggressive growth was the 1920s, as table 3-1 shows.[9] Pioneering chains like A&P in groceries and Woolworth's in variety stores grew substantially during this period, but the biggest growth came from smaller stores like Kroger and Safeway in groceries, Kresge in variety stores, J. C. Penney in apparel, and Walgreen's in drug stores.

While J. C. Penney's was a major new retailing force, it paled in significance compared to Sears, Roebuck.[10] Founded as a mail-order house,

TABLE 3-1

GROWTH OF SEVEN LEADING CHAIN STORE COMPANIES, 1920–30

Name of Chain	Type of Store	No. of Stores, 1920	No. of Stores, 1930
A&P	Grocery	4,544	15,737
Kroger	Grocery	799	5,165
Safeway	Grocery	191	2,202
F. W. Woolworth	Variety	1,111	1,881
Kresge	Variety	184	678
J. C. Penney	Apparel	312	1,452
Walgreen	Drug	23	440

SOURCE: Godfrey M. Lebhar, *Chain Stores in America, 1859–1959* (New York: Chain Store Publishing Corporation, 1959), 53.

Sears made large investments in retail stores in the 1920s and after, far surpassing leading pioneer Montgomery Ward (which unfortunately followed a very conservative expansion strategy after World War II, fearing the reemergence of the Great Depression). Its operations were viewed as a lower-price alternative to the traditional department stores, offering good and dependable (if not always extremely stylish) merchandise to customers, either through the mail or through their outlet stores. The Sears catalogue became a salvation to people in rural areas and small towns, and the retail outlets, located often in medium-sized and even larger cities, offered the urban shopper a convenient alternative to the more pricy department stores. Even as late as the early 1980s, Sears was the nation's leading retailer in volume, until surpassed first by Kmart and then Wal-Mart.[11]

The department stores, which originally were mostly retail operations centered in single major cities, started to merge early in the twentieth century to form chains as well. The venerable R. H. Macy's, founded in 1858, expanded beyond New York, adding such regional icons as Bullock's and I. Magnin on the West Coast. David May, who started a store in the mining town of Leadville, Colorado, in 1877, ultimately built a chain that encompassed such names as Kaufman's (Pittsburgh), Hecht's (Washington), Foley's (Houston), Wanamaker's (Philadelphia), and Marshall Field's (Chicago).

Smaller regional chains evolved, such as Dillard's (now national in scope) and Belk's in the South. The biggest of them all, particularly since its recent purchase of May Department Stores, is Federated Department Stores. Founded as a holding company in 1929 with such stores as F&R Lazarus (Columbus, Ohio), Abraham & Straus (Brooklyn, New York), and Filene's (Boston), the chain grew over time to include such prominent retailers as Bloomingdale's (New York), Burdines (Miami), and Rich's (Atlanta).[12]

Department stores were opposed by smaller, independent retailers. These merchants sometimes tried to curtail the growth of their bigger competitors through legislation. In 1897, for example, the Chicago City Council passed an ordinance restricting the ability of department stores to sell liquor and meats.[13]

Hostility to chain stores in the middle third of the twentieth century was in many ways similar to the anti–Wal-Mart feelings today, and partly for the same reason. Small local stores could not match the efficiency of the chains, and fought to stop their growth. A comment by the speaker of the Indiana house was not atypical of those fighting the chain stores: "The chain stores are undermining the foundations of our entire local happiness and prosperity. They have destroyed our home markets and merchants."[14] It is no wonder that pleas for "retail price-maintenance" (price-fixing), designed to keep chains from undercutting the prices of the less efficient local providers of goods, were commonplace. Several states tried, with varying degrees of success, to limit chain store growth through legislation. In 1929 and 1930 alone, over 140 anti-chain-store bills were introduced into state legislatures.[15] One successful effort (from the smaller retailer's standpoint) was the passage in 1936 of an amendment to the Clayton Antitrust Act of 1914, called the Robinson-Patman Act. The act was designed to prohibit price discrimination among buyers if the impact of that discrimination was to reduce competition substantially. The companion Miller-Tydings Act of 1937 permitted manufacturers to set retail prices. Advocates called this a "fair trade" law.

Other things being equal, these laws probably had the effect of slowing down chain store growth, but not dramatically. Retailers found ways around them, and the courts were not inclined to fine or jail persons for offering customers a good bargain. For example, in an important 1951 decision, the U.S. Supreme Court ruled for a defendant who had posted liquor prices below the "fair trade" price dictated by the manufacturer. The Court argued that the antitrust laws prohibiting restraint of trade took precedent over the Miller-Tydings Act.[16] An attempt to resurrect the law, the McGuire Act, was similarly left unenforced by the courts and ultimately repealed in 1975.[17] Given the reasoning in chapter 1 above, these so-called fair trade and resale maintenance laws could well be considered protectionist legislation to protect relatively less efficient retailers and reduce the consumer welfare of customers.

Retailing at the Beginning of the Discount Age

In the 1960s, a new type of retail outlet began to develop. Discount stores were relatively large stores which sold a wide variety of goods. A sort of cross between an old general store and a modern department store, discount stores did not offer some of the amenities of department stores, such as free gift-wrapping, home delivery, or stylish in-store restaurants, but they had low prices—and free parking. In time, they came to surpass other forms of retailing. Their story will be told in the next two chapters.

What was American retailing like in, say, 1965, at the very beginning of the era of discount stores? Table 3-2 shows the sales of all retailers with revenues in excess of $1 billion. Since consumer prices have risen more than sixfold since 1965, that is perhaps the equivalent of $6 billion today—large operations even by today's standards.[18] Sears, Roebuck sales were slightly less than 1 percent of total output (GDP), about one-half the size of Wal-Mart's domestic sales in relation to GDP today. Thus Sears was an important national institution, although considerably less dominant in retailing than Wal-Mart is now.

Six of the eleven billion-dollar retailers were in the grocery business (A&P, Safeway, Kroger, Acme, National Tea, and Food Fair). When people "went to the store" they usually were buying groceries and related items. By far, the number one general retailer was Sears, Roebuck, with sales nearly triple those of nearest rival J. C. Penney. The variety store chains, such as F. W. Woolworth, and department store chains like Federated, while not insignificant by any means, were relatively less important. The striking difference from today was the absence of the large, big-box discount

TABLE 3-2
U.S. RETAIL OUTLETS WITH SALES OVER $1 BILLION, 1965

Rank	Company	Sales (in millions of $)
1	Sears, Roebuck & Co.	$6,390
2	A&P	5,119
3	Safeway Stores	2,939
4	Kroger Co.	2,555
5	J. C. Penney Co.	2,289
6	Montgomery Ward	1,748
7	F. W. Woolworth	1,443
8	Federated Dept. Stores	1,331
9	Acme Supermarkets	1,201
10	National Tea	1,162
11	Food Fair	1,120

SOURCE: Information Please, *Information Please Almanac, 1967* (New York: Simon and Schuster, 1966), 607.

chains which dominate the retail scene, or specialty retailers like Home Depot or Best Buy.

The retail-trade industry grew over time with the economy, with retailing becoming somewhat more important over time relative to total employment, in part because of the decline in agricultural work. Figure 3-1 looks at employment in the retail industry for various years in the twentieth century before the discount store revolution.

Employment in retail trade quadrupled between 1900 and 1965, implying a compounded annual growth of over 2 percent a year. The growth in the relative importance of retail trade in the overall labor force is shown in figure 3-2. Employment grew in the period 1900–1965 from 10.2 to 13.6 percent of the labor force, with the relative growth a bit faster in the first three decades than after 1929. It is not likely, however, that the sector's contribution to total output grew quite as fast, as productivity of workers in retailing probably rose less than that of workers in the overall economy because of greater technological advances in other sectors, notably manufacturing. Data limitations, however, restrict our ability to measure precisely the output effects of changes in retail trade.[19]

FIGURE 3-1

EMPLOYMENT (IN THOUSANDS) IN RETAIL TRADE, 1900–1965

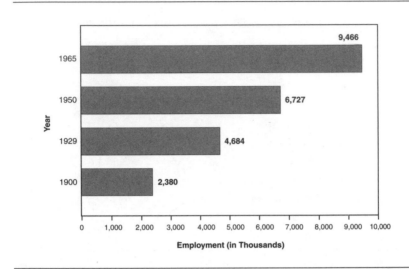

SOURCE: U.S. Bureau of the Census, *Historical Statistics of the United States, Colonial Times to 1970* (Washington, D.C.: Government Printing Office, 1975), 141–42. The 1900 numbers are partially estimated from decennial census data that were classified differently than the later data, and thus are less reliable.

Conclusions

What can we learn from this history? First and foremost, retailing of goods is constantly changing. The farmers' markets, peddlers, and general stores of old, while not completely extinct, have shrunk into insignificance. The variety stores like Woolworth's that were important just forty years ago are largely gone or diminished in importance. As people's incomes and living habits change, so do their shopping habits, and merchants have to change to keep up with tastes and preferences or face oblivion.

The two words key to describing historical trends in American retailing are "growth" and "change." Retailing evolved with rising incomes, improved transportation and communication, and urbanization. From small displays of merchandise by door-to-door salespersons to large department and variety stores with massive quantities of goods on display, retailers changed the scope and nature of their operations to meet

FIGURE 3-2

RETAIL TRADE EMPLOYMENT AS PERCENT OF TOTAL U.S. EMPLOYMENT, 1900–1965

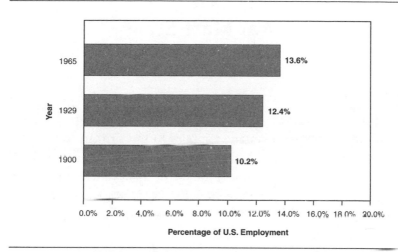

SOURCE: U.S. Bureau of the Census, *Historical Statistics of the United States, Colonial Times to 1970* (Washington, D.C.: Government Printing Office, 1975), 141–42.

the changing demands of a public with rising incomes. Attempts by traditional retailers to slow change through legislation had little effect in the long run. The evolution continues, as the story of Wal-Mart and its imitators discussed in coming chapters indicates.

4

The Wal-Mart Story

The French have a sagacious saying: "The more things change, the more they remain the same." This certainly applies to modern American retail trade. Things have changed enormously in the last generation—but the same thing could have been said about the rise of chain variety and grocery stores around 1930, or the explosive growth of Sears, Roebuck and Montgomery Ward dating still earlier. Change is the norm in retail trade in America. With rising incomes, technological innovations, and different patterns of behavior, American tastes for buying goods have changed.

While there are many dimensions to the change, the rise of the modern, large-scale discount store is easily the most important in recent times. And within that sector, the huge market leadership of Wal-Mart Corporation stands out. After providing a bit of information on the general growth of retail trade since the 1960s (picking up where we left off in the last chapter), we will turn to telling the story of arguably the greatest entrepreneur of the late twentieth century, Sam Walton, and of the highly successful company he and his associates built.

Retail Trade Growth Since 1965: An Overview

Both the dimensions and the nature of retail trade have changed greatly in the past four decades or so. Figure 4-1 shows that, in an inflation-adjusted sense, retail trade has grown considerably, as measured by its contribution to national income. Figure 4-2 shows that as the national income has risen, retail trade's share has remained roughly constant, meaning that retailing has been a fairly dynamic part of a growing economy in a country whose population rose 60 percent in the same time period.

FIGURE 4-1

REAL CONTRIBUTION OF RETAIL TRADE TO U.S. NATIONAL INCOME,
1960–2004 (IN BILLIONS)

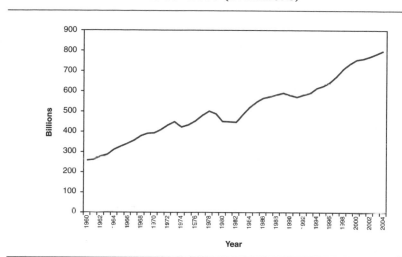

SOURCE: Author's calculations using data from U.S. Department of Commerce, Bureau of Economic Analysis, table 6.1B, "National Income and Product Accounts Table: National Income Without Capital Consumption Adjustment by Industry," *National Economic Accounts*, www.bea.gov/bea/dn/nipaweb/TableView.asp?SelectedTable=168&FirstYear=1985&LastYear=1987&Freq=Qtr (accessed August 13, 2006), and U.S. Department of Labor, Bureau of Labor Statistics, *Consumer Price Index*, ftp://ftp.bls.gov/pub/special.requests/cpi/cpiai.txt (accessed August 13, 2006).

Before turning to discount stores, the single most important innovation and the focus of this book, it should be noted that discounting is certainly not the only new approach to selling goods in modern times. In the 1970s and '80s, a relatively new breed of sophisticated mail-order houses grew greatly in importance, selling clothes (Land's End, Orvis, L. L. Bean, Talbots, and Eddie Bauer, to name a few), electronic and household gadgets (Hammacher Schlemmer, Brookstone, Sharper Image, Frontgate), and a variety of other often unique items to generally upscale customers (Harry and David, with its high quality fruit). In the 1990s, the QVC and Home Shopping networks became important sellers of jewelry and other items over television. And, most significant, of course, Internet selling grew extraordinarily rapidly, especially after 2000, with companies such as Amazon.com and eBay becoming huge successes. Particularly interesting is eBay, which not only uses home shopping through

FIGURE 4-2

RETAIL TRADE SALES AS A PERCENT OF NATIONAL INCOME, 1960–2004

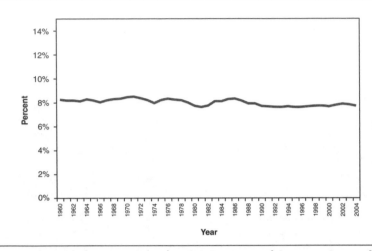

SOURCE: Authors' calculations using data from U.S. Department of Commerce, Bureau of Economic Analysis, table 6.1B, "National Income and Product Accounts Table: National Income Without Capital Consumption Adjustment by Industry," *National Economic Accounts*, www.bea.gov/bea/dn/nipaweb/TableView.asp?SelectedTable=168&FirstYear=1985&LastYear=1987&Freq=Qtr (accessed August 13, 2006).

electronic means, but has virtually created a whole new industry in retailing used merchandise.

Even traditional retailing underwent some serious changes, with the rise of chain stores relative to independent operators in a variety of specialty businesses, such as pharmacies and shoe stores, not to mention department stores. Indoor shopping malls became larger with more attractions—the Mall of America near Minneapolis, for one, drew crowds from around the country—and, as tastes changed in the past decade, they began to be supplemented by malls with detached structures, resembling small downtown areas. But all of these were quantitatively small developments compared with the rise of the large discount store.

Although Sam Walton with his Wal-Mart stores eventually emerged as the king of American discounting, he was not the originator of the concept, nor even an important player during the first two decades of the industry's evolution. If there were a triumvirate of pioneers in the industry, it would probably comprise Marty Chase, Sol Price, and Harry Cunningham.

A Ukrainian immigrant, Martin Chase might have a claim to opening the first discount store.[1] He bought an old abandoned textile mill in Cumberland, Rhode Island, and in late 1953 and early 1954 developed what some regard as the first discount house. His Ann & Hope operation became a small chain that by 1969 did $40 million in sales. Ann & Hope used the then-novel self-service concept, greatly lowering personnel costs. It had ample parking, a relatively rare phenomenon at the time, and the use of central checkouts instead of many smaller ones throughout the store saved labor costs as well. Ann & Hope had a reputation for integrity and a liberal return policy. These, plus large quantities of low-priced goods, made it a hit.

While Marty Chase might have been the first, a far more important industry pioneer was Sol Price, still living at this writing. Price began an operation known as Fed Mart in 1954 in California, and ran it successfully for twenty years, selling out to a German company in 1975. In 1976, Price and his son Robert started Price Club, the first warehouse-style discount firm, which merged into Costco a few years later and remains, somewhat ahead of Sam's Club, the largest warehouse-style retailer in America.

The third of the triad of early pioneers was Harry Cunningham.[2] Sam Walton had enormous respect for Cunningham, saying he was the one "who really designed and built the first discount store as we know it today, and who, in my opinion, should be remembered as one of the leading retailers of all time."[3] Cunningham became CEO of S. S. Kresge, the perennial runner-up to Woolworth's in the variety store business, in 1959. Cunningham brilliantly foresaw the coming demise of variety stores and made massive investments in discount stores, beginning with his first Kmart store in Garden City, Michigan, in 1962. He opened his store the same year that Sam Walton began Wal-Mart but, unlike Walton, was the chief executive of a large corporation with substantial resources. He opened 18 stores in 1962 alone, and by 1966 he had 162 stores, with sales more than doubling in four years and exceeding $1 billion. (Wal-Mart was less than 1 percent of that size at the time.) Kmart continued to grow even after Cunningham retired in 1972, reaching $13 billion in sales by 1980, and briefly surpassing Sears, Roebuck to become America's largest retailer.[4]

Sam Walton

No person has done more to revolutionize modern American retailing than Sam Walton, and no company is nearly as important in contemporary retail history as Wal-Mart. Born in 1918, Walton entered the retail business by opening a Ben Franklin variety store in 1945. An energetic and highly successful operator, Walton started Wal-Mart in 1962. Within a generation, the company was the largest retail firm in the United States, and within a decade of Walton's death in 1992 it had ascended to the top spot of the Fortune 500 list of top corporations, where it remains today.

The accolades used to describe Sam Walton are extraordinary. The former CEO of General Electric, Jack Welch (himself one of the great business leaders of the late twentieth century), said that "Sam Walton understood people the way Thomas Edison understood innovation and Henry Ford, production. He brought out the very best in his employees, gave his best to his customers, and taught something of value to everyone he touched."[5] And, as his longtime business competitor Harry Cunningham of Kmart Stores said, "Sam's establishment of the Walton culture throughout the company was the key to the whole thing. It's just incomparable. He is the greatest businessman of this century."[6]

Walton, arguably the most successful American entrepreneur a decade before the end of the twentieth century, was in many ways uncannily similar to the individual who was the most successful entrepreneur ten years after the beginning of that century, John D. Rockefeller.[7] Let us list twelve:

- Both men were innovators. They did not start the first businesses in their fields, but they were able to take a basic idea and find ways significantly to reduce costs to gain a competitive advantage.

- Both personified the American ideal of working hard, putting in long hours in a passionate pursuit of their goals, and saving large portions of their income.

- Neither Rockefeller nor Walton put on airs, nor lived lavish lives. For example, neither bought luxurious "toys" like big yachts or (in Walton's case) a luxury private jet. They lived very comfortably in very nice homes, but far more modestly than many other businessmen of far smaller wealth.

- Both ran businesses that were vilified as evil by many important writers, business leaders, labor unions, and others, although in Walton's case the criticism intensified after his death, whereas in Rockefeller's case, it came long before.

- These otherwise very shrewd men were slow to engage in public relations work to counteract the criticism of their businesses, even though both had engaging personalities and were actually quite skilled at dealing with criticism. Both thought, more or less, "Our record speaks for itself."

- Both had a very strong desire to succeed, to rise to the top, to be number one. In keeping with the ethics of his times, Rockefeller was far more ruthless in his methods than Walton, but both were very ambitious.

- Both men were religious, attending church regularly. Rockefeller was far more demonstrative in his religious devotion, but both sincerely believed in God and gave time and resources to the church.

- Both were good bosses, excellent in discerning first-rate talent and recruiting and nurturing it. While Walton in particular was an extraordinary motivator of human beings, Rockefeller was good at it as well.

- Both were extremely skilled and tough in dealing with suppliers and getting the best deals possible. Rockefeller negotiated unbelievably favorable deals with railroads, just as Walton did with major suppliers of products. Both were skilled at minimizing transportation costs, Rockefeller through his famous (or infamous) deals with railroads and the adroit purchase of pipelines, Walton through operating a highly efficient nonunion trucking fleet.

- Both men heartily disliked labor unions and were generally successful in keeping them out of their operations.

- Both were dedicated family men, with large numbers of children and devoted wives. Neither had any hint of personal scandal outside his marriage.

- Both were good with numbers, able to calculate the financial impact of potential business decisions accurately and shrewdly.

To be sure, there were differences between the two. Sam Walton was more of an extrovert, serving in his younger years, for example, as the president of service clubs and chambers of commerce in the small towns in which he lived, whereas Rockefeller was more introverted and craved privacy. While both came from ordinary, even moderately poor, backgrounds, Rockefeller's family was poorer, with a more checkered past; Walton's wife came from a prosperous family that provided some financial help to him in the early years.

Far more than Rockefeller, Walton studied his competitors' operations religiously, adopting good ideas and improving upon them. As Sol Price, pioneer in both discount retailing and the warehouse retail store concept has said, "Sam phoned to tell me he was going to start a wholesale club. It was no surprise. He is notorious for looking at what everybody else does, taking the best of it, and then making it better."[8]

One factor Sam Walton himself considered a major contributor to Wal-Mart's success was the beginning of a profit-sharing plan in 1971, which he said "was without a doubt the single smartest move we ever made at Wal-Mart."[9] While profit-sharing was offered partly to help keep out unions, Walton believed that the carrot of building an ownership interest in the company (financed by company contributions) did more to increase loyalty, stimulate innovation, and reduce employee turnover (and therefore training costs) than anything else he ever did.

Like Rockefeller, Walton was incredibly tight—cutting costs to the bone. For example, he forbade employees traveling in groups to have single hotel rooms because of the added expense. He resisted buying a corporate jet until the company was quite large. He combed expense accounts for examples of conspicuous and expensive consumption. He tried, most often successfully, to cut out the expenses of dealing with wholesalers by going directly to manufacturers to buy products. In a business where profit margins tended to be small, a series of seemingly little cost-cutting moves could have a big impact on profits. He also realized that the sensitivity of customers to prices was pretty high, and that most often you could make a greater profit by accepting a small (say, 15–20 percent) markup on goods and having a huge volume, than by marking them up 35–40 percent or more and selling few of them. In the jargon of economics, he realized the demand for most goods he sold was highly elastic. Walton never lost sight of the most important factor in his success—namely, having satisfied customers.

The Growth of Wal-Mart

Sam Walton was in business for seventeen years before he opened his first Wal-Mart. After attending college (where he worked his way through school with a variety of small business ventures) and serving in World War II, Walton entered the retail business by buying a Ben Franklin franchised store in Newport, Arkansas, in 1945 for $25,000, mostly borrowed from his wife Helen's parents. He used zany promotions (for instance, putting popcorn or ice cream machines on the street in front of the store) and attractive pricing, got some merchandise cheap from suppliers other than Ben Franklin itself, and worked very hard. In these ways, Walton increased the sales of that first Ben Franklin from $72,000 in the year before he owned it to $105,000 in the first year of operation, growing to $175,000 within a couple of years. After the lease on the building was not renewed in 1950, Sam moved to Bentonville, Arkansas, and began a Ben Franklin store there. Using a self-service approach to reduce labor costs, along with publicity-creating promotional activities, Walton again was successful, and within a few years was expanding his variety store operations to new locations. Always the innovator, by the late 1950s Sam had bought a small airplane to scout out locations for new stores from the air. In 1960, the Walton operation had expanded to fifteen variety stores with sales of $1.4 million.

Sam Walton was increasingly interested in the discount house concept that was beginning to develop a significant presence in some parts of the country. After flying around the nation investigating various operations, he decided to open a Wal-Mart store in 1962. The first Wal-Mart in Rogers, Arkansas, was less than one-tenth the size of many of today's modern "supercenters." But it did a million dollars in sales annually, several times the volume of other Walton stores. By opening this (and most other Wal-Mart stores for many years) in small towns rather than larger cities, Wal-Mart attained a very strong market position, without serious local competition. This flew in the face of conventional retail wisdom, which suggested that large stores were not viable in less than medium-sized cities—say, of fifty thousand or more people.

Wal-Mart instituted a number of practices that permitted it to sell goods at lower prices than competitors and still make a nice profit. These included ruthlessly bargaining with suppliers, cutting out wholesalers, and doing little advertising. The company began operating its own nonunionized and efficient trucking fleets, using computers to order and keep track of inventories and sales (thus minimizing inventories and increasing customer satisfaction), and cutting travel and other costs to the bone.

With the passage of time, the geographic area of Wal-Mart stores expanded. In the 1972 fiscal year (mostly calendar year 1971), a decade after the Wal-Mart concept was introduced into Arkansas, the firm operated in five states—Arkansas, Kansas, Louisiana, Missouri, and Oklahoma—with only a minor presence in Louisiana and Kansas. It expanded, however, both intensively (building more stores in existing market areas) and extensively (adding new states). For example, by 1975, the year the company passed one hundred stores, it had developed a modest presence in Kentucky, Mississippi, and Tennessee. But Wal-Mart also greatly increased saturation of existing states. For example, in fiscal year 1972, Wal-Mart had six stores in Oklahoma; three years later, the number had grown to fifteen. One factor constraining the growth of new stores was that Sam Walton wanted to build them within three hundred to three hundred fifty miles from the distribution center in Bentonville, to minimize transportation costs and allow merchandise to reach the stores quickly after being ordered. The long-run solution to this problem, of course, was the opening of more distribution centers.

Table 4-1 shows the growth in sales of the company from its last years as a private firm (technically, the operation was a series of companies, one for each store, with store managers having a financial interest in the operations they managed), through its move to a public company in 1970 and, in 1972, as a company traded on the New York Stock Exchange. During the

TABLE 4-1

SALES, PROFITS, AND PROFIT MARGINS, WAL-MART STORES,
FISCAL YEARS 1968–75

Fiscal Year	Sales	After-Tax Profits	Profit Margins[1]
1968	$12,618,754	$481,754	3.82%
1969	21,365,081	605,211	2.83
1970	30,862,859	1,187,764	3.85
1971	44,286,012	1,651,599	3.73
1972	78,014,164	2,907,354	3.73
1973	124,889,141	4,591,469	3.68
1974	167,560,892	6,158,520	3.68
1975	236,208,880	6,353,336[2]	3.68[2]

NOTES: 1. After-tax profits divided by sales. 2. Earnings lowered because of an accounting change. Profit margins are stated based on the old accounting rules for comparability purposes.
SOURCES: Wal-Mart, *Wal-Mart Annual Report, 1972,* 6, walmartstores.com/Files/1972AR.pdf; Wal-Mart, *Wal-Mart Annual Report, 1975,* 2, walmartstores.com/Files/1975AR.pdf (both accessed June 29, 2006).

space of seven years in the late 1960s and early 1970s, the company's sales grew at an extraordinary compounded annual rate of 52 percent. Profits rose in lockstep with sales, with profit margins in all years save one ranging in the very narrow range of 3.68 to 3.85 percent of sales.

Two things are striking about the data in table 4-1, in addition to the remarkable growth. First, as indicated, Wal-Mart's profits grew with sales— but there is no indication that the company "exploited" customers by extracting ever-greater profit margins as it gained certain economies of large-scale operation. Second, the company grew through slow years (a recession in 1970, a bigger recession in 1974) as well as good ones, seeming invulnerable to economic downturns.

Despite an almost exponential growth in sales and profits in the early years, Wal-Mart was not an enormously hot stock after it went public. In the first five years of being listed on the New York Stock Exchange, the price of the stock did not move upward, despite sharply rising profits and sales. Interestingly, the stock price at the opening bell on August 25, 1972, the first day of Big Board trading, was $32.50—almost precisely what the opening

Figure 4-3

The Price of Wal-Mart Stock, August 1972 to August 1977

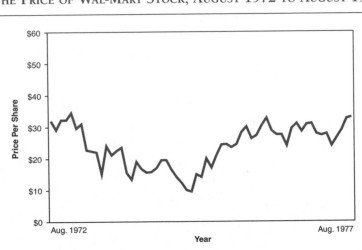

Source: Yahoo Finance, "Historical Prices," http://finance.yahoo.com/q/hp?s=WMT (accessed June 29, 2006).

price would be (after adjusting for a stock split) five years later, on August 25, 1977. As figure 4-3 indicates, the price showed little change over the period, actually trending down for a time in inflation-adjusted terms in the inflationary, high-unemployment environment of the 1970s. There appears to have been no awareness among mainstream investors that Wal-Mart was more than a temporarily successful regional phenomenon as investors, like competitors, consistently and persistently underestimated Sam Walton and his company.

While the thirteen years after the opening of the first Wal-Mart were a time of great accomplishment, even at the beginning of 1975 the company was a very small operator compared to such retail giants as Sears, Roebuck, Kmart, and J. C. Penney. A decade later, however, Sam Walton was acknowledged as America's richest man, and Wal-Mart had moved from successful regional discounter to the most highly regarded and profitable retail firm in the world.

The financial dimensions of the progression are documented in table 4-2. Profits in 1985 were greater than *sales* a decade earlier. Sales growth slowed to an average annual compounded rate of "only" 39.2 percent a

TABLE 4-2

SALES, PROFITS, AND PROFIT MARGINS, WAL-MART STORES,
FISCAL YEARS 1975–85

Fiscal Year	Sales[1]	After-Tax Profits[1]	Profit Margins[2]
1975	$236,209	$6,353	2.69%
1976	340,331	11,132	3.27
1977	478,807	16,039	3.35
1978	678,456	21,191	3.12
1979	900,298	29,447	3.27
1980	1,248,176	41,151	3.30
1981	1,655,262	55,682	3.36
1982	2,462,647	82,794	3.36
1983	3,398,687	124,140	3.65
1984	4,702,940	196,244	4.05
1985	6,453,028	270,767	4.20

NOTES: 1. All dollar amounts in thousands. 2. After-tax profits divided by sales.
SOURCES: Wal-Mart, *Wal-Mart Annual Report, 1975*, 2, http://walmartstores.com/Files/1975AR.pdf; *Wal-Mart Annual Report, 1985*, 14–15; http://walmartstores.com/Files/1985AR.pdf (both accessed June 29, 2006).

year. Profits grew even faster as profit margins rose, although the 1985 figure of 4.2 percent was not dramatically higher than the 1968 figure of 3.8 percent.[10] Stores grew in size and in numbers, adding one or two states per year in the early 1980s, with Wal-Marts opening in twenty states, mostly in the South and Midwest, by 1985. There were now 745 stores in place—seven times as many as a decade earlier—with average sales per store of around $8.7 million, compared to less than $2.3 million a decade earlier. Even allowing for the considerable inflation of this period, per-store sales approximately doubled.

While a large part of the growth was simply a matter of more stores being opened in more locations, there were also continual efforts to refine the business model and improve upon it.[11] Both stores and distribution centers became bigger, and the move to the innovative Wal-Mart computerized inventory control system was well under way. Wal-Mart could operate with low in-store inventories in relation to sales, conserving working

FIGURE 4-4

VALUE OF $1,000 INVESTED IN WAL-MART STOCK ON AUGUST 25, 1972

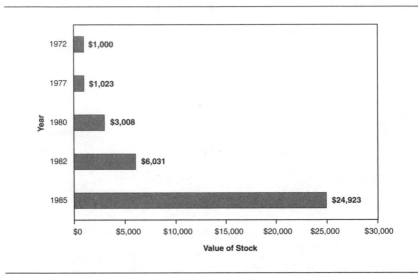

SOURCE: Yahoo Finance, "Historical Prices," http://finance.yahoo.com/q/hp?s=WMT (accessed June 29, 2006); authors' calculations.

capital. But the company also started the first of three major departures from the traditional business model when it added Sam's Club in 1983. As Sol Price observed, Sam Walton was not shy about adopting ideas of competitors, in this case Price Club (later Costco). Starting in the early 1980s, he opened large, warehouse-style discount operations designed more for small businesses than individual consumers.

What a difference a decade made. As figure 4-4 shows, investors in Wal-Mart were richly rewarded after 1977, with nearly a twenty-five-fold appreciation in the stock price by August 25, 1985, the thirteenth anniversary of the stock's listing on the Big Board. By then, Wal-Mart was a major American corporation highly valued by investors.

If the decade of 1965–75 was the time when Wal-Mart became a significant regional chain, and 1975–85 was spent achieving national prominence, 1985–95 was when the company became America's dominant retailer. While these last years were somewhat bittersweet because of the death of founder Sam Walton in 1992, sales continued to grow rapidly, though at a considerably less torrid pace of 23.7 percent a year (see table 4-3). Profit growth was

TABLE 4-3

SALES, PROFITS, AND PROFIT MARGINS, WAL-MART STORES,
FISCAL YEARS 1985–95

Fiscal Year	Sales[1]	After-Tax Profits[1]	Profit Margins[2]
1985	$6,401	$271	4.23%
1986	8,451	327	3.87
1987	11,909	451	3.79
1988	15,959	628	3.94
1989	20,649	838	4.06
1990	25,811	1,076	4.17
1991	32,602	1,291	3.96
1992	43,887	1,609	3.67
1993	55,484	1,995	3.60
1994	67,344	2,333	3.46
1995	82,494	2,681	3.25

NOTES: 1. All dollar amounts in millions. 2. Profits divided by sales. A restatement of 1985 sales leads to slightly different sales and profit margins from those reported in table 4-2.
SOURCE. Wal-Mart, *Wal-Mart Annual Report, 1995*, 12–13, http://walmartstores.com/Files/1995AR.pdf (accessed June 26, 2006)

slightly less rapid as well, as profit margins tended to fall, but they never deviated from the 3.2–4.2 percent range, consistent with earlier periods. The company gained greater efficiencies from greater scale economies, improved inventory controls, and made other changes, but these measures did not increase profit margins. Rather, the gross margin in the entire discount industry (the markup on merchandise) declined sharply—to the benefit of customers. Sam Walton put it well shortly before his death in 1992 when he observed, "The percentage of gross margin in this industry . . . has dropped steadily from around 35 percent in the early sixties to only 22 percent today."[12]

It was during 1985–95 that Wal-Mart truly went national, expanding by the 1995 fiscal year to forty-nine states (all but Vermont). As late as 1990 there were no Wal-Mart stores in California. Five years later there were seventy-eight, not to mention twenty-six Sam's Club outlets. Additionally during this period, the company undertook a second significant alteration

FIGURE 4-5

VALUE OF A 1972 WAL-MART STOCK INVESTMENT IN 1985–1995

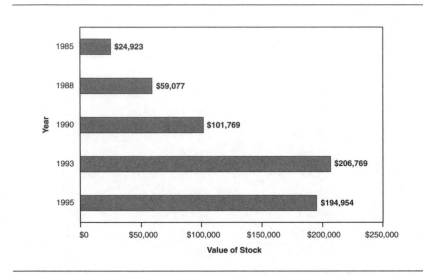

SOURCE: Yahoo Finance, "Historical Prices," http://finance.yahoo.com/q/hp?s=WMT (accessed June 29, 2006); authors' calculations.

to its business model, expanding beyond the nation's borders into Canada, Mexico, and Hong Kong.

The third major change in the original business model also occurred at this time: the introduction of Wal-Mart Supercenters. Supercenters were even larger than traditional Wal-Mart discount stores, adding groceries to general merchandise. This bold move eventually made Wal-Mart the largest grocery operation in the country, larger than such mainstay chains as Kroger, Safeway, and Albertsons.

Investors in Wal-Mart stock shared mightily in the company's prosperity, aided by a general rise in the stock market. As figure 4-5 shows, an initial $1,000 investment in Wal-Mart stock in 1972, worth nearly $25,000 by 1985, had increased roughly eightfold in value again by a decade later (to nearly $200,000), despite some moderate decline in the stock's price in 1993–95. On the whole, Wall Street was high on the company, finally realizing that the long record of double-digit growth in sales and profits might be far more enduring than earlier pundits had predicted.

TABLE 4-4

SALES, PROFITS, AND PROFIT MARGINS, WAL-MART STORES,
FISCAL YEARS 1995–2005

Year	Sales[1]	After-Tax Profits[1]	Profit Margins
1995	$82,494	$2,681	3.25%
1996	93,627	2,740	2.93
1997	104,859	3,056	2.91
1998	117,958	3,526	2.99
1999	137,634	4,430	3.22
2000	165,013	5,377	3.26
2001	180,787	6,235	3.45
2002	204,011	6,592	3.23
2003	229,616	7,955	3.46
2004	256,329	9,054	3.53
2005	285,222	10,267	3.60

NOTE: 1. All dollar amounts in millions.
SOURCE: Wal-Mart, *Wal-Mart Annual Report 2005*, 22–23, www.walmartstores.com/Files/2005AnnualReport.
pdf (accessed August 11, 2006); authors' calculations.

In the last decade (1995–2005), the company continued to grow, becoming the largest corporation in the world in terms of sales. Yet at the same time, continued expansion became more challenging. Sales growth slowed substantially to 13.2 percent a year, barely half that of the previous decade (see table 4-4). The company was still very prosperous, exhibiting profit increases every year, and actually increasing profit margins a bit during this period, although the 2005 figure was almost precisely the same as for 1968—before Wal-Mart was even a publicly held corporation. By fiscal year 2005, the corporation's after-tax profits of over ten billion dollars were seventh among U.S. corporations, behind only two petroleum companies, which had a boom year because of high oil prices (Exxon Mobil and Chevron Texaco), two financial service companies (Citigroup and American International Group), and General Electric and Pfizer.[13] Its profits were several times those of such former industrial icons as General Motors and Ford.

With the passage of time, the retail emphasis changed. By 2005, there were significantly more supercenters than conventional discount stores. Together, however, Wal-Mart stores in the United States (including supercenters and "Neighborhood Markets," which are smaller, grocery-oriented stores) constituted barely two-thirds of the company's total sales, although they had nearly 460 million square feet of selling space, the equivalent of over ten square miles.[14] And while Sam's Club contributed 13 percent of sales, nearly 20 percent were international (compared with none thirteen years earlier, before Sam Walton's death).

Clearly, the growth area of the firm was the international sales, which far more than doubled from 2000 to 2005. The company has a major presence in Brazil, Britain, and Germany and has been in Argentina, Canada, and Mexico, although, in a rare retreat, it recently pulled out of Korea. There are clearly major hopes for expansion in China, where a modest joint-venture investment has already been made. About 30 percent of the increase in operating income from 2000 to 2005 came from international operations, a proportion that inevitably will grow in the future.

With growth and increased prominence come problems and challenges as well as power and affluence. Like the Standard Oil Trust run by John D. Rockefeller at the beginning of the previous century, Wal-Mart's number one position in terms of sales makes it a highly visible target for those unhappy with American capitalism, or with specific business practices. The increase of Wal-Mart critics in number and visibility imposes costs on the company for lawyers, public relation firms, lobbyists, and advertising, as well as sometimes preventing it from taking advantages of opportunities (as when a community or even a nation passes laws or zoning restrictions that are targeted at Wal-Mart).

Additionally, the company has largely saturated the American market. The average American household today spends about two thousand dollars annually in Wal-Mart stores. While this may grow with time with population and economic growth, the possibilities of huge percentage increases in sales have peaked domestically. Internationally, the opportunities are large (particularly with the company moving into China in a major way), but differences in laws, customs, political risks, and consumer tastes put Wal-Mart at some disadvantage relative to local entrepreneurs, who know the business and political environment better.

Another challenge faces Wal-Mart in the domestic market that still provides the vast majority of the company's profits and revenues. As Americans become more affluent, they become a bit more upscale, wanting more stylish clothing, demanding tidier and less cluttered stores, and being slightly less sensitive to prices. Wal-Mart has stuck to Sam Walton's old policy of minimizing prices to customers, a policy that had much to commend it (and still does, probably), but which may need to be modified as the economy itself changes. As we will see in the next chapter, some other retail chains have actually had better records of growth in domestic sales than Wal-Mart in recent years. Wal-Mart itself is not oblivious to this, and in 2005 began what has been termed a "big makeover," introducing more upscale merchandise in an attempt to reach out to more middle- and upper-income shoppers, a move that has both considerable potential and considerable risk.[15]

Sam Walton himself was concerned about the problems of "bigness." As he said late in his life, "The bigger Wal-Mart gets, the more essential it is that we think small. . . . Even by thinking small, can a $100 billion retailer really function as efficiently and productively as it should? Or would maybe five $20 billion companies work better?"[16] Also relevant today with respect to competitors' recent gains relative to Wal-Mart was Sam's observation that "those companies out there who aren't thinking about the customer and focusing on the customer's interests are just going to get lost in the shuffle."[17]

A look at the behavior of Wal-Mart stock shows how perceptions have changed, reflecting some of the concerns cited above. Figure 4-6 shows what a $1,000 initial investment in Wal-Mart stock in 1972 would be worth on August 25 (the date the company's stock initially went on the Big Board) of several recent years. The value of the stock continued to surge in the late 1990s, quadrupling in five years. Yet since 2000, though the price showed a modest increase for a time, it subsequently tumbled some, and as of late 2005 was below what it was five years earlier. There is a growing perception that Wal-Mart is vulnerable, either because of the rise in criticism, the slowdown in sales growth, the insurgence of competitors, or a combination of all of these things.

To be sure, the price of Wal-Mart stock reflects, in addition to fundamental financial conditions at the company and perceptions about its future, the overall mood of the nation regarding common stocks. In figure

FIGURE 4-6

VALUE OF $1,000 OF WAL-MART STOCK PURCHASED ON AUGUST 25, 1972

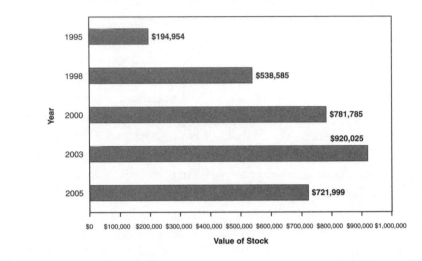

SOURCE: Yahoo Finance, "Historical Prices," http://finance.yahoo.com/q/hp?s=WMT (accessed June 29, 2006); authors' calculations.

FIGURE 4-7

CHANGING PRICE OF WAL-MART STOCK VS. THE S&P 500 INDEX, 1995–2005

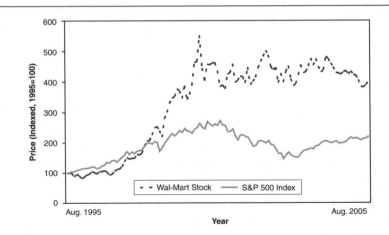

SOURCE: Yahoo Finance, "Historical Prices," http://finance.yahoo.com/q/hp?s=WMT (accessed June 29, 2006).

4-7, we look at the price of Wal-Mart stock over the period 1995–2005 (adjusted for a stock split in 1999), relative to the Standard & Poor's 500 stock index.

While over the long run (the entire period), Wal-Mart easily outperformed the overall market, that has not continued to be true in recent years. Since hitting an all-time high in March 2002, the price of stock (as of this writing) has actually declined well over 25 percent, while the broader-based S&P index rose more than 10 percent. While this is not the first time Wal-Mart has had a relative decline in stock price, it is a rather long and quantitatively large one, with the stock currently selling at a lower price in relation to earnings than that of many competitors, such as Target Stores.

Having pointed out the negatives, however, it is worth noting that Wal-Mart remains an enormously successful company, one whose earnings have grown every single year for at least thirty-seven years. (Though we lack data to confirm it, earnings probably have grown every year since Sam Walton set up shop in Bentonville, Arkansas, in 1960.) The rate of return on stockholder equity has been around 20 percent a year—a very high return compared to the typical firm. In the twenty-one fiscal years from 1985 to 2005, the rate of return varied from 18.7 percent to 37.1 percent. The 2005 return of 22.1 percent was the second highest in the past decade.[18] In short, there is still a lot of life, vitality, and profitability to the company, even as it passes through corporate middle age.

Conclusions

The retail trade industry has continued to grow with the economy as a whole over the past several decades. Like the rest of the economy, retailing has seen massive amounts of change, including such new concepts as online and television shopping, specialty mail-order companies, and so forth. Most important, however, is the rise of the modern general merchandise discount store.

Wal-Mart is the foremost operator in the discount store industry. Sam Walton worked hard to find ways to maintain low prices, including operating an outstanding computerized system for controlling inventories, keeping a tight rein on expenses, and eschewing heavy advertising. He used his entrepreneurial talents to make Wal-Mart the market leader in retailing, far outdistancing older icons like Sears, Roebuck and other new upstart discounters like Kmart.

The history of the retail trade industry, however, is a history of change. Those who are slow to embrace change, like Sears was in the 1970s and 1980s, will get lost in the shuffle. Perhaps Wal-Mart needs to spin off Sam's Club into a separate corporation, aggressively push Internet shopping, open an upscale chain that offers value but pushes more expensive merchandise, or even buy specialty retailers.

The more things change, the more they remain the same. Among the recent changes has been the emergence of a whole class of strong competitors to Wal-Mart, many of whom have emulated its techniques, just as Sam Walton did with earlier competitors in the process of building his retail empire. To the followers and imitators of Wal-Mart we now turn.

5

Imitators and Innovators

The Rise of Big-Box Stores: Wal-Mart's Competitors

As indicated in the previous two chapters, Wal-Mart did not rise in isolation as a new concept in retailing. Some of today's major names in big-box discounting, such as Target, actually predate Wal-Mart as a corporation. Today's largest retail operators are just another innovation in a dynamic industry that has seen many companies come and go, and big-box stores, having grown with the American suburbs, represent the latest iteration. This chapter is about some of the firms other than Wal-Mart and their role in the industry's development.

In fiscal year 2005 (2004/2005) there were eleven big-box retailers in the United States with annual revenues exceeding $10 billion. Table 5-1 provides summary financial information on the largest U.S. big-box operators.[1] (Some of the world's largest big-box store operators are headquartered outside the United States. These are described in chapter 10.)

Of course, Wal-Mart is by far the largest big-box operator. It is not the most profitable, however, in relation either to sales or invested capital. In 2005, the consumer electronics operator Best Buy earned the highest ratio of net profit to invested capital. (Although Kmart's ratio was actually higher, this was apparently something of a statistical anomaly related to its recent emergence from bankruptcy protection.) Wal-Mart and Home Depot had returns on invested capital almost as high as Best Buy's, followed closely by Lowe's and Staples.

Further, Wal-Mart is not the fastest growing big-box operator. Over the past five years, Best Buy and Lowe's have grown faster, and Target has achieved growth only slightly below that of Wal-Mart. Over the past ten

TABLE 5-1

BIG-BOX RETAILERS WITH MORE THAN $10 BILLION IN SALES,
FISCAL YEAR 2005

	Annual Volume (Billions)	Net Profit (Billions)	Return on Invested Capital	Compound Average Annual Growth (5 Years)	Compound Average Annual Growth (10 Years)	Inventory Turn
SUPERCENTER						
Wal-Mart	$285.2	$10.3	20.8%	12.8%	13.8%	7.5
Target	$46.8	$3.2	14.5%	11.7%	NA	5.8
Kmart	$19.7	$1.1	24.7%	−11.9%	−4.9%	4.5
MEMBERSHIP						
Costco	$52.9	$1.1	12.0%	10.5%	11.2%	11.5
HOME IMPROVEMENT						
Home Depot	$73.1	$5.0	20.7%	9.8%	19.3%	4.8
Lowe's	$36.5	$2.2	18.9%	18.0%	19.6%	4.0
CONSUMER ELECTRONICS						
Best Buy	$27.4	$1.0	22.1%	17.1%	18.4%	7.3
Circuit City[1]	$10.5	$0.1	3.0%	−0.1%	NA	5.4
OFFICE SUPPLIES						
Staples	$14.4	$0.7	17.2%	6.2%	15.0%	6.5
Office Depot	$13.6	$0.3	10.4%	5.7%	12.3%	6.6
OTHER						
Toys R Us	$11.1	$0.3	5.8%	−1.7%	2.3%	4.0

NOTE: 1. Growth rate is over four years.
SOURCE: Annual reports of relevant corporations 2004/2005.

years, Lowe's, Home Depot, Best Buy, and Staples all experienced faster growth than Wal-Mart. The imitators and followers of the Wal-Mart big-box model are slowly closing the gap between themselves and the retail giant.

A majority of the big-box retailers other than Wal-Mart are *not* in the business of being the equivalent of discount department stores, selling many different types of goods, ranging from clothing to snow shovels to picture frames. Rather, they are specialty retailers, emphasizing electronics or office supplies or home improvement products or toys, or selling in large quantities via the warehouse store concept.

One of the principal keys to success in retailing is maximizing "inventory turn," the ratio of annual sales to the cost of merchandise ("cost of sales") on hand at any given time. Different sectors of the big-box industry experience different inventory turn ratios because of variations in product mix and corporate strategy. This is evident from the data in table 5-1. Membership warehouses tend to have the highest inventory turns because of their more limited product selection, which is skewed toward merchandise that sells quickly. The world's leading membership warehouse, Costco, illustrates the point, with by far the best inventory turn ratio among the large big-box operators.

Within the categories, there is also a clear relationship between higher inventory turn and performance. Among the supercenter operators, Wal-Mart (7.5) and Target (5.8) are the leaders in inventory turn, as well as profitability. In other words, Wal Mart "turns over," or sells items in stock, an average of 7.5 times a year, compared with 5.8 times for Target. Put differently, the stock of goods that Wal-Mart needs to maintain on hand is smaller in relation to its annual sales (since the goods sell quicker), reducing its capital costs in terms of inventory. To be sure, Wal-Mart's better inventory turn ratio among the general merchandise retailers reflects, in part, the higher product turnover rate inherent in the membership warehouse business, with Sam's Club representing approximately 13 percent of sales. On the other hand, recently bankrupt Kmart has historically experienced and continues to experience inferior inventory turn ratios.

Table 5-2 shows the recent movement of several top retail companies, including some that are not big-box discounters, in the Fortune 500 rankings. Note that while some retailers such as Wal-Mart, Home Depot, Best Buy, and, to a lesser extent, Costco have moved up sharply over time, others, including Sears, Kmart, and J. C. Penney have declined significantly. As a general proposition, the big-box retailers have shown marked gains, relative both to the economy as a whole and to other retailers. Some of the traditional retailers that have remained fairly stable in the Fortune 500 rankings over time, notably Federated Department Stores, have done so only by making big acquisitions that have disguised otherwise notable downward trends.

TABLE 5-2
FORTUNE 500 RANKINGS OF TEN LEADING RETAILERS, 1995–2005

Company	1995	1998	2002	2005
Wal-Mart	4	4	1	1
Home Depot	77	44	18	13
Kroger	25	36	22	21
Target	30	34	34	27
Costco	47	53	44	29
Sears[1]	9	16	32	45
J. C. Penney	32	25	42	74
Best Buy	373	199	131	77
Kmart[1]	15	23	40	113
Fed. Dept. Stores	141	83	118	133

NOTE: 1. Before the merger of Sears and Kmart.
SOURCE: *Fortune Magazine*, "Fortune 500: 1995–2005," http://money.cnn.com/magazines/fortune/fortune500_archive/full/1995/ (accessed September 8, 2006).

Discount Department Stores and Supercenters

Wal-Mart, Target Stores, and Kmart are the largest national operators of discount department stores and supercenters, although others, such as Meijers and Fred Meyer, are important in some regions of the country. Wal-Mart is by far the largest, with annual sales now exceeding $300 billion, including foreign sales. This greatly exceeds the combined total of its next five highest-volume competitors. (That is especially true if one measures bigness by profits—two of the next five largest retailers lost money in 2005, although some, such as Home Depot, actually had considerably higher profit margins on sales than Wal-Mart.)

Target. Target is the second-largest operator of discount department stores and supercenters in the United States, with 2004/2005 sales of $47 billion. In 2004, net profits were $3.2 billion, representing a 14.5 percent return on stockholder's equity—a perfectly respectable return, although well below that of Wal-Mart. Target has experienced fairly strong growth, about equaling that of Wal-Mart over the past five years. Sales volumes have doubled since the late 1990s, when Target's annual volume was a full one-third below that of Kmart. Target has now more than doubled Kmart's volume.

Target has a distinguished pedigree, having descended from well-known names in U.S. retailing. Target was established as a unit of Dayton's, the large Minneapolis area department store chain. Dayton's later merged with Detroit's J. L. Hudson to form Dayton-Hudson, which eventually purchased Chicago's Marshall Field's. In 2000, the company was renamed "Target Stores." It divested itself of conventional department stores when it sold its Dayton-Hudson operations to May Department Stores (itself acquired by Federated Department Stores the following year) in 2004. Thus, the company has gone from being a department store chain that also operated a discount operation to a discount retailer that has shed its sluggish and less profitable department stores. In this sense, Target's transformation is much like that of Kmart a generation earlier, when the S. S. Kresge company, a variety store chain, opened a discount division and later got out of the variety store business.

Though less than one-fourth the size of Wal-Mart, Target has managed to differentiate itself from its bigger rival in several ways. It places less emphasis on groceries in its supercenter-sized stores. Most importantly, it appeals to a somewhat more affluent class of customers than Wal-Mart, and sells somewhat more upscale goods, particularly apparel items. It is not as small-town in its origins as Wal-Mart, growing out of an operation centered in major metropolitan areas.

In recent years Target's same-store sales growth has often exceeded Wal-Mart's, and the bigger retailer is taking countermeasures to try to imitate its smaller competitor. For example, Target created "Global Bazaar" stores, based on the concept of selling chic home furnishings in a strikingly handsome setting. Wal-Mart's prototype response to this highly successful innovation was Wal-Mart Store #5260. The venture has won kudos from at least one veteran industry observer, who offers "condolences-in-advance to Target when roll-out meets rollback!"[2]

Kmart. Kmart was established by the S. S. Kresge Company, the nation's third-largest operator of variety stores. At the beginning of the 1960s, it started in the discount store business at almost exactly the same time Sam

Walton began in rural Arkansas. Through Kmart, Kresge made the transition from pre–World War II–style retailing to the big-box model that was to become dominant by the late twentieth century. This was an impressive feat, in light of the inability of other firms, such as W. T. Grant, G. C. Murphy, McCrory, Kress, and Newberry, to make the transition. F. W. Woolworth, which had previously been the largest variety store operator, established its own Woolco stores division to compete in the discount department store market, but it closed the chain in 1984. Its Canadian Woolco operation was sold to Wal-Mart in 1994. Woolworth's has since become the "Foot Locker," specializing in sports apparel.

For many years before Wal-Mart eventually surpassed it, Kmart was the nation's largest discount department store chain. With sales peaking in 2000 at $37 billion, Kmart employed more than 230,000 people at its height. However, one successful transition was not enough. In the 1990s and early 2000s, Kmart encountered serious difficulties. The company had invested in a number of firms outside its core business, once owning, for example, a controlling stake in Borders, OfficeMax, the Sports Authority, and various international concerns. Each of these interests was sold along with such core business units outside the United States as Kmart of Canada, Kmart of Mexico, a chain of Eastern European stores, and the company's automobile service centers.

The 1995 annual report indicates that the company had experienced a high rate of "stockouts," which encouraged people to shop at competitors whose inventory control was better. Moreover, the company had accumulated a large amount of "aged, discontinued inventory." The same letter contains a hint of what was to come. In describing the fact that more than two hundred stores had been closed, the chairman commented, "Some people have asked why we don't close another 500 stores; the answer is because we don't need to, with the exception of 30 to 50 more stores that we plan to close this year."[3]

In fact, six hundred additional store closings were eventually to follow. There was some progress late in the 1990s, but by 2002, the company filed for Chapter 11 bankruptcy. Significant retrenchment became necessary. After emerging from bankruptcy, Kmart purchased Sears to become the Sears Holdings Corporation. The combined Sears and Kmart sales are approximately $55 billion, which now makes Sears Holdings the second-largest general retailer in the United States—larger than Target, although smaller than specialty retailer Home Depot. The sales of Kmart Stores, however, have fallen to below $20 billion.

In the years of the company's decline, Kmart stores came increasingly to be viewed as overcrowded, dirty, and stocking merchandise that people were not too interested in, while not having adequate quantities of currently popular goods. In a sense, Kmart was the biggest victim of Wal-Mart's famous inventory control system, and because of its own inadequacies in this area, was unable to compete on equal terms with its once much smaller competitor.

Membership Warehouses

The membership department store industry has become largely concentrated in two operators, Costco and Sam's Club, a unit of Wal-Mart. The much smaller BJ's Wholesale Club is the third-largest operator, with stores concentrated in the eastern United States.

Costco. Costco is the world's largest membership department store operation and has sales similar to Sears/Kmart, behind Wal-Mart and Home Depot. Costco started its operations in the Seattle area, merging eventually with Price Club. In 2004/2005, sales were $53 billion, somewhat less than one-fifth of Wal-Mart's worldwide sales volume. The company earned a net profit of nearly $1.1 billion, representing a 12 percent return on stockholders equity—markedly lower not only than Wal-Mart, but than other big retailers such as Home Depot and Target.

The Costco membership warehouse operation, through Price Club, actually predated Sam's Club by many years. As recalled earlier, Sam Walton borrowed the wholesale warehouse concept and ran with it. Yet this is an area where Wal-Mart's acclaimed efficiency did not lead to its becoming the dominant retail player, and it appears that Sam's Club's volume has been growing more slowly than Costco's in recent years.

Costco's stores tend to be larger and have higher volume than Wal-Mart's, and located in more upscale areas (see chapter 8). Accordingly, they are more likely to sell somewhat luxurious merchandise, such as fairly high-quality wines and fancy dessert items. Costco has expanded outside the United States and now has stores in Canada, the United Kingdom, Japan, Taiwan, and South Korea, and a joint venture in Mexico.

Costco attributes its success in large part to the careful selection of products that are in high demand, thereby achieving an inventory turnover of 11.5 annually. As noted in table 5-1 above, this is the highest among the large big-box stores, both in the United States and internationally. The 2004 Costco annual report indicates that its volume per store is twice that of Sam's Club, its nearest competitor. The company has been particularly successful in identifying product lines that have high turnover, becoming, for example, the nation's largest wine retailer.

Another factor contributing substantially to Costco's profitability is its lower labor costs relative to the volume of sales. According to a November 12, 2004, "10-K" filing, this is due to its shorter hours of operation as compared to traditional wholesalers, discount grocery retailers, and supermarkets, and "to other operational efficiencies inherent in a warehouse-type operation."

Finally, Costco's wages and benefits are reputedly higher than at Sam's Club, a subject to which we turn in the next chapter.

Specialty Big-Box Stores: Home Improvement

Two of the largest U.S. big-box store operators are in the home improvement business. Home Depot and Lowe's are both highly profitable, with Lowe's growing somewhat faster than market leader Home Depot in recent years. The third-largest home improvement company, Menards, is much smaller and operates principally in the Midwest.

Home Depot. Home Depot has grown rapidly and is reputed to have reached the $50 billion revenue mark earlier than any other retailer. The company is the world's largest operator of home improvement warehouses, which average 160,000 square feet. In 2004/2005, the company had $74 billion in revenues, making it second in retailing in the United States to Wal-Mart, and it had approximately one-fourth of Wal-Mart's volume. Only France's Carrefour and Germany's Metro AG (see chapter 10) are larger among the international big-box operators.

Home Depot, like Wal-Mart, is much larger than any of its direct competitors, being nearly double the size of second place Lowe's, and it is more than double the size of the second-largest specialty big-box retailer, Best Buy. Home Depot's net profit was $5.8 billion in 2005/2006, with a hefty 22.8 percent return on stockholder's equity. Its rate of sales increase averaged about 19 percent annually over the past ten years, well above Wal-Mart's 13.8 percent. Sales growth has slowed in the last five years, with an annual increase of about 11 percent. Home Depot has an inventory turnover rate of 4.8, higher than that of its principal competitor, Lowe's.

Home Depot began in 1978 with stores in Atlanta. By 1990, there were 145 stores generating a sales volume of $3.8 billion. In the late 1990s, Home Depot surpassed Kmart as the second-largest big-box retailer in the United States, and it now operates about two thousand stores. With a big presence already established in Canada and a growing one in Mexico, Home Depot has announced plans to open stores in China, a market in which European big-box home improvement stores already operate.

Recently, Home Depot has been "reinventing" itself to make up for lost ground and momentum in its core home improvement business.[4] Company founders Bernie Marcus (who was quite fond of Sam Walton) and Arthur Blank ran the company on a decentralized, entrepreneurial basis. In late 2000, a new CEO, Robert L. Nardelli, formerly of General Electric, took charge. Nardelli moved the company to a more centralized, almost military operation (it brags about the number of ex-military personnel it has), and became very aggressive in cutting costs. Where the management style at Lowe's is demanding but rather low-key and collegial, Home Depot under Nardelli presents a disciplined, high-pressure environment.

Nardelli, seeing the growth in traditional home improvement stores slowing and a rising encroachment by traditional general merchandise retailers like Wal-Mart in its mainline business, has announced a sharp slowdown in new store openings in the United States but has moved aggressively to expand in other ways, particularly overseas and by moving into wholesaling goods to building contractors. While many on Wall Street are more optimistic about Lowe's because of its high sales growth, Home Depot is one of the most profitable retail firms around, and is flourishing by most standard measures.

Lowe's. Lowe's, the second-largest operator of home improvement ware-houses, had its beginnings as a local hardware store in North Wilkesboro, North Carolina, in the late 1940s and opened hardware stores over the next three decades. During the 1980s, Lowe's began building large home improvement centers that were eventually more than ten times the size of its previous hardware stores. In the fiscal year ending in early 2006, Lowe's had a volume of $43 billion, with a net profit of nearly $2.8 billion and a return on stockholder equity of over 21 percent. Lowe's has increased its revenues by nearly 20 percent annually over the past ten years, the fastest growth rate of any U.S. big-box store operation with more than $10 billion in sales. Though only slightly above that of Home Depot, Lowe's growth rate has been faster than its larger competitor in recent years.

With well over 1,100 stores in the United States and new operations beginning in Canada, Lowe's is a darling on Wall Street. The price of its common stock more than doubled in the five years from early 2001 to early 2006. The company has a great combination of high growth in sales and very high rates of return on equity. Its stores are large and airy, and customers like the "feel" of Lowe's, perhaps more than that of other discount houses.

Specialty Retailers: Consumer Electronics

The consumer electronics field has two main operators, Best Buy and Circuit City.

Best Buy. Best Buy was established by Richard M. Schultze in the Minneapolis-St. Paul metropolitan region. After some years in more general retailing, Schultz focused on consumer electronics and opened the first Best Buy store in 1983. The chain has grown to more than nine hundred stores, located in both the United States and Canada. (Most of its Canadian stores trade under the name "Future Shop.") Best Buy's annual sales volume is approximately $27 billion, with a net profit of nearly $1 billion in 2005/2006. The return on stockholder equity is a very impressive 23 percent. Best Buy has experienced some of the strongest growth among big-box operators, which has no doubt contributed to the sharp rise in its stock price over time, as outlined earlier. Over the past ten years, sales have risen 18.4 percent annually, a close third to Home Depot and Lowe's. In the past five years, sales have increased 17.1 percent annually. The company is the largest speciality consumer electronics retailer in North America, second overall only to Wal-Mart.

Best Buy's great success has spurred an impressive imitator: Wal-Mart itself. Seeing the high profit margins and rapid sales growth Best Buy commands, Wal-Mart, the mother of all big-box discounters, has remodeled a large proportion of its stores' electronic areas, widening aisles and putting in more upscale merchandise, including sleek, new high-definition television sets and upscale notebook and laptop computers.[5] Even more ominously for Best Buy, Wal-Mart is going after the highly profitable extended-warranty business.

But Best Buy is meeting the challenge by exhibiting a trait of all highly successful retail entrepreneurs: the ability to follow the pulse of consumer tastes and alter its investments to meet them constantly. Intending not only to compete vigorously in the electronics goods business it now dominates, the chain is expanding into other lines. Its Eq-life stores, for example, sell products in the rapidly expanding health and wellness area.[6] And within its core electronics area, the firm is trying to focus on small-business customers, a category it thinks has been relatively neglected.[7]

The Competition: Circuit City. Founded in 1949, and with six hundred stores in the United States and Canada, Circuit City is the second-largest consumer electronics specialty retailer. Circuit City's financial performance has lagged far behind that of its larger competitor, Best Buy. Its annual volume of about $11 billion, with a net profit under $100 million, represents only a low, single-digit return on stockholder equity, less than one-fourth that of such peer powerhouses as Best Buy, Home Depot, Lowe's, or Wal-Mart. Over the past four years,[8] Circuit City has experienced little sales growth, and among the largest big-box store operators, only Kmart and Toys R Us have performed more poorly. Circuit City's inventory turnover rate is 5.4, a full one-quarter less than that of Best Buy.

The electronics retailing business is a good example of what Joseph Schumpeter once famously called "creative destruction."[9] In any business, there is a failure for almost every success story, and, indeed, the two are very often correlated. Best Buy did a better job than Circuit City of building stores in the right locations, providing goods that consumers wanted, and pleasing customers with good service. They were rewarded, and Circuit City is paying the price, although there are some signs of a rebound in the older retailer.[10]

Specialty Stores: Office Supplies

There are three large national office supply big-box stores: Staples, Office Depot, and OfficeMax. As did the home improvements and electronics companies, these firms have taken a concept originated by retailer pioneers like Fred Meyer and Harry Cunningham and perfected by Sam Walton and adapted it to a specialty area.

Table 5-3 gives some key statistics on the three competitors as of early 2006. Collectively, they have about $40 billion in sales, less than 20 percent the domestic sales of Wal-Mart and far less than Home Depot. While Staples and Office Depot are close to each other in size, Staples is three times as profitable, with a highly respectable return of stockholder equity approaching 20 percent, similar to that observed by companies like Wal-Mart, Home Depot, and Best Buy. By contrast, Office Depot's returns are far lower, making less than a 10 percent return on stockholder equity—a low number by any accounting.

OfficeMax is even more marginal, barely breaking even in 2005 (it actually lost money because of some one-time expenses; but excluding them, it made a small profit). A good measure of the effectiveness of a company might be the ratio of the value of its stock to each dollar of sales. The figure for Staples is a very high $1.12—that is, there is $1.12 worth of Staples stock outstanding for every $1.00 worth of products sold in 2005. The figure for Office Depot is 30 percent less, at $0.78, and for OfficeMax it is almost 80 percent less, at $0.23. Wall Street is very high on Staples, lukewarm on Office Depot, and frigid in its views toward OfficeMax.

Just because three firms are in the same business using roughly similar business models does not mean all are perceived as having roughly equal prospects. Leadership, it seems, makes a big difference in retail trade, a point made early by people like James Cash Penney, somewhat more recently by Sam Walton, and today by a new generation of entrepreneurs. The devil is in the details, and some are better at dealing with them than others.

TABLE 5-3

CHARACTERISTICS OF THE THREE LEADING BIG-BOX OFFICE
SUPPLY RETAILERS, 2006[1]

Statistic	Staples	Office Depot	OfficeMax
Sales	$16.08	$14.28	$9.16
Net Income (Profits)	0.834	0.274	0.023[2]
Return on Equity	19.54%	9.18%	1.00%[2]
Capitalization	$18.06	$11.08	$2.11
Capitalization/Sales	$1.12	$0.78	$0.23

NOTES: 1. Sales, net income, and capitalization numbers are in billions. 2. Excludes non-recurring losses; return on equity is partially estimated.
SOURCES: Staples, *2005 Annual Report*, C 1, http://ccbn.mobular.net/ccbn/7/1793/1971/; Office Depot, *2005 Annual Report*, 14, http://ccbn.mobular.net/ccbn/7/1648/1814/; Office Max Inc. *2005 Annual Report*, 14, http://investor.officemax.com/downloads/OMX_AR_2005.pdf (all reports accessed on August 11, 2006).

Other Specialty Operators

There are a number of smaller specialty chains with stores that are, on average, considerably smaller than a Wal-Mart Supercenter or a Home Depot or Lowe's but which nonetheless are large by standards of the specialty, and these might be characterized as "big-box" stores in some sense. A few examples give some flavor of the diversity of the big-store concept that has come to dominate modern American retailing.

Toys R Us was the pioneer specialty big-box retailer. Though battered severely by competition from the general merchandise big-box operators, especially Wal-Mart, in recent years its sales have been a respectable $11 billion. In the business of selling housewares are stores like Bed Bath & Beyond, Linens 'n Things, and Crate and Barrel. Some chain lumber companies slug it out with the likes of Home Depot, notably 84 Lumber. In the bookstore business, the leaders are Barnes and Noble and Borders, having supplanted earlier small retailers like Waldenbooks that did not aggressively adopt the big-box approach to retailing with associated amenities like coffee bars and reading areas. Several firms operate in the pet business, including Petsmart and Petco. Sports Authority has tried the big-box concept in sporting goods. The "big-box discount concept," pioneered especially well by Wal-Mart and extended to specialty areas like home improvement by companies like Home Depot, continues to expand into ever more narrow areas of product specialization.

The Next Generation of Retailing?

Retailing goes through cycles, with new forms supplanting the old. The general stores and peddlers of the early nineteenth century were replaced by specialty stores and, later, department stores. Mail-order retailing and chain variety stores became important in the early twentieth century, a period of continued growth of department stores. The rise of the discount house and its evolution into the large big-box operation represent merely another stage in the evolution of retail trade. What will be the next big wave of innovation?

While a fuller discussion of this comes in chapter 12, the most certain answer is Internet shopping. Virtually all of the big-box operators have established Internet sales sites. In a sense, Internet sales represent a resurgence of long-distance shopping, similar to the mail-order shopping that was so prevalent before World War II. Web-based sales have boomed because they can be more convenient in many circumstances.

The big-box stores face growing competition from Internet-based retailers. Amazon.com is probably the best-known. Having started in 1995 as a bookseller and diversified into music and other fields in more recent years, Amazon has nearly $7 billion in revenues, with a net profit of $600 million— a very high profit margin by retail standards. The company has 9,000 employees and is now the largest retailer of books in the United States. Dell Computers may demonstrate the potential for Internet sales in electronics. Its online sales volume has been estimated at $9.7 billion in 2004[11]—nearly as large as the entire volume for Circuit City, the second-largest consumer electronics operation. The large Internet sales of retailers such as Amazon and Dell would seem to indicate that big-box stores are already facing considerable competition from the "next wave" of retail innovation.

An especially vibrant example of Internet shopping growth is the remarkable eBay phenomenon. eBay makes its money selling used goods, serving as a market-maker by bringing buyers and sellers together. In fiscal year 2005, the company made over $1 billion in profit on $4.552 billion in sales volume—easily the highest profit margin of any major retail-related business, with earnings and sales growing very rapidly. Its novel and innovative concept of retailing reminds us that change is the one constant of American retailing.

Conclusions

Imitation is the sincerest form of flattery, and Wal-Mart is probably a better and more efficient company because others have followed its lead, even as it has followed the lead of others. Wal-Mart was the biggest of the late twentieth century retail innovators, but by no means the only one to make large profits. It is interesting to note the large number of firms making 20 percent rates of return on their stockholders' equity. While most people think of retailing as sort of old-fashioned, low-tech, and slow-growing, in recent times it has been vibrant and dynamic. Yet, as in other businesses, there are winners and losers. Best Buy is a winner while, relatively speaking, Circuit City is a loser. Similarly, OfficeMax has been unable to match the leadership of Staples. In the long run, the one big winner is the American consumer, who has benefited mightily from the large selection of reasonably priced goods available in nice, clean stores.

PART III

Wal-Mart: Good or Bad?

6

Employment and Wage Effects
of Discount Stores

Many critics have argued that Wal-Mart, and by extension other big-box discount stores, have hurt American workers. Allegedly, this has come about in two ways: First, the growth of the large discount houses has cost jobs, and second, workers are receiving relatively low or substandard wages and benefits. The lost jobs argument assumes that employment created by the opening of new discount stores and any firms that might be established or expanded in conjunction with them is insufficient to compensate for reduced employment from existing retailers and other local businesses. Alternatively or additionally, it is argued that workers in other (nonretail) industries lose jobs, because Wal-Mart (or Target, or whatever) sells largely foreign-made goods, and, in the absence of the discount stores, customers would more likely buy American-made goods. So there is "stealth," or unseen job loss, as well.

In this chapter, we evaluate these arguments and show that it is hard to find much support for them. Indeed, with respect to job loss, the evidence probably goes more the other way—the innovations in retailing have, on balance, created new jobs. By effectively raising real incomes of Americans by offering goods at lower prices, the discount stores have enhanced the demand for a variety of goods and services. In the era of rapid proliferation of discount stores, the growth of retail trade employment has been relatively robust. And as the American economy has become more "discount-store intensive," the overall unemployment rate has tended to fall somewhat—hardly consistent with a massive net loss of jobs to foreign workers. Moreover, workers in the newer discount stores do not seem to be underpaid relative to other, comparable workers. And it is notable that it is not the workers themselves, by and large, who are concerned about their wages—

these complaints come mostly from others (for example, labor unions) who have a vested interest in organizing these workers into unions, something that the workers, by and large, have strongly opposed doing.

Employment in Retail Trade

Critics of Wal-Mart and other big-box discount stores argue that these stores are job-killers. Whatever jobs are created at Wal-Mart are cancelled out by jobs lost at smaller local stores smashed by the Wal-Mart competition. What has really happened to employment in the Wal-Mart part of the retail trade sector in recent years?

Figure 6-1 looks at changes in employment in the "general merchandise stores" component of retail trade—the part that includes Wal-Mart—for the nation over the period 1998–2004. (The comparable historical data are limited to that period because of changes in the way businesses were classified, beginning with 1990.[1])

Employment in the United States rose slightly over 4 percent from 1998 to 2004, while it rose more than twice as fast (9 percent) in the general merchandise stores component of retail trade. From 2000 to 2004, total U.S. employment actually declined slightly, leading to the "jobless recovery" arguments prominently heard in the 2004 presidential election. Yet, during this same time period, employment rose nearly 3 percent in the general merchandise store category. Far from being job-killers, these retail outlets were a source of some job growth in a period of employment stagnation.

In general, the vibrant retail trade industry has been an important contributor to economic growth in recent years. Figure 6-2 shows the average annual real increase in the value added to the gross domestic product for the retail trade industry, all private industry, government, and all of GDP over the years 2001–4. Note that the growth in retail trade was over twice as great as that for the entire GDP or for the whole private sector, and four times that of government. Looking more closely at specific sectors, we find that the percentage growth of retail trade was greater than for *any* other sector of the economy, including financial services, professional and business services, manufacturing, construction, and so forth.[2] It is no wonder that retail trade was a bright spot in an otherwise dismal employment picture.

FIGURE 6-1

U.S. EMPLOYMENT, 1998–2004 (1998=100)

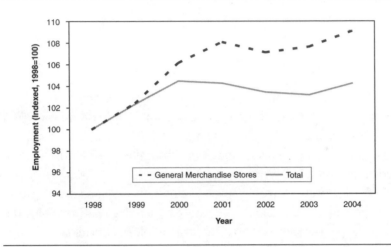

SOURCE: Authors' calculation, using U.S. Department of Commerce, Bureau of Economic Analysis, table 6.4D, "National Income and Products Table: Full-Time and Part-Time Employees by Industry," www.bea.gov/bea/dn/nipaweb/TableView.asp?SelectedTable=182&FirstYear=2004&LastYear=2005& Freq=Year (accessed August 11, 2006).

FIGURE 6-2

AVERAGE ANNUAL REAL OUTPUT GROWTH, 2001–2004

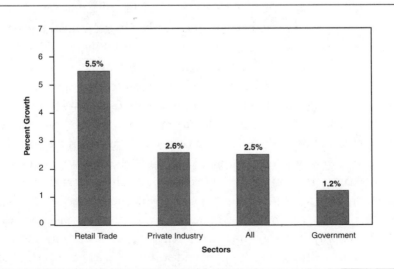

SOURCE: Authors' calculations using Bureau of Economic Analysis.

While the federal data do not separate out Wal-Mart, by using some information from Wal-Mart annual reports on the number of associates, and by making certain assumptions about the sales-to-employee ratio at international outlets relative to domestic ones, we can estimate the change in Wal-Mart versus non-Wal-Mart employment for the three-year period 1998–2001. (Data on the number of associates were not reported after the 2002 annual report, which covers mostly calendar year 2001.)[3] Under a reasonable set of assumptions, the number of Wal-Mart domestic employees grew by over 160,000—but the number of non-Wal-Mart employees working in general merchandise stores also grew, although by only slightly over 30,000. Job creation at Wal-Mart was in no way matched by job destruction at competitive stores.

Employment Effects of Wal-Mart

A more sophisticated approach to analyzing the impact of Wal-Mart on employment levels would be to look at variations in employment growth by state as they relate to the intensity of Wal-Mart's presence. Accordingly, we calculated for the years 1998 and 2004 the numbers of Wal-Mart stores per million people in each state, and, using multiple regression analysis, related that to various measures of the increase in job opportunities by state. If the critics of Wal-Mart are correct, there should be a negative relationship between the presence of Wal-Mart and job growth (however measured).

We performed some sixteen different statistical tests, using various measures of job growth (for example, the percentage growth in employment and the change in the number of jobs related to the change in the population ages sixteen years or older), in most cases introducing other potential explanatory variables (such as the extent of unionization, the proportion of workers in manufacturing, and the tax burden) into the analysis for control purposes. In only five of the sixteen tests did we observe a negative relationship between the intensity of Wal-Mart's presence and employment growth, and in none of those cases was the relationship even close to being statistically significant at the 10 percent level—itself a low standard for evaluating the validity of the hypothesis that Wal-Mart lowers employment opportunities. By contrast, in eleven of the tests a positive relationship was observed, in some cases statistically significant at the 10 percent level. These tests lead us to reject the hypothesis that Wal-Mart on balance is a destroyer of jobs, and to assert that they even provide some very modest support for the opposite hypothesis—that Wal-Mart on balance is job-creating.

It can be argued that the use of state data might fail to capture some of the negative employment effects of Wal-Mart. For example, even if Missouri (a Wal-Mart-intensive state) does not suffer any employment loss, the mere fact of Missouri stores selling a lot of Chinese-made goods may lead to job loss in other states among manufacturing workers who otherwise would be providing goods to retail customers throughout America, including Missouri. Accordingly, perhaps the geographical frame of comparison should be the entire nation, not individual states.

It is possible to look at America at different points of time and observe unemployment rates (or other measures of labor force involvement) as they relate to the relative importance of Wal-Mart in the economy. We might ask, for example, has unemployment become a bigger problem in the years since the company has had a large national presence?

In figure 6-3, we look at the period 1974–2004 (thirty-one years), and calculate the median unemployment rate in the years 1974–84, when Wal-Mart's presence in the economy was small (less than $2 in domestic sales for each $1,000 of national output), in 1985–93, when the Wal-Mart presence was moderately large (between $2 and $10 in sales per $1,000 in output), and in 1994–2004, when the Wal-Mart presence was quite large (more than $10 in sales per $1,000 in output).

The evidence is quite striking. As Wal-Mart became a larger presence in American life, the unemployment rate fell. The typical rate in the modern era of giant Wal-Mart presence is about two full percentage points smaller than in the early years, when the company had only a regional presence. The evidence supports the view that Wal-Mart, if anything, is job-enhancing, and its presence reduces unemployment.

Yet we would be the first to admit that many factors other than Wal-Mart's growth could have explained the downward drift in unemployment rates over time. To cite just one example, in the period of Wal-Mart's emergence as a major discounter, inflation has cooled dramatically, and the altered inflationary expectations of individuals, have, in turn, reduced wage and salary increases. There are good theoretical reasons to believe wage and

FIGURE 6-3

MEDIAN AMERICAN UNEMPLOYMENT AND WAL-MART'S PRESENCE

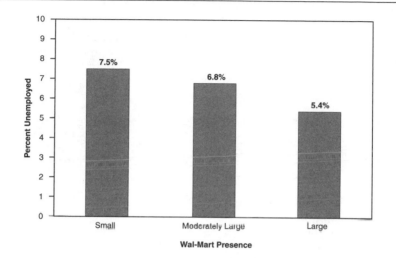

SOURCES: Information on Wal-Mart size comes from Wal-Mart, *Wal-Mart Annual Report 1984*, 14–15, www.walmartstores.com/Files/1984AR.pdf (accessed August 13, 2006); *Wal-Mart Annual Report 1993*, 6–7, www.walmartstores.com/Files/1993AR.pdf; *Wal Mart Annual Report 2004*, 17–18, www.walmartstores.com/Files/annualreport_2004.pdf (all accessed August 13, 2006); Bureau of Labor Statistics, as reported in the *Economic Report of the President* (Washington, D.C.: Government Printing Office, 2006), 324–25.

price variables are critical in influencing the demand and supply of labor, and thus the rate of unemployment. Accordingly, we performed some more extensive multivariate analysis incorporating other variables. Of particular importance are the labor market variables that comprise what Vedder and Gallaway have termed the "adjusted real wage." Extensive earlier research demonstrated that unemployment is strongly positively correlated with the adjusted real wage and also is correlated with its components, namely the price level, wage level, and degree of labor productivity growth.[4]

With this in mind, we ran seventeen different variants of regression models, attempting to explain measures of job availability in terms of the presence of Wal-Mart and other factors and to explicitly test the hypothesis, "Wal-Mart on balance has improved job opportunities." Looking again at the period 1974–2004, we used different measures of employment opportunity (the unemployment rate, changes in the unemployment rate,

TABLE 6-1

ORDINARY LEAST SQUARES REGRESSION RESULTS,
EMPLOYMENT–WAL-MART RELATIONSHIP

Variable or Statistic	Dependent Variable:[1]	
	Unemployment Rate	Employ.–Pop. Ratio[2]
Constant	−65.991	122.250
	(3.217)	(3.574)
Wal-Mart Sales Per $1000 GDP	−0.082	0.081
	(2.279)	(3.713)
Labor Share of National Inc. (−1)	0.633	−0.576
	(3.179)	(1.588)
Labor Share of National Inc. (−2)	0.484	−0.388
	(2.904)	(1.419)
% Change, Real GDP	−0.097	0.113
	(2.253)	(1.665)
MA(1)	1.037	1.226
	(1,799.2)	(4.549)
MA(2)	0.047	0.276
	(0.380)	(16.536)
MA(3)		0.003
		(0.010)
R^2	.859	.905
D-W Statistic	1.984	1.858

NOTES: 1. Numbers in parentheses are t-values. 2. Employees as a percentage of the population over the age of sixteen.
SOURCES: Information on Wal-Mart size comes from Wal-Mart, *Wal-Mart Annual Report 1984*, 14-15, www.walmartstores.com/Files/1984AR.pdf; Wal-Mart, *Wal-Mart Annual Report 1993*, 6-7, www.walmartstores.com/Files/1993AR.pdf; Wal-Mart, *Wal-Mart Annual Report 2004*, 17-18, www.walmartstores.com/Files/annualreport_2004.pdf (all accessed August 13, 2006). Employment and economic data are from U.S. Bureau of Economic Analysis and Bureau of Labor Statistics; see *Economic Report of the President* (Washington, D.C.: Government Printing Office, 2006).

and the employment to population ratio), different measures of labor costs (the adjusted real wage or components, using Bureau of Labor Statistics or Bureau of Economic Analysis data), and, in some equations, a business cycle variable (the growth in real GDP), along with differing lag structures for variables or alternative approaches to dealing with statistical problems.

In all seventeen instances, the expected relationship between Wal-Mart's presence (as measured by domestic sales as a percentage of gross domestic product) and the job opportunity variable was obtained. In thirteen of the seventeen, the findings were statistically significant at the 1 percent level, the highest standard conventionally used to evaluate hypotheses. In a large majority of statistical estimations, then, the hypothesis, "Wal-Mart increases job opportunities" was solidly confirmed. In two of the other four cases, the relationship was statistically significant at least at the 10 percent level. All in all, the findings rather strongly supported the hypothesis that Wal-Mart has had a positive impact on employment opportunities in the United States.

In table 6-1, two representative regression results are presented for readers with some technical understanding of the technique. The results suggest that well over a one-percentage-point fall in the aggregate unemployment rate can be associated with the large growth in Wal-Mart relative to the national economy over time. Alternatively, well over one new worker was added for each one hundred persons over the age of sixteen as a consequence of the growth of Wal-Mart. While that result might seem rather strong, the fact is that over 1 percent of American workers are employed at Wal-Mart today, suggesting the result is quite plausible if Wal-Mart has done relatively little "crowding out" of other workers.

These findings are not the last word.[5] Some statistical issues suggest they might tend to overstate Wal-Mart's positive employment contribution.[6] Nevertheless, the results increase our feeling that the critics who argue that Wal-Mart destroys jobs are simply wrong, and that the evidence is far stronger that the company has had a positive impact on job opportunities for American workers. We hope other objective researchers will explore this issue further.

In the next chapter, we revisit this issue on a more "micro," or community, level, but again the evidence is similar: Wal-Mart's entry into a community has an overall positive employment effect.[7]

Are Wal-Mart Workers Underpaid?

Labor unions and some others have long argued that Wal-Mart employees are exploited, receiving low wages for their labors. Compared with other businesses, Wal-Mart, or so it is argued, pays a smaller amount, leading in some cases to poverty for its workers.

Before turning to the empirical evidence, it should be pointed out that there are several logical problems with the "Wal-Mart employees are underpaid" argument. First, it is worth noting that no one is forced to work at Wal-Mart. The people holding jobs there do so voluntarily, and have the legal right simply to quit and go to work elsewhere. Situations today are not like a century or more ago, when workers of firms in small isolated towns could not easily travel to locations where other jobs were available, leading to what economists call "monopsonistic exploitation."[8] Today, it is a rare situation where within thirty minutes of home there are not at least some alternative employers offering jobs with skill requirements similar to those at Wal-Mart.

Similarly, when asked if they want to have collective bargaining, Wal-Mart workers have consistently said "no."[9] The employees themselves have shown little evidence of profound disenchantment or a sense of exploitation. While Wal-Mart management has clearly wanted to keep unions out, they have not actively coerced workers into staying out of them, or illegally tried to subvert the nation's laws with respect to collective bargaining.[10]

Finally, retail trade has always been a relatively low-paying field. Jobs are, for the most part, unskilled in nature and do not require advanced educational training. Workers are paid according to their contributions to store revenues, which are typically relatively modest. Merely showing that Wal-Mart employees make less than, say, the average pay in all occupations says little about Wal-Mart's compensation relative to comparable firms in retail trade.

With that by way of background, let us look at some evidence regarding Wal-Mart workers. The company asserts that, as of this writing in late 2005, "Wal-Mart's average full-time hourly wage nationally is $9.68 an hour."[11] This compares with an average hourly wage reported by the Bureau of Labor Statistics (BLS) for those in the occupation group "service" in private industry in the United States of $9.14 an hour.[12] The Wal-Mart figure exceeds the national average by about 6 percent. Yet the Wal-Mart figure is well below some other data showing an average wage in retail trade of slightly over $12 an hour.[13]

The average Wal-Mart figures are depressed by the fact that Wal-Mart stores are relatively highly concentrated in nonmetropolitan areas where wages are relatively low, as well as in states with relatively low income levels. For example, using state data, we find a rather strong statistically significant (at the 1 percent level) negative correlation (about –0.52) between the number of Wal-Mart stores per one million population and the proportion of the population living in metropolitan areas. The simple correlation between the density of Wal-Mart stores and per-capita income is even more strikingly negative (–0.59) and equally significant statistically.[14] This is not surprising, given the fact that Wal-Mart has been particularly popular among people of modest income for whom price sensitivity is high.

The point we are making here is that wages are most relevantly compared to those of other workers in the labor market in which they are employed. Service industry employees in metropolitan areas typically make a dollar or so more hourly than the average for nonmetropolitan areas.[15] Similarly, employees in low per-capita income areas typically have lower wages. Adjusting for these factors, it is probable that the Wal-Mart wage is noticeably higher relative to reported national averages.

Wal-Mart helpfully publishes average hourly wage data by state.[16] As of this writing, average hourly wages vary from a low of $8.75 an hour in West Virginia to a high of $10.94 in New Hampshire. The New Hampshire average wage is fully 25 percent above that of West Virginia. To be sure, the geographic variation of Wal-Mart wages is less than for workers as a whole, reflecting perhaps in part the possibility that unskilled workers have less wage variation, and perhaps also some company policy implicitly setting a minimum wage that benefits workers in lower-paying states. Regression analysis shows a strong positive statistical relationship between Wal-Mart average wages by state and the state-average wages of workers in general— Wal-Mart is heavily influenced by local labor market conditions in determining its wage rates.

The earlier point that Wal-Mart stores are concentrated in lower-wage areas, thereby driving down the reported average system-wide wage relative to national averages, can be demonstrated by a simple arithmetic exercise. In figure 6-4, we compare the ten most "Wal-Mart-intensive" states in early 2005 (based on stores per one million persons, as listed in the 2005 *Annual Report*), with the ten least Wal-Mart-intensive states. We look at the average wage level prevailing in the state for all workers, according to Bureau of Labor Statistics data.[17]

FIGURE 6-4

AVERAGE WEEKLY WAGES, 10 MOST AND LEAST INTENSIVE
WAL-MART STATES, FALL 2004

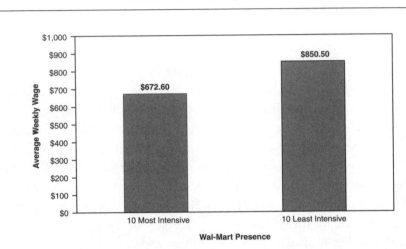

SOURCES: Wal-Mart, *Wal-Mart Annual Report 2005*, 53, www.walmartstores.com/Files/2005AnnualReport.
pdf, (accessed August 13, 2006); U.S. Department of Labor, Bureau of Labor Statistics, table 4, "Covered (1) Establishments, Employment, and Wages by State, third quarter 2005 (2)," www.bls.gov/
news.release/cewqtr.t04.htm (accessed August 13, 2006); authors' calculations.

Wages are strikingly (26.4 percent) higher in states where Wal-Mart has
a very limited presence than in states where it is relatively ubiquitous. An
analysis that incorporates the nonmetropolitan-area orientation of Wal-Mart
would no doubt further demonstrate that, even today, its stores are concentrated largely in rather small, semi-rural areas where wages tend to be low.
Even if the average wage for retail workers were close to $12 hourly while
Wal-Mart paid about $10 nationally, most of that differential would probably
be explained by the stores' uneven distribution across the nation's landscape.

To test this hypothesis, we took data on the distribution of Wal-Mart
employees by state and calculated the proportion working in each state. We
used those proportions to calculate the distribution of the entire U.S. labor
force if its interstate distribution were precisely the same as Wal-Mart's, and
then calculated the impact that changed distribution would have on average U.S. weekly wages in the fourth quarter of 2004. We concluded the
average U.S. wage would have fallen by 6 percent. That explains at least

one-third of the difference between the reported Wal-Mart average wage and national estimates for all retail trade.

There are other issues involved in comparing the reported Wal-Mart average wage to national data. First, the Wal-Mart data are based on full-time workers. While the company asserts that, unlike most of the industry, a majority of its employees are full-time, there are still a substantial number of part-time employees, a majority of whom probably make less than the typical full-time employee. The Wal-Mart figure also excludes supervisory personnel working on a salary (not hourly) basis, who are generally paid more than the average of hourly workers. If both part-time and salaried workers were included in our calculations, it is our suspicion that the resulting average wage would likely still be at least in the $10 hourly range, and possibly higher—highly competitive with service industry employees generally.

Still other data leave us with the impression that Wal-Mart's pay for employees is not strongly out of line with the industry standards. To mention one source, data from the U.S. Bureau of Labor Statistics National Compensation Survey for some occupations common at Wal-Mart are compatible with the Wal-Mart average. For example, the national average pay in July 2003 for "cashiers" was $8.40 an hour. Even allowing for some increases since then, the current figure for cashiers is still no doubt below the Wal-Mart average wage. The average for "service occupations except private household" from the same survey was $10.40 hourly, slightly above the Wal-Mart norm, but probably not so after appropriate adjustments for local labor market conditions are made.[18]

An ironic and even amusing recent incident helps make the case that Wal-Mart indeed pays its workers in line with labor market conditions. A nemesis of Wal-Mart, the United Food and Commercial Workers Union, went out to hire protesters at new Wal-Mart grocery stores (called Neighborhood Markets) in the Las Vegas area. One of the store managers noted that while the average rate of pay for Nevada Wal-Mart workers was $10.17 an hour, the paid picketers were only paid $6.00 an hour—with no benefits. Wal-Mart's fiercest union critic was hiring workers to protest Wal-Mart at compensation levels more than 40 percent lower than those earned by the allegedly oppressed Wal-Mart workers. And the UFCW workers did not receive 401K plans like the Wal-Mart workers, health insurance (like many of them), or the like. One of the walkers on the picket line revealed to a reporter that he once worked for Wal-Mart, noting, "I can't complain. It wasn't bad. They started paying me at $6.75, and after three months I was already getting $7, then I got Employee of the Month, and by the time I left (in less than one year), I was making $8.63 an hour."[19] His comment illustrates another fact: the lifetime earnings of many Wal-Mart employees are enhanced through promotions, and many of the relatively highly paid management workers begin as rank and file employees earning hourly wages.

To be sure, while Wal-Mart appears to pay wages not greatly out of line with industry standards, the company does not claim to be the industry leader in providing high wages or benefits for its employees. Some unions have championed the role of Costco in that regard, as that company proclaims as one of its goals making its associates (employees) content and satisfied. Wages are said by some to be as high as $15 an hour on average. While we could not verify that claim, even if true it raises an interesting question. Is Costco paying more in wages and benefits than necessary to acquire reliable employees, and, if so, is it violating a fiduciary responsibility to its stockholders by, in effect, giving away some of the fruits of their investment? The return on stockholder equity at Costco is typically in the 10–12 percent range, well below the Wal-Mart norm and also below that of all American industry. If the reason for this is making payments to workers beyond those reasonable to maintain their loyalty, it is reducing the wealth of the owners of the company and the company's ability to expand its services to consumers (which provide them welfare in the form of consumer surplus) as rapidly as it otherwise would. Whatever gains are provided to workers are offset by losses in wealth and welfare to consumers and investors.

Fringe Benefits

A favorite line of criticism of Wal-Mart detractors is that the firm does not provide benefits for its employees. Especially egregious in their eyes is that Wal-Mart pushes health care costs onto the general taxpayer, which, aside from being callous and exploitive of its employees, burdens the taxpayer and gives the firm an unfair advantage over other firms that allegedly do not engage in this practice.

While complete data are not available to analyze these criticisms fully, limited information suggests that the charges are largely without merit. First of all, the notion that "Wal-Mart does not provide health care benefits" is simply fallacious. As of late 2005, the company was insuring nearly a million people, including 568,000 employees.[20] While these plans require payments by individuals, they are heavily subsidized by the company.

One might note that Wal-Mart has a total of well over one million domestic employees, so it is true that less than one-half (slightly over 43 percent by our calculations) receive health benefits from the company. These statistics, however, are similar to those for American industry as a whole. While the proportion of all workers in private industry receiving health care benefits is slightly higher (53 percent), the proportion with wages of less than $15 an hour having such benefits is less (39 percent).[21]

Not only is Wal-Mart not markedly different from typical employers of low-wage workers regarding health insurance, but it is extremely unlikely that a majority of its employees are, in fact, dependent on Medicaid, as some critics claim. Large numbers of employees are part-time workers who are seldom insured by employers, even in the public sector. Many, if not most, of these employees are secondary earners in households where a spouse or parent has family health insurance coverage. Some older Wal-Mart employees work at the company part-time to supplement pension income and are part of the Medicare program to which they contributed through their taxes before retirement (and also now while working at Wal-Mart). One study estimates that over 90 percent of Wal-Mart workers are insured in some manner.[22]

Is it possible that some part-time Wal-Mart employees have such low incomes that they receive Medicaid? Of course it is, just as it is true for workers at Target, in hospitality businesses (where average wages are lower than at Wal-Mart), and for a host of other employments. But it seems unlikely that the proportion of Wal-Mart employees receiving Medicaid is as high as the proportion of Medicaid recipients in the total U.S. population (15–20 percent).[23]

Critics of Wal-Mart's benefits program tend not to take into account a significant fringe benefit offered by the company that has greatly enriched some senior employees. Wal-Mart contributes to a profit-sharing plan that, with provisions for bonuses for good performance, can be a healthy addition to compensation, particularly if capital gain income is included. The company claims that a majority of its employees own stock in it, which no doubt contributes to an apparent lack of hard evidence that, as a group, Wal-Mart workers are generally unhappy with their employer. For more than three decades, Wal-Mart has been justifiably proud of this plan. As Sam Walton himself put it, "I guess it's the move we made that I'm proudest of . . . [and] without a doubt the single smartest move we ever made at Wal-Mart."[24]

An additional benefit that is hard to quantify but nonetheless real is the 10 percent discount employees receive on merchandise purchased at Wal-Mart. For some, the discounted price of stock or merchandise could well be worth a dollar an hour or more.

All told, Wal-Mart currently claims it spends more than $4.2 billion annually on employee benefits. That is at least $3,200 per employee. If the average employee, including part-time workers, works thirty hours a week and earns $10 an hour, each earns about $16,000 in annual wages. Thus, benefits are equal to about 20 percent of wages, a figure that appears to be roughly in line with the average for American industry.[25] Wal-Mart does not stand out as a company with unusual employee compensation and benefit practices.

Conclusions

Critics of big-box retail stores, most notably Wal-Mart, claim that these stores treat workers poorly. They cost jobs and offer substandard wages and benefits. A review of the evidence, however, provides very little support for that position. With respect to employment, the evidence suggests, if anything, that the expansion of the discount retail trade industry has been associated with a net creation of jobs in America. There is no reliable evidence that Wal-Mart, for example, has been a job-killer.

Wages and benefits have to be placed in the context of the labor market in which workers compete. As a general proposition, a majority of Wal-Mart employees are relatively unskilled and are working in an industry that historically has paid low wages relative to other sectors of the economy. The evidence suggests that Wal-Mart wage policies are not significantly out of line with industry averages. Moreover, the allegations that Wal-Mart dumps its health care costs onto the governmental welfare system appear to be egregious distortions of facts. Just as Wal-Mart has been good for consumers and investors, it has been good for its employees and labor in general as well.

7

Competition and Communities

Critics of Wal-Mart and some other big-box retailers argue that these stores destroy competition and communities, forcing the closure of beloved local businesses. Moreover, this destruction of competition has several deleterious effects: the loss of jobs, the weakening of the local economic base, and the destruction of a very sense of community. Often, critics argue, with the arrival of Wal-Mart, the downtown business district will become a pale imitation of its former self, and with that the locals will lose their geographic bearings, no longer gathering informally to discuss and ultimately solve the community's problems.[1]

Some of these arguments are difficult to evaluate conclusively. The "sense of community" or "community spirit" is particularly elusive when it comes to measurement, for example. However, there are some things that can be quantified or evaluated, and in this chapter we set out to do so. For example, is the arrival of Wal-Mart in a community accompanied by economic improvement or decline? Does employment rise or fall? How about income? Do competitors wither away and the new big-box discounter become a monopolist that tends to raise its prices relative to earlier stores in the long run?

Some Analysis of Store Openings

In order to get some sense of the answer to these questions, we decided to take a sample of new Wal-Mart Supercenters and look at basic indicators in the communities that host them, before and after Wal-Mart's opening. Specifically, we picked twenty-five towns with stores that opened in the year 2002 and looked at the changes in a number of economic variables for those communities in the two full years prior to the store opening, specifically 1999–2001. We then compared these findings to data for the next two years, including the year the store opened and the first full year afterward (2001–3).

While this is not a full-blown examination of the entire population of Wal-Mart openings, it is a good-size sample. The stores were located in seventeen states in all sections of the country, including four in the East (Palmyra and Mexico, Maine, and Bradford and Punxsutawney, Pennsylvania); seven in the Midwest (Bemidji, Minnesota; Mason City, Iowa; Petoskey, Michigan; Athens and Napoleon, Ohio; and Hayward and Plake Delton, Wisconsin); nine in the South (Seneca, South Carolina; Bushnell and Palatka, Florida; Columbia, Tennessee; Batesville, Oxford, and Waynesboro, Mississippi; Laurinburg, North Carolina; and Lebanon, Virginia), and five in the West (Perry and Price, Utah; Hobbs, New Mexico; Del Rio, Texas; and Evanston, Wyoming).

Since Wal-Mart's impact on communities is likely to be greatest in smaller towns where the store is a relatively large presence, we confined our analysis to towns of under 35,000 population in counties with fewer than 75,000 residents, located in nonmetropolitan areas.[2] In fact, the population of the towns in our sample varied between 1,953 and 33,864, with most towns having fewer than 10,000 residents (the median was 9,175) and most counties having fewer than 45,000 inhabitants (the median was 44,810). In short, we looked mostly at small towns in semi-rural counties located a good distance from a large city. This has historically been the prime market for Wal-Mart and is even today, as the company increasingly enters metropolitan areas.

Total Employment. First, we asked, was the picture with respect to total employment in the county with the new Wal-Mart Supercenter better or worse in the period after it opened than in the period before it opened? To answer that question, we needed to do some sort of control for general macroeconomic conditions affecting employment. Nationally, the unemployment rate rose from 4.7 percent in 2001 to 6.0 percent in 2003, and employment rose four times as much in 1999–2001 (before the store openings) than after.[3] So one would expect a poorer record of employment growth in the period of and following the Wal-Mart opening compared with 1999–2001. The macroeconomic changes arising from the mild 2001 recession, however, were quite

FIGURE 7-1

MEDIAN EMPLOYMENT GROWTH, 25 FUTURE WAL-MART TOWNS AND
NON-METRO AREAS OF THE SAME STATES, 1999–2001 (PERCENT)

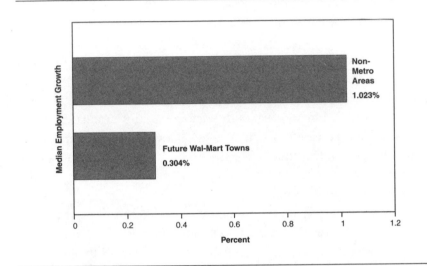

SOURCES: U.S. Department of Commerce, Bureau of Economic Analysis, "Regional Economic Profiles" www.bea.gov/bea/regional/reis/default.cfm?catable=CA30 (accessed August 13, 2006); new Wal-Mart store opening information found at www.walmartfacts.com/FeaturedTopics/?id=8 (accessed August 13, 2006).

diverse across the country. Accordingly, we decided to compare the growth (or decline) in employment of the county in which the new store opened with that in the entire nonmetropolitan region of the relevant state.

In deciding whether a county had an improved employment record after its Wal-Mart opening, we applied a high standard. The county's total employment had to increase more in 2001–3 relative to 1999–2001 than in the nonmetropolitan areas of the state as a whole. In fourteen (56 percent) of the cases, the pace of employment growth in the Wal-Mart counties increased relative to the control group. Moreover, in four of the other eleven cases, the experience following the store opening was probably at least as positive as it was negative, with the employment growth higher in the Wal-Mart county than in other nonmetro areas of the state (but with a relative slowdown in employment growth compared to the earlier period). Only in two cases—Hobbs, New Mexico, and Laurinburg, North Carolina—was there evidence solidly consistent with the views of Wal-Mart critics that

FIGURE 7-2

MEDIAN EMPLOYMENT GROWTH, 25 FUTURE WAL-MART TOWNS AND NON-METRO AREAS OF THE SAME STATES, 2001–2003 (PERCENT)

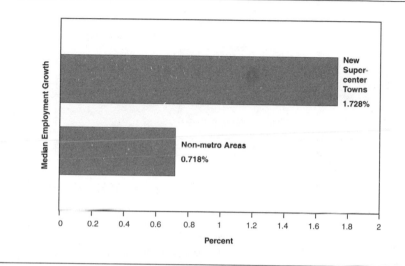

SOURCES: U.S. Department of Commerce, Bureau of Economic Analysis, "Regional Economic Profiles," www.bea.gov/bea/regional/reis/default.cfm?catable=CA30 (accessed August 13, 2006);Wal-Mart Stores opening information found at www.walmartfacts.com/FeaturedTopics/?id=8 (accessed August 13, 2006).

Wal-Mart's opening had a sharp adverse employment effect, with employment growth going from positive to negative, both absolutely and relative to the rest of the state's nonmetropolitan areas. The cases of clear pickup in job growth were at least twice those of relative job decline. On balance, the evidence supports the view that, as a rule, Wal-Mart adds to job opportunities in communities that it enters.

This is best demonstrated by looking at the median employment-rate experience of the twenty-five counties. In figure 7-1, we look at the median employment growth of the twenty-five Wal-Mart counties from 1999 and 2001—immediately prior to the opening of the new supercenters—as compared to the median employment growth in the nonmetropolitan areas of the same states. Note that the median future Wal-Mart community had significantly *lesser* job growth than other nonmetropolitan areas in the same states.

Now compare that with figure 7-2, which makes the same comparison for 2001–3, a period beginning with the year preceding the Wal-Mart opening

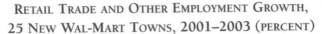

FIGURE 7-3

RETAIL TRADE AND OTHER EMPLOYMENT GROWTH,
25 NEW WAL-MART TOWNS, 2001–2003 (PERCENT)

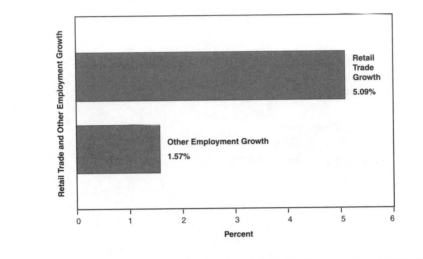

SOURCES: U.S. Department of Commerce, Bureau of Economic Analysis, "Regional Economic Profiles," www.bea.gov/bea/regional/reis/default.cfm?catable=CA30 (accessed August 13, 2006); Wal-Mart stores opening information found at www.walmartfacts.com/FeaturedTopics/?id=8 (accessed August 13, 2006).

and ending the year after. During this time, the median Wal-Mart county had more than double the employment growth of the other nonmetropolitan parts of the state. Moreover, employment growth accelerated between 1999–2001 and 2001–3 in the Wal-Mart counties, while it fell in the non-metropolitan areas of the same states (and, for that matter, in the nation as a whole). The evidence, then, clearly does not support the "Wal-Mart destroys jobs" thesis, but is supportive of the opposite hypothesis, namely that the opening of Wal-Mart stores is consistent with an improving employment picture in the communities in which they operate.

Next we looked at employment growth in retail trade. Detractors argue that the new jobs created at Wal-Mart are more than offset by the jobs destroyed by the closing of competing stores. It might be argued that Wal-Mart, with its renowned efficiency, has a high sales-to-employee ratio relative to its competitors, and the substitution of sales at Wal-Mart for sales elsewhere means moving from more to less labor-intensive modes of retail distribution.

We calculated employment growth in retail trade in the period 2001 (before the Wal-Mart Supercenters opened) and 2003 (the first full year of operation) for the twenty-five selected counties, and then compared it with employment growth in occupations other than in retail trade. In doing the calculations, we simply added together the numbers for all twenty-five counties in which the new Wal-Marts opened. The results, shown in figure 7-3, are interesting. Non-retail-trade employment grew by 1.57 percent in the relevant counties, more than in the nation as a whole (possibly suggestive of some positive spillover effects from the new Wal-Mart, and/or possibly reflecting the fact that Wal-Mart located its stores in counties with perceived promise), but employment in retail trade rose by a robust 5.09 percent, more than three times as much. About 30 percent of total employment growth in the twenty-five counties was attributable to retail-trade employment growth—a huge proportion, considering that only about 12 percent of employees worked in retail trade nationwide. On the basis of this, we would conclude that the evidence supports the conclusion that Wal-Mart is a net creator of jobs.

Income and Compensation Growth. Analysis similar to that above was performed for the twenty-five selected communities, using personal income growth as the measure of economic performance. The results were not quite as telling as those for total employment, but still tended toward refuting the contention that Wal-Mart had adverse aggregate economic effects on communities. In a bare majority of cases, Wal-Mart's introduction was associated with an improving income growth picture relative to the nonmetropolitan areas of the state. However, in fully seven of the twelve other communities, income growth in the era after Wal-Mart opened was greater than in the nonmetro areas of the same state. All told, in 80 percent of the cases a good argument could be made that the opening of Wal-Mart was associated with relatively high income growth.

A major argument of labor unions is that Wal-Mart depresses wages. We have earlier argued that relatively low Wal-Mart wages are explainable by general labor market conditions, that workers in retail trade are historically relatively low-paid, and that Wal-Mart stores are located disproportionately in low-wage and low-income areas. But we have not looked directly at total compensation (wages and fringe benefits) in retail trade in the communities in which Wal-Mart locates.

FIGURE 7-4

PERCENT CHANGE IN ANNUAL COMPENSATION, RETAIL TRADE,
2001–2003, WAL-MART COUNTIES (PERCENT)

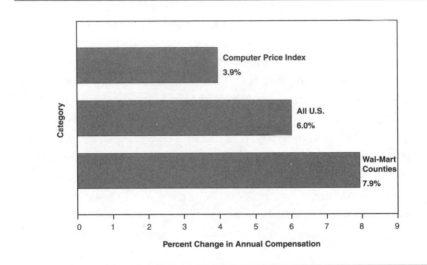

SOURCES: U.S. Department of Commerce, Bureau of Economic Analysis, "Regional Economic Profiles," www.bea.gov/bea/regional/reis/default.cfm?catable=CA30 (accessed August 13, 2006); U.S. Department of Labor, Bureau of Labor Statistics, *Consumer Price Index*, ftp://ftp.bls.gov/pub/special.requests/cpi/cpiai.txt (accessed August 14, 2006); Wal-Mart stores opening information found at www.walmartfacts.com/FeaturedTopics/?id=8 (accessed August 13, 2006).

We remedied that defect for our sample of twenty-five new Wal-Mart communities by calculating average annual compensation of workers in retail trade for the year 2001, before Wal-Mart had begun business, with that for the year 2003, after Wal-Mart began. If Wal-Mart were paying wages below the norm for retail trade in the communities in which it operated, we would expect average annual compensation to decline, or at least remain stagnant (falling in inflation-adjusted terms). In fact, in a solid majority of communities, retail trade wages and benefits rose. Adding together the twenty-five counties as if they were one economic unit, we found that average annual compensation in retail trade rose an impressive 7.93 percent, going from $16,937.82 to $18,282.57 (see figure 7-4)—this at a time when the Consumer Price Index rose 3.94 percent. In short, real annual wages (broadly defined to include fringe benefits) rose 3.84 percent, or nearly 2 percent annually. There is no support for the hypothesis that Wal-Mart depresses wages in retail trade.

To be sure, the twenty-five communities selected were relatively healthy economically—no doubt both a cause and a consequence of Wal-Mart's arrival in them. As noted above, overall employment growth in these counties was more robust than the national average. It is possible that rising real wages in retail trade were actually dramatically less than in other occupations. That, however, was not the case. Compensation in nonretail occupations rose only slightly more (8.27 percent), not a meaningful difference. Moreover, the increase in retail trade compensation in the Wal-Mart counties considerably exceeded the national increase for the same period, 6 percent.

Certainly, this is not the last word on this subject. At least three criticisms might be leveled against the analysis above. First, the sample of twenty-five counties, while fairly large and geographically dispersed, might somehow not be representative of the nation as a whole. Second, the Bureau of Economic Analysis data are annual compensation figures, and it is theoretically possible that a significant increase in average hours worked annually in retail trade could have occurred between 2001 and 2003, meaning that the trend in hourly wages would be different than for annual wages. Third, the data are for all retail trade, not just the big-box discount category. If wage trends in the discount stores are fundamentally different from those in other retail trade, this would distort the results. The probabilities of any or all of these happening to a significant enough magnitude to fundamentally alter the findings are, in our judgment, pretty small, but they are clearly not zero.

Findings of Other Scholarly Researchers

If we were to summarize in a single sentence the preponderance of scholarly work on the economic impact of Wal-Mart, it would be that Wal-Mart's impact is more positive than negative, and that the negative consequences of its expansion touted by its critics are, at the minimum, overstated, and sometimes downright wrong. To be sure, not all the studies reach a positive conclusion about Wal-Mart, and there are some nuances and qualifications that need to be pointed out; but on balance the evidence more often finds Wal-Mart's economic impact to be positive or relatively benign.

Consumer Welfare. As discussed in chapter 1, any assessment of Wal-Mart on communities must look at the impact of product prices on buyers. Here the evidence is clear and relatively unambiguous. Consider, for example, the findings of Emek Basker of the University of Missouri. Speaking of Wal-Mart's prices to consumers, she concludes, "I find robust price effects for several products, including shampoo, toothpaste, and laundry detergent; magnitudes vary by product and specification, but generally range from 1.5–3 percent in the short run and four times as much in the long run."[4] Basker looked at ten widely used consumer products (aspirin, cigarettes, Coke, detergent, Kleenex, shampoo, toothpaste, men's dress shirts, pants, and underwear), using standardized brand names (such as Arrow shirts, Levis 501 jeans, and Crest toothpaste). The analysis was very extensive, involving some 165 sample cities over an extended time period. While for some products, such as cigarettes and Coke, the Wal-Mart price advantage was essentially nonexistent, for others prices were reduced in the long run by 8–13 percent from what would have existed without Wal-Mart.

The distinguished MIT economist Jerry Hausman, along with Ephraim Leibtag, found even greater price effects—approaching 25 percent in the aggregate—and they emphasize that these price advantages create very significant amounts of surplus to consumers, running literally into the hundreds of billions of dollars in the period of Wal-Mart's existence. This is particularly true for the lower-income consumers who frequent Wal-Mart Supercenters.[5] Hausman and Leibtag add that "a significant decrease in consumer surplus arises from zoning regulations and pressure group tactics that restrict the entry and expansion of supercenters into particular geographic markets."[6]

Global Insight, a large and prestigious private economic consulting firm, estimated the impact of Wal-Mart's prices on the *entire* Consumer Price Index for about two dozen large metropolitan areas for which the U.S. Labor Department's Bureau of Labor Statistics constructs price indices.[7] They estimated that Wal-Mart's impact (as measured by store square footage) was to lower overall prices by somewhere between 1 and 4 percent.[8] For the entire economy, they estimated that Wal-Mart has lowered consumer prices (as measured by the Consumer Price Index for All Urban Consumers) by 3.1 percent. Other things being equal, this implies a vast welfare gain and a rise in real incomes measured literally in the hundreds of billions of dollars

The Global Insight study was conducted at Wal-Mart's request with Wal-Mart financial support, and thus its objectivity may be subject to question. Yet three highly respected and disinterested scholars, Marvin Kosters of the American Enterprise Institute, Isabel Sawhill of the Brookings Institution, and Robert Parry, retired president of the Federal Reserve Bank of San Francisco oversaw the study's execution and then, attending a conference on Wal-Mart in November 2005, generally found the study to be methodologically sound.[9]

Wal-Mart's positive contributions to consumer welfare are reflected in favorable public attitudes toward Wal-Mart. The Pew Research Center polled over 1,500 adults in late 2005, and reported that 81 percent of respondents found Wal-Mart a good place to shop.[10] Moreover, lower-income groups found the store an especially good place to shop, even more so than relatively affluent customers. Even 73 percent of union members agreed.[11]

Employment and Wage Effects. The Global Insight study did very extensive analysis of wage and employment effects of Wal-Mart at both the national and local levels. A rather extensive and sophisticated general equilibrium model of the entire economy was utilized, which allows for secondary and tertiary effects of policies to be analyzed. For example, it is possible that lower Wal-Mart prices increase disposable incomes, which in return raises the savings rate, which then lowers interest rates and stimulates capital formation. The standard partial equilibrium approach used in most studies does not pick up the many spillover effects of Wal-Mart policies.

Global Insight estimates that Wal-Mart on net was responsible for 210,000 new jobs by 2004, lowering the unemployment rate by 0.14 percent from what it otherwise would have been.[12] Moreover, it estimates that given Wal-Mart's comparative efficiency, total factor productivity (a comprehensive measure of the increased efficiency of all inputs used in the production process) was raised by a nontrivial 0.75 percent by 2004. With respect to wages, Global Insight concludes that Wal-Mart's total effect was to lower wage levels somewhat in nominal terms (2.2 percent), but given that the downward price effects of Wal-Mart are even greater, in an inflation-adjusted effect, real disposable income is estimated to rise by 0.9 percent from what it would be in the absence of Wal-Mart. That conclusion is generally consistent with the findings with respect to productivity.

At the local level, Global Insight estimates that the overall short-run impact of Wal-Mart in a typical community is to create 137 jobs. This suggests some loss of non-Wal-Mart jobs (since the typical store employs somewhere between 150 and 350 persons), but not enough to offset the new employment. Some net decline in jobs in some forms of retailing, such as food stores, is more than offset by increases elsewhere. In the longer term, the employment effects are slightly smaller but still positive. Wal-Mart is not a net job-killer; indeed, the opposite is closer to the truth.

Similar to the Global Insight findings are results of studies conducted in 2005 by, respectively, Hicks and Basker, and in 2001 by Hicks and Wilburn. For example, using quarterly data and looking at new store openings in Pennsylvania, Hicks concludes that "Wal-Mart . . . has a longer term effect on net employment of a little more than fifty jobs in a year."[13] Particularly interesting are Hicks's findings regarding worker turnover in retail trade. He observes a dramatic (over 40 percent) decline in job turnover in retail trade after Wal-Mart enters markets—which completely contradicts the claims of critics that Wal-Mart is an unfair, hostile employer. Where employers are disliked or morale is low, job turnover tends to be high. The decline in turnover rates is thus particularly revealing. Indeed, these results hint that the relatively low turnover rates at Wal-Mart may be a factor in that firm's high productivity and efficiency.

A recent study by Russell Sobel and Andrea Dean is not only generally consistent with the evidence of Hicks, but it goes even further in denying that Wal-Mart has adverse effects. The authors find that most of the loss to non-Wal-Mart businesses cited by critics and acknowledged by writers like Hicks is illusory. They conclude that "contrary to popular belief, our results suggest that the process of creative destruction unleashed by Wal-Mart has no statistically significant impact on the overall size of the small business sector in the United States."[14]

With respect to wages, Hicks's recent study finds only very modest effects, consistent with the general notion that Wal-Mart pays roughly the market wage. Actually, the entrance of Wal-Mart into retail markets has, according to Hicks, a positive impact on wages of new hires (about $90 per month), but the impact on existing workers is statistically insignificant. Overall, Hicks's study cannot find any support for those who believe public policy in communities should be to discourage (or encourage, for that matter) Wal-Mart, a finding observed a decade earlier by Kenneth Stone.[15]

Hicks's overall conclusions on employment effects are remarkably similar to those of Emek Basker. For a study appearing in the prestigious *Review of Economics and Statistics*, Basker used a huge sample with over 40,000 observations—data on 1,749 Wal-Mart counties (with over 2,300 Wal-Mart stores) for the twenty-three years from 1977 to 1999.[16] Basker concludes that the job gains from Wal-Mart during that period were largely, but not completely, offset by job losses elsewhere, leaving an average net gain of fifty jobs per store—uncannily similar to Hicks's finding. Factoring in the loss of twenty jobs in wholesaling arising from Wal-Mart's high use of vertical integration (that is, less reliance on wholesalers), there is still a net job gain, albeit a very small one.

While the preponderance of evidence, including our findings, supports the position that Wal-Mart, on balance, has very small but mostly positive effects both on the total level of employment and wages, one study reaches somewhat different conclusions. The findings of Neumark, Zhang, and Ciccarella seem somewhat puzzling to us.[17] As in the other studies, much of the evidence cited by these authors shows that Wal-Mart has a positive impact on *total* employment, by around 2 percent, which is actually a sizable proportion in relation to countywide employment. Since mean county employment was over twenty thousand for the largest of three samples used, this implies net job creation of four hundred jobs or so—far more than in the other studies. Since Wal-Mart itself typically employs roughly three hundred workers, it also implies significant gains elsewhere, suggesting something of a job multiplier effect. At the same time, however, Neumark and colleagues find a significant decline in retail jobs, implying a very sizable increase in nonretail jobs. While these results are counterintuitive, they are marginally plausible. They are, however, quite different from those of all the other researchers mentioned above. Moreover, the Neumark study finds that payrolls fall after Wal-Mart opens, which implies a drop in compensation per worker—something not found elsewhere.

The disparity in results reflects the use of different samples, as well as differences in procedures used to control for the myriad of factors that explain employment and payroll growth. A statistical problem arises because Wal-Mart obviously picks communities to locate in where they think they might be profitable, and those often have a bright economic future independent of Wal-Mart itself. Does Wal-Mart raise economic growth, or does it locate where economic growth is already high? Is Wal-Mart the cause or the effect? In attempting to correct for what most researchers refer to as the "endo-geneity problem," the analysis gets rather complicated, and we wonder in this case if the cure is worse than the disease.

Moreover, a closer look at the data leads us to conclude that the Neu-mark results, aside from bordering on bizarre in some respects, are also quite mixed. The authors' use of relatively straightforward regression pro-cedures (ordinary least squares) tends to show positive employment effects, but the introduction of instrumental variables (IV) to control for the endo-geneity problem reverses the relationship. Further, the so-called baseline findings, even using the IV approach, for the two samples that are reported show a very robust positive relationship between "general merchandise" retailing employment and Wal-Mart openings, implying the loss of jobs outside general merchandising is truly substantial, far greater than what others observe.[18]

Finally, quite different conclusions are reached about the aggregate retail employment effects, using what are termed the "B sample" and the "C sam-ple." Using what economists term "sensitivity analysis" (using different approaches to evaluate evidence), the results reported by Neumark and col-leagues seem to be all over the map—not something that inspires confidence.

That said, the researchers are solid scholars (Neumark, for one, is a noted labor economist), so these results cannot be dismissed out of hand. Nonetheless, when weighed against the predominance of evidence, we would conclude that the majority of the research on Wal-Mart suggests that it has had, on average, modestly positive effects on community employ-ment and little impact on wage levels or income. Most of the evidence flatly contradicts the complaints of the company's critics. Moreover, the reader is reminded that even if there are, in fact, modest negative labor market effects, they still have to be weighed against the sizable gains in consumer welfare associated with what Wal-Mart terms "everyday low prices."

Despite the strident and persistent attacks on Wal-Mart as an employer, it is interesting that a solid majority (56 percent) of Americans still consider Wal-Mart to be a good place to work, according to a Pew Research Center poll, with the numbers particularly high (62 percent) among low income households. Interestingly, the positive reactions are nearly as strong in union households (52 percent) as nonunion ones (57 percent).[19]

Impact on Governments. One criticism of Wal-Mart that has received relatively little attention by us so far is that the company imposes a burden on taxpayers. At the national level, that arises partly because some Wal-Mart workers are on Medicaid, allegedly as a result of the hard-nosed approach of the company to providing medical benefits (a criticism which we believe is largely invalid, as discussed earlier). At the local level, Wal-Mart supposedly increases welfare rolls and has other adverse fiscal effects that force local governments either to reduce services or raise taxes.

Before we even look at some evidence on fiscal impacts, it should be pointed out that some of the more strident critics only selectively look at the fiscal effects, citing possible expenditures effects that the company has on governments while ignoring the added revenues that Wal-Mart often brings into communities through sales and property tax receipts.

Moreover, the critics sometimes make absolutely unrealistic assumptions: that lower-income Wal-Mart workers would be in fine financial shape (or at least not in need of public assistance) if Wal-Mart did not exist. Implicit is the assumption that in the absence of Wal-Mart, workers would be making $12 or $14 hourly wages instead of $9–$10 and that their other employers would provide full benefits. For example, on one anti–Wal-Mart website it is claimed that "one 200 employee Wal-Mart store may cost federal taxpayers $420,750 a year."[20] It is alleged that federal spending for free and reduced lunches, low-income housing assistance, energy assistance, health care costs, and so on soar in the presence of Wal-Mart.

The above criticism is particularly applicable with respect to Medicaid benefits. Joe Hansen, president of the United Food and Commercial Workers Union, has opined that "a company that reflects America's values doesn't have 660,000 of its employees without company-provided health insurance."[21] Yet, as discussed earlier, a large proportion of those uninsured are covered by other insurance, typically provided through a spouse's employment or the Medicare program universally available to citizens over age sixty-five. Moreover, in response to criticisms, Wal-Mart has announced new insurance programs designed to lower costs for its employees.

Even more important, the evidence above, while not unanimous, generally argues that Wal-Mart does not lower compensation levels for workers, and actually modestly increases employment, meaning some otherwise unemployed persons are on the job because of Wal-Mart, which should reduce welfare expenditures. As will be discussed in chapter 9, Wal-Mart's efficiency raises worker productivity, which unquestionably has positive long-run compensation effects for the entire economy. Other things being equal, this should lower public assistance costs.

So what is the net fiscal impact of Wal-Mart on communities and the nation as a whole? According to Michael Hicks, it is probably *positive*.[22] For example, Hicks finds that Wal-Mart stores in Ohio enhance property tax revenues somewhere between $350,000 and $1.3 million annually and raise labor force participation. He concludes that while Medicaid expenditures average around $651 per worker, the cost nationally may be more like $900. And these figures may be high: Sonya Carlson, for example, estimates in a 2005 study that Medicaid costs per worker in Oregon were only $311.[23] Some, such as Dube and Jacobs, have attributed to Wal-Mart a low-wage policy subsidized by governmental public assistance that potentially has given it an unfair competitive advantage over other firms. As Hicks observes, however, the study does not actually "provide unassailable evidence that Wal-Mart practices differ systematically from other similar firms."[24] Moreover, it is probably true that in retail trade in general, Medicaid subsidies per worker are likely to be several hundred dollars a year, so the Wal-Mart statistic is hardly startling. In any case, the appropriate question is: What would Medicaid subsidies have been if Wal-Mart did not exist? Given the company's likely overall neutral-to-positive impact on employment and wages, it is hard to believe that national Medicaid costs would be much lower (and, indeed, might be a bit higher) in the absence of Wal-Mart.

Wal-Mart and Its Suppliers

Wal-Mart deals with literally thousands of suppliers, and, given its sales volume, it is very often the leading customer for many of them. Inevitably, this leads to complaints that Wal-Mart squeezes its suppliers, demanding low and discounted prices from prevailing levels. There is plenty of anecdotal evidence confirming that Wal-Mart is very aggressive in demanding low prices from suppliers. The company also engages in various cooperative strategies to track inventories and products in the supply chain with major suppliers, such as Procter & Gamble. By sharing data from its acclaimed inventory system with them, Wal-Mart helps large suppliers get merchandise quickly to the appropriate stores.

Of course, Wal-Mart is not alone in being aggressive with suppliers to obtain a competitive price advantage. One of the authors asked a large supplier to several big-box discount chains, "Is Wal-Mart peculiarly aggressive and brutal in negotiating contracts with you?" The respondent answered, "Wal-Mart is bad, but Home Depot is the absolute worst to deal with." It is worth noting, however, that, whatever his complaints, the supplier reluctantly admitted he made money dealing with both Wal-Mart and Home Depot, and that profit margins were not so small that he was seriously considering abandoning the business with the big-box retailers.

It is no doubt true that one of the many factors in the success of Wal-Mart, Home Depot, and other big-box retailers is their ability to reduce significantly the costs of getting goods from the manufacturer to the store. While driving very hard bargains with suppliers is part of the story, more important is the fact that Wal-Mart (and now other discounters) are dealing directly with manufacturers, eschewing to a large extent the wholesale operators that traditionally have been the source of supplies in retail trade. With high volumes, Sam Walton correctly thought, he could reduce distributional costs by carrying out the traditional wholesale function himself, using company-owned trucks to reduce transportation charges. That model is now followed by several of the big-box discounters.

Conclusions

Does Wal-Mart hurt communities economically? In scientific research involving human behavior, it is usually very difficult to control for the myriad of things that affect phenomena beyond the key variable under study, and this is no exception. To answer the question, "What is the economic impact of Wal-Mart?" one must ask a difficult, counterfactual question: "What would economic life have been like in the absence of Wal-Mart?"

With this caveat in mind, we did some simple analysis of twenty-five communities that opened Wal-Mart Supercenters in 2002, and concluded that their opening had more positive than negative economic consequences, independent of the unquestioned gains in consumer welfare associated with lower prices of goods. Employment growth tended to be somewhat higher in new Wal-Mart communities, for example. It does not appear that wage levels in retail trade fell on average—indeed, it is more likely they rose.

A review of bigger and more sophisticated studies by others shows mixed results, but the majority of the truly well-designed academic studies show that Wal-Mart does not have deleterious economic effects. Most of the evidence suggests that Wal-Mart, on balance, increases employment, for example. The impact on wages is questionable, but in any case is not dramatically positive or negative, probably because Wal-Mart seems to pay roughly the going wage for local labor conditions. It is doubtful that Wal-Mart has any strong net fiscal effects on communities, but the more convincing evidence suggests those effects, if anything, are positive.

The net result? Wal-Mart is a plus for American society. The huge gains in consumer welfare, measured by Hausman and Leibtag to be in the billions of dollars annually, are unquestionably greater than the other, relatively small net economic costs (which the evidence suggests are probably close to zero and more likely negative) that Wal-Mart imposes on society. In our judgment, it is hard to conclude that Wal-Mart has not been good for America.

8

Wal-Mart and the Poor

Wal-Mart, and to a lesser extent, other big-box discount stores, have been charged with being indifferent and insensitive to the needs of the poor and disadvantaged. For example, it is argued that by paying substandard wages, Wal-Mart hurts the most vulnerable members of our society.

In this short chapter, we argue that Wal-Mart's benefits have disproportionately aided those with limited income. Poor people have been the primary beneficiaries of "everyday low prices" and the employment opportunities that would otherwise have been unavailable. Rather than being part of the problem facing the poor, Wal-Mart is part of the solution to the problem of poverty in America.

Wal-Mart's Customers

Who are Wal-Mart's customers? They are spread across every socioeconomic category, from very poor to highly affluent, but the firm has always located the majority of its stores in relatively nonaffluent (and even poor) communities, has stressed "everyday low prices," and has not emphasized expensive brand names. Sam Walton's business vision was based on offering consumers lower prices, an approach that appeals more to lower-income individuals than more affluent customers.

Evidence for this is offered in figure 8-1, which looks at shopping habits of Americans by income category. According to Pew Research Center survey data, people from low-income households are far more inclined to shop regularly at Wal-Mart than those from families with above-average incomes. Indeed, there is a striking correlation: As income rises, the proportion of regular Wal-Mart shoppers falls. Wal-Mart caters to, and successfully

FIGURE 8-1

REGULAR WAL-MART SHOPPERS AS A PERCENTAGE OF GROUP,
BY INCOME CATEGORIES (PERCENT)

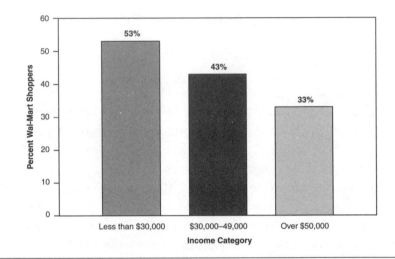

SOURCE: Pew Research Center, *Wal-Mart a Good Place to Shop But Some Critics Too*, December 15, 2005, http://people-press.org/reports/display.php3?ReportID=265 (accessed August 13, 2006).

attracts, customers of modest means.

Since Wal-Mart's strategy is to appeal to more price-conscious consumers, it is hardly surprising that their stores are disproportionately located in less affluent communities. To verify that thesis, we examined all of the Wal-Mart Supercenters that opened in 2001, 2002, and 2003—a total of 450 stores. We compared the average income level in the counties where these Wal-Mart stores were located with the average income of counties where seventy-two new Costco stores had opened in the same time period. (Costco is Wal-Mart's biggest competitor in the warehouse-store category, and critics of Wal-Mart often cite Costco as a model of what these stores should be.)

As figure 8-2 shows, however, even correcting for population size, Wal-Mart stores are, on average, located in significantly less affluent areas than Costco stores. The Costco counties have, on average, nearly 30 percent higher incomes than the Wal-Mart ones. The nearly $8,000 per-capita income differential is huge. For example, looking at the fifty states for 2003,

FIGURE 8-2

AVERAGE PER-CAPITA INCOME, COUNTIES WITH NEW WAL-MART
SUPERCENTERS AND NEW COSTCO STORES, 2001–2003

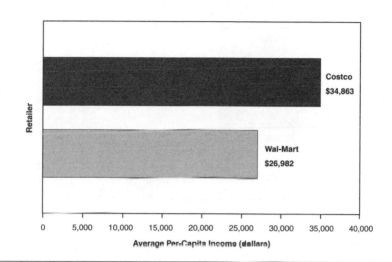

SOURCES: Author's calculations; Wal-Mart stores opening information found at www.walmartfacts.com/FeaturedTopics/?Id=8, Costco stores opening information found at: www.costco.com/Warehouse/Location.aspx?country=United%20States (information obtained by clicking on each individual store location); U.S. Department of Commerce, Bureau of Economic Analysis, "Regional Economic Profiles," www.bea.gov/bea/regional/reis/default.cfm?catable=CA30; and U.S. Bureau of the Census, "State and County QuickFacts," http://quickfacts.census.gov/qfd/index.html (all sources accessed August 13, 2006).

the standard deviation on variations in per-capita income was only $4,288. Based on state data, average incomes in Costco counties are nearly two standard deviations higher than those in Wal-Mart counties. The typical Wal-Mart store was located in an area with average incomes similar to Alabama, Oklahoma, or Arizona; the typical Costco went into areas with average incomes like those in Colorado or New York.

Wal-Mart's critics may tout the virtues of Costco but they are ignoring an important difference between the companies: Wal-Mart makes a greater effort to cater to the most cost-conscious consumers—the less affluent. Costco may be a fine alternative for more affluent consumers, but people tend to shop near their homes. Wal-Mart serves less affluent neighborhoods far better than Costco. Whether it offers lower prices than Costco is an empirical question that future researchers might wish to examine.

FIGURE 8-3

PERCENT OF NEW OPENINGS IN LOWER INCOME COUNTIES, 2003

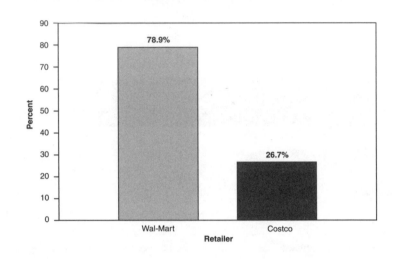

SOURCES: Author's calculations; Wal-Mart stores opening information found at www.walmartfacts.com/ FeaturedTopics/?id=8; Costco stores opening information found at www.costco.com/Warehouse/Location. aspx?country=United%20States (information obtained by clicking on each individual store location); U.S. Department of Commerce, Bureau of Economic Analysis, "Regional Economic Profiles," www.bea. gov/bea/regional/reis/default.cfm?catable=CA30; and U.S. Bureau of the Census, "State and County QuickFacts," http://quickfacts.census.gov/qfd/index.html (all sources accessed August 13, 2006).

The use of average figures sometimes disguises nuances in the data because of unusual distributions of observations around the average. To partially test for that, we did a very simple analysis. We divided the counties where Wal-Mart and Costco opened stores in 2003 into two categories—those with incomes above the national average of $31,487, and those with lower incomes. As figure 8-3 shows, an overwhelming majority of the Wal-Mart stores were located in the relatively low-income counties, while only a small minority of Costco stores were. A look at the poverty rate for 2000 for the counties in which the sample of twenty-five new Wal-Mart stores discussed in chapter 7 were located shows the average poverty rate was 13.92 percent, compared with an average of 12.24 percent for the states in which the stores were located.[1]

Moreover, not only does Wal-Mart locate in relatively low-income areas, it reaches out specifically to members of minority groups with disadvantaged socioeconomic status. To appeal to Hispanics, for example, Wal-Mart generally uses Spanish-language signage, and even has a quarterly magazine with a circulation of over 500,000 provided free in its 1,400 stores with a large Hispanic clientele.[2] While motivated by profits, not altruism, Wal-Mart nonetheless is trying to connect with a large group of persons that, on the average, have low incomes and modest educations, and are considered poor or near-poor.

Implications for Policy

States or localities that try to keep Wal-Mart out either directly (by use of zoning laws or similar means) or indirectly (by punitive legislation that raises costs, such as mandatory insurance not required of competitors, or very high minimum wages for employees, as recently enacted in Chicago) are hurting their poor citizens, as they are the prime beneficiaries of Wal-Mart. Earlier, we argued that the "consumer surplus" arising from low Wal-Mart prices provides literally tens of billions of dollars of annual welfare benefits to its customers. A large proportion of those benefits accrue to the poor. When Wal-Mart announces, for instance, that it will provide a large number of generic drugs to the public for $4 each, it is aiding all Americans, but especially the poor.

A little arithmetic exercise makes the point. Suppose Wal-Mart provides $50 billion in annual benefits in the form of consumer surplus, with $20 billion of that surplus going to the poor, $20 billion to the middle class, and $10 billion to the rich. Those numbers are plausible, given the empirical evidence introduced earlier. Suppose there are 60 million poor Americans with incomes averaging $10,000 ($30,000 for a family of three), 175 million middle-class Americans with average incomes of $30,000 per person, and 60 million upper income Americans with per-capita incomes averaging $60,000.

The poor would receive Wal-Mart-generated consumer surplus equaling $333 a person ($1,000 for a family of three) per year, or 3.33 percent of their average income of $10,000 a person. The middle class would receive surplus equaling $114.29 per person, which is about 0.38 percent of income, while the rich would receive surplus equaling only 0.28 percent of their income.

The actual distribution of the burden may be somewhat different than this exercise suggests, but the benefits of Wal-Mart almost certainly disproportionately accrue to the lower-income members of the population. Thus, any policy move that reduces Wal-Mart's incentives or ability to operate will hurt the poor more than the rich. That means that preventing Wal-Mart from operating in a community is the equivalent of imposing a highly regressive tax on the population—a tax that is disproportionately paid by the poor. But taxes at least have the virtue of providing income to the government that could conceivably provide some welfare-enhancing services (perhaps mainly for the poor); that is not the case with most anti–Wal-Mart policies that have been proposed to date. Indeed, they are probably revenue reducing, inasmuch as they would reduce sales (and thus sales tax and maybe income tax revenues) to the relevant community.

Of course, we have been looking only at consumers. Wal-Mart (and other big-box discounters) employs large numbers of workers, as well. We do not have good family income data available for Wal-Mart workers, but since those individuals work in generally low-income areas and receive compensation that, while competitive for the retail industry, is lower than typical of all American workers, it is reasonable to assume that family income of new Wal-Mart workers is significantly less than the average for the American population (although it is enhanced by employment at Wal-Mart). In short, Wal-Mart provides income and job opportunities for relatively less-affluent citizens.

Let us look at the impact of legislation on workers. The State of Maryland mandated health care benefits for its workers, although the law was later invalidated by a federal court. Suppose, however, that the law is ultimately enacted in a form that meets judicial approval. Assume that before the mandate, Wal-Mart workers cost the company on average $10 an hour in wages and $2 in fringe benefits—a total of $12 an hour—and that the new mandate will add $1 an hour to the fringe-benefit costs. One or more of the following four outcomes will occur.

- Wal-Mart will simply swallow the added costs and receive lower profits.

- Wal-Mart will raise its prices to cover the new expense.

- Wal-Mart will reduce openings of new stores in Maryland and abandon plans to open a large distribution center there, preferring to put its resources in communities where profit opportunities are greater.

- Wal-Mart will reduce wages to employees to cover the added personnel costs, either immediately or in the long run, by reducing pay for new hires.

With three of these four outcomes, poor persons in general and Wal-Mart workers in particular are likely to be either neutrally or negatively affected. Only in one scenario might there be gains to Wal-Mart workers (and, marginally, to the poor as a whole), and that would probably only hold in the short run. That optimistic scenario occurs where Wal-Mart pays higher employee compensation, sees its labor costs rise, and sees its profits fall. In the short run, Wal-Mart workers receive a benefit previously not received, and thus gain by the outcome.

There are several problems with this scenario. First, since many Wal-Mart workers already receive the benefits offered through their spouses or Medicare, only a portion of the workforce is positively affected. Moreover, the lower profits will almost certainly have a negative impact on the price of Wal-Mart stock. Since a majority of Wal-Mart employees are also stockholders, they lose wealth. Indeed, for workers for whom the health insurance benefit has no value, the net effect of Wal-Mart's new government-mandated benefits would be negative.

If the health care benefit increases the number of employee applicants, Wal-Mart almost certainly will reduce wages for new employees, offsetting the benefit—the fourth option cited above. If Wal-Mart raises prices (option two above), the huge consumer welfare gains to customers—gains that accrue disproportionately to the poor—will be reduced. Sales will also fall, forcing Wal-Mart to lay off some employees and reduce its work force. Almost certainly, Wal-Mart will reduce its investments in the state imposing restrictions (in this case, Maryland), since the prospective rate of return will fall below those in other states or countries.

Problems exist with other forms of restricting Wal-Mart. Zoning laws designed to keep out big-box retailers raise the cost of shopping to citizens of a community, as they either have to pay higher prices for goods from other local merchants, or they have to incur significant transportation costs to travel longer distances to shop at stores like Wal-Mart. There is no way to know the true motives of Wal-Mart's opponents, but certainly their actions tend to benefit competing local merchants and the affluent members of the community who don't want stores catering to lower-income people.

Wal-Mart and Public Assistance

As was mentioned previously, some critics argue that Wal-Mart increases the cost of public assistance. There are two ways that could be happening. First, Wal-Mart workers are probably on average relatively poor, and some use Medicaid insurance benefits. Second, Wal-Mart workers' low wages could make them eligible for other forms of welfare; if there was no Wal-Mart, critics believe these workers would have better-paying jobs.

These arguments were largely addressed earlier. The appropriate question is not whether some Wal-Mart employees receive some public assistance; rather, we should ask whether total public assistance payments are greater because Wal-Mart exists. The same question could be asked about other big-box discounters as well.

Almost certainly the answer to the question is no. Wal-Mart's overall economic impact is clearly positive, raising total incomes above what would otherwise exist. The underlying reason for this is the fact that Wal-Mart has fostered greater productivity growth (as will be discussed in the next chapter), and productivity growth raises output per capita. For Wal-Mart's success to create higher public assistance payments, the entire incremental income associated with the store would have to go to upper- and middle-income people, with lower-income people receiving none of the financial benefits, and, indeed, even losing income because of Wal-Mart.

That outcome seems highly implausible. Wal-Mart serves low-income communities, and many of its employees are from low-income backgrounds; without Wal-Mart, at least some of them would probably be unemployed.

We cannot know all the causes of changes in poverty levels and the relative importance of different factors, but it does seem relevant to us that we see Wal-Mart's rise has coincided with a generally falling national poverty rate. Over the two decades from 1984 to 2004, the five-year moving average of the poverty rate fell about two and one-half percentage points—a significant decline.[3] The number of households receiving cash assistance fell significantly between 1985 (early in the Wal-Mart revolution) and 2002 (while the population itself grew).[4] This is surely not mainly due to Wal-Mart's success, but it does make one wonder how much of a *negative* effect on poverty Wal-Mart could have had.[5] We also note that, as indicated earlier, while some Wal-Mart employees do receive Medicaid benefits, the incidence is not significantly different from that found among the general population or among other retail-trade employees.

Conclusions

Wal-Mart is more a friend than an enemy of the poor. To be sure, there are some Wal-Mart employees who might be considered poor. But through its low prices and its hiring of hundreds of thousands of low-skilled workers, the company has, on balance, done a lot to make life better for low-income Americans. A disproportionate share of Wal-Mart shoppers are relatively less affluent, and the low prices and greater choice the store offers materially improve their lives. Taxing or regulating Wal-Mart out of business would have the same impact as an extremely regressive tax—burdening the poor far more than the rich. Wal-Mart's rise is generally coincident with a decline in poverty and the amount of public assistance in the United States; although we cannot prove there is a causal relationship between those trends, we suspect it is not entirely coincidental.

9

The Discount Revolution in Broader Economic Context

While we have made some mention of the international dimensions of the revolution in big-box discounting in the United States and its spread around the world, most of this book's emphasis is on specific, fairly narrow economic aspects of the changes that have occurred within the United States. For example, we have looked at the impact of price changes on consumers and of Wal-Mart on community employment, and at whether suppliers to the big-box discounters like Wal-Mart are being unduly abused. In this chapter we do a somewhat broader, necessarily more speculative, exploration. Has the discount revolution had a measurable economic impact on our rate of economic growth, our overall prosperity—indeed, on our way of life?

Accordingly, we make some reasonably educated speculations as to the impact of Wal-Mart and its imitators on national productivity and thus on our total output. How much of modern economic growth is attributable to this retail revolution? So as not to mislead, we will state up front that it is very difficult, arguably impossible, to come up with a precise measure of the aggregate economic impact of innovations like Wal-Mart supercenters. We think, however, that using reasonable assumptions, we should be able to present a range of possible effects.

Estimating Broader Economic Effects: Some Issues

When someone asks the question, "How much have big-box discount stores enhanced American economic well-being?" they are implicitly posing what Robert Fogel once famously called a "counterfactual proposition."[1]

What would the world have been like in the absence of such stores? Answering that question is inherently difficult, and inevitably involves making a number of assumptions that, while perhaps reasonable, can lead to material errors in estimation if they are, in fact, erroneous. Moreover, given the enormous potential spillover effects of any economic change on a large variety of economic activities, the most sophisticated method of estimating economic effects involves constructing vast, general equilibrium models with scores, if not hundreds, of equations. Unfortunately, the complex interrelationships in the American economy are not all precisely known and are constantly changing. Even large econometric models are prone to error—often as much so as less-sophisticated "partial equilibrium" analysis, such as we attempt in a somewhat rudimentary form below.

To get a sense of the multisector potential spillover effects of innovations in retail trade, consider the impact of, say, Wal-Mart stores on national savings. If, as empirical evidence suggests, Wal-Mart has lowered retail prices and increased the true disposable income of individuals, then it is likely to have increased personal savings as well. Other things being equal, that alone would lower interest rates which, in turn, would lead to some increase in investment spending and an accompanying rise in productivity, which, in turn, would lead to greater wage growth and future rises in consumer spending, savings, and so on. These secondary and tertiary effects of new stores, though perhaps rather small, might cumulatively be quite meaningful.

It is very difficult to trace all of these effects; for example, the sensitivity of investment spending to interest rates has varied historically and with different types of investment. Also, the rise in the supply of loanable funds associated with big-box discounters may be offset by a rise in the demand for such funds which, for example, prevents interest rates from falling. In short, trying to draw conclusions about the precise economic impact of some innovation on society is tricky business, and is prone to error.

Despite that huge caveat, we should not simply abandon any effort to make a reasonable guess as to the impact of stores like Wal-Mart on the economy. We should, at the very minimum, be able to assert the *direction* of the impact—positive or negative—and make some reasonably accurate assessments as to the extent of the aggregate impact.

The Big-Box Discount Revolution and Productivity Change

Let us start our exploration by turning specifically to increases in the productivity of labor resources—an increase in output per unit of labor inputs used. When productivity rises, wages and standards of living go up. The long-term rise in labor productivity in the United States is the single most important factor in America's exceptional affluence.

It is roughly true that labor productivity in the United States rose 2 percent a year from 1870 to 1945, by about 3 percent a year from 1945 to around 1970, by a bit over 1 percent a year from 1970 to the early 1990s, and well above 2 percent a year in the last decade or so.[2] The long-term average since 1870 is about 2 percent growth.

Labor productivity growth tends to be somewhat volatile, rising sharply during boom periods and languishing during recessions. For that reason, it is probably best to look at a moving average of productivity change in order to get a better picture of long-run trends. In figure 9-1 we observe the five-year annual moving average of productivity growth for the United States for three years—1980, 1992, and 2004—and relate that, in figure 9-2, to the growth in the relative importance of Wal-Mart (as measured by domestic sales as a percentage of gross domestic product). The rise in productivity over time occurs at the same time that Wal-Mart grows from being a relatively minor force in retail trade to becoming the nation's largest corporation based on employment or sales.

Of course, merely demonstrating that two statistics both trend upward does not prove any sort of causation. Moreover, there are literally hundreds of factors other than big-box discount houses that might explain productivity growth. Nonetheless, the fact that enhanced productivity growth happens at the very time that important innovations are occurring in retail trade raises at least the possibility that the two are causally related. Moreover, it adds to the other evidence that contradicts the hypothesis of critics of big-box retailing that these stores have adverse economic effects.

To carry the analysis further, we looked in greater depth at productivity *within* the nation's leading retailer, Wal-Mart. We calculated sales per employee over the 1990s to see if it was sizable enough to have some material broader effects on the economy. In inflation-adjusted terms, sales per worker at Wal-Mart rose 2.78 percent a year from fiscal year 1990 to fiscal

FIGURE 9-1

FIVE-YEAR MOVING AVERAGE OF ANNUAL PRODUCTIVITY GROWTH,
1980, 1992, 2004 (PERCENT)

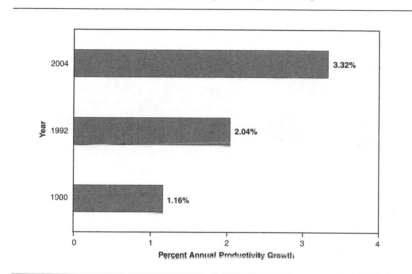

SOURCE: U.S. Department of Labor, Bureau of Labor Statistics, as reported in the *Economic Report of the President* (Washington, D.C.: Government Printing Office, 2006), 341.

year 2000. In the 1990s, productivity per worker in the entire business sector rose by 2.06 percent a year, a good deal less than the Wal-Mart gain. During the same period, the annual increase in value-added output per worker in all retail trade was 2.04 percent in inflation-adjusted terms.[3] ("Value-added" refers to the dollar value of the distributional services provided by the retailer; it is total sales minus the cost of goods purchased.)

The Wal-Mart data, however, are not a direct measure of productivity. If average hours per worker remained unchanged as well as the ratio of value-added output to total sales, and if international sales per worker were immaterial, then the 2.78 percent statistic would be a good indicator of productivity change. We suspect that that assumption may be reasonably good with respect to hours worked and the ratio between value-added output and sales, but are certain that it is not with respect to overseas stores. The calculations were derived by dividing Wal-Mart sales by total (including international) employment. For the years 1990–94, when fewer than 1 percent of Wal-Mart stores were overseas, the growth in sales per worker in

FIGURE 9-2

**WAL-MART DOMESTIC SALES AS A PERCENT OF GDP,
1980, 1992, 2004 (PERCENT)**

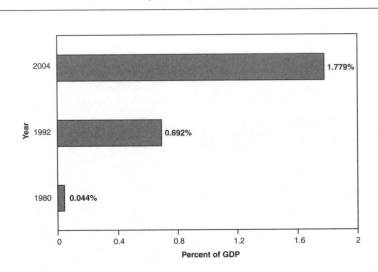

SOURCES: Author's calculations using data from Wal-Mart, *Wal-Mart 1980 Annual Report*, 3, www.walmartstores.com/Files/1980AR.pdf; *Wal-Mart 1992 Annual Report*, 3, www.walmartstores.com/Files/1992AR.pdf; *Wal-Mart 2004 Annual Report*, 17, www.walmartstores.com/Files/annualreport_2004.pdf; U.S. Department of Commerce, Bureau of Economic Analysis, table 1.1.5, "National Income and Product Accounts Table: Gross Domestic Product," *National Economic Accounts*, www.bea.gov/bea/dn/home/gdp.htm (all accessed August 13, 2006).

inflation-adjusted terms exceeded 4 percent a year. International operations were immaterial.

The growth in foreign operations after 1994, however, complicates the calculations of productivity growth per domestic employee. If one assumes that overseas sales per worker were as high as domestic, we would estimate real domestic sales per worker rose 3.59 percent from 1990 to 2000. If anything, the figure is likely to be higher, as sales per worker likely are somewhat lower overseas. Thus it is plausible, even likely, that domestic productivity growth at Wal-Mart was at least 4 percent a year—dramatically higher than for either the economy as a whole, or for the non-Wal-Mart component of retailing, where sales growth per worker probably was modestly under 2 percent a year. Admittedly, if there have been dramatic changes in hours worked per employee or if the markup of goods sold has changed a lot, these calculations could be seriously in error, but we find it highly unlikely that measurement errors were so large that true productivity growth was trivial or nonexistent.

Service industries have historically had lower productivity growth than goods industries, where the substitution of machinery for labor has allowed rapid advances. For example, productivity in manufacturing has risen far more than in the total (largely service-oriented) economy in recent decades.[4] For a significant and growing segment within a major service sector (retail trade) to have productivity growth much higher than the norm for the whole economy suggests that this growth might have had important effects in the aggregate productivity statistics.

Moreover, Wal-Mart's productivity advance did not occur in a vacuum. The increased competitive pressures fostered by the company's efficiency no doubt increased efforts of competitors to raise their productivity, as well. Thus, Target, Home Depot, Best Buy, Costco, retail grocery chains, and many other retailers have no doubt had productivity advances necessitated by the Wal-Mart competitive threat. Having said that, a cursory look at changes in sales per employee over time at two competitors (Target and Home Depot) does not show the significant gains observed at Wal-Mart, although that may very well reflect data problems (for example, no correction for changing hours of work per employee) rather than genuine stagnation.[5]

The rise in productivity at Wal-Mart in the 1990s (and, no doubt, earlier and later) reflected two major trends. First, Wal-Mart's relentless pursuit of efficiency had big payoffs, especially as the company refined and extended its famous distribution and inventory control systems. Second, the mix of types of stores changed, with supercenters and, to a lesser extent, Sam's Club stores growing vastly in importance compared to the smaller, original Wal-Marts. Presumably, output per worker was higher in the larger, higher-volume stores.

By looking at data on value-added sales per worker and making some adjustment for changing average hours in retail trade (which tended to decline steadily from 1947 until about 1990), we can get a general picture of productivity change in retail trade by decades.[6] The trickiest part of making such calculations is adjusting for inflation, which was particularly substantial in the 1970s and early 1980s, but was continuous to some degree throughout the postwar era. As discussed earlier, there is virtually universal agreement that the Consumer Price Index (CPI) overstates inflation. For the estimates reported below, we accordingly constructed our own price index based on the CPI–All Urban Consumers (CPI-U), adjusting for what we believe was probably the average amount of inflationary bias for that index in various periods.[7]

During the 1960s, the discount house, typified by Kmart but including many smaller regional names, including Wal-Mart, revolutionized retailing by supplanting the older variety stores and traditional department stores in general merchandising. Productivity per worker is estimated to have risen sharply—over 2 percent a year. By 1970, the discount store was well-established, and over the next two decades, productivity growth was modest, averaging perhaps one-half of 1 percent annually. In the 1990s, as the Wal-Mart revolution became more apparent, productivity growth again rose, with value-added output per worker in all of retail trade rising by about 1.2 percent a year, more than double the rate prevailing in the preceding two decades. The estimate for the 1990s is somewhat lower than obtained above using an alternative estimation procedure, but not wildly different. By any measure we use, productivity growth in retail trade accelerated after 1990.

Statistics indicate that productivity advance accelerated again after 2000, with retail employment showing very modest change while sales rose robustly. Thus, any analysis of post-1990 productivity growth would lead to higher estimates than reported above for the 1990s alone.

The U.S. Department of Labor's Bureau of Labor Statistics, with far more comprehensive and refined data than those readily available to us, has estimated industry productivity changes for years. They show considerably greater growth than indicated above, concluding that "from 1987 to 2004, labor productivity rose at an average annual rate of . . . 3.4 percent a year in retail trade."[8] This is markedly greater than productivity in American industry as a whole, as indicated in figure 9-3. Moreover, if one disaggregates the data further to include only the part of retail trade encompassing most big-box discount merchandising, the productivity gains are even more startling, as shown in figure 9-4. In the NAICS classification code 4529, which includes essentially general merchandise operations other than department stores (such as warehouse clubs and superstores), productivity growth was an astonishing 7.6 *percent* a year for the seventeen-year period 1987–2004. Put differently, the typical employee working in these stores in

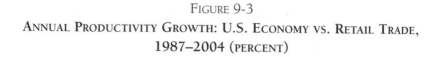

FIGURE 9-3

ANNUAL PRODUCTIVITY GROWTH: U.S. ECONOMY VS. RETAIL TRADE,
1987–2004 (PERCENT)

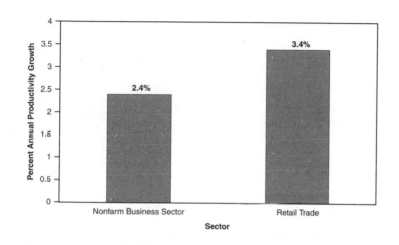

SOURCES: Nonfarm business sector data are drawn from historic data in U.S. Department of Labor, Bureau of Labor Statistics, "Archived News Releases for Productivity and Costs," www.bls.gov/schedule/archives/prod_nr.htm#2006 (accessed August 13, 2006); retail trade data is found in the BLS's "Productivity and Costs By Industry: Wholesale Trade, Retail Trade, and Food Services and Drinking Places, 2004," September 27, 2005, ftp://ftp.bls.gov/pub/news.release/History/prin.09272005.news (accessed June 27, 2006).

2004 added nearly 3.5 times as much output to the economy for each hour worked as did her or his counterpart seventeen years earlier.

As figure 9-4 shows, productivity advance in the big-box category is also vastly greater than in many other traditional retail categories, including grocery and department stores. The grocery store comparison is particularly interesting and may explain why Wal-Mart has risen to the top in grocery sales in the U.S.: the company is simply more efficient. Moreover, since the most intense opposition to Wal-Mart is being heavily funded by the United Food and Commercial Workers, a union whose membership is largely in the traditional grocery industry, it appears that much Wal-Mart bashing is coming from segments of the relatively less productive and inefficient traditional retail sector—fighting a war of words against a competing sector that is more innovative and productive.

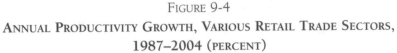

FIGURE 9-4

ANNUAL PRODUCTIVITY GROWTH, VARIOUS RETAIL TRADE SECTORS,
1987–2004 (PERCENT)

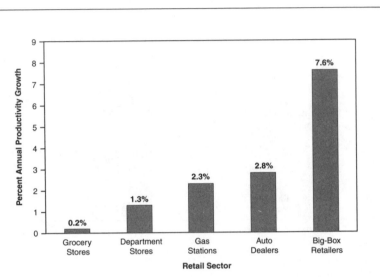

SOURCE: U.S. Department of Labor, Bureau of Labor Statistics, "Productivity and Costs by Industry:
Wholesale Trade, Retail Trade, and Food Services and Drinking Places, 2004," September 27, 2005,
http://www.bls.gov/news.release/archives/prin_09272005.pdf (accessed August 13, 2006).

Broader Economic Effects: Social Savings of
Modern Discount Stores

Traditionally, retail trade has not been considered a cutting-edge sector of
the economy in terms of productivity advance. For example, in the first
generation after World War II, when productivity in the economy as a
whole was rising at a rate of 3 percent a year, it is likely that growth in
retail-trade productivity was far less, probably in the 1–2 percent range.
The results shown in figure 9-3—indicating that productivity growth in
recent years has actually been far higher in retailing than in the economy
as a whole—thus represent a bit of an aberration that is largely a consequence of the Wal-Mart revolution and, more recently, gains from Internet-
based shopping.

Let us ask the counterfactual question: What if the big-box discount revolution, embodied and led by Wal-Mart, had not occurred? How would American society today be different? If retailing had followed historic patterns and showed modest innovation (with productivity growing as it has in the department store sector in the past two decades), total productivity growth in retail trade would likely have been something like one percentage point lower than the average for the economy as a whole rather than one point above. What would have happened if we had had 1.4 percent instead of 3.4 percent retail trade productivity growth from 1987 to 2004?

Since more than one-tenth of the American labor force is employed in retail trade, this difference of two percentage points in the growth of retail trade productivity (consistent with there being no efficiency-enhancing big-box discounting trend) would translate into more than two-tenths of a percentage-point drop in overall labor productivity, sending it from 2.4 to 2.2 percent a year. The cumulative impact of that over seventeen years would be to lower overall productivity in 2004 by about 3.5 percent.

If one believes that at least some of the productivity-enhancing gains from big-box discounting had already been achieved by 1987, it is easy to conclude that the big-box revolution has raised labor productivity in the entire economy by 5 percent over time—and that is without considering any possible effect that big-box retailers may have had on the productivity of their suppliers. If we tried to take that effect into account, it is possible that overall productivity has risen by as much as 7 percent, and overall gross domestic product by 5 percent, as a result of big-box discounting. That translates into over $600 billion in annual output, or over $2,000 for every man, woman, and child in the United States.

One might argue that 5 percent of GDP is not a huge proportion, and that in the absence of the big-box discount revolution, America would still have experienced economic growth. That is true, but the growth certainly would have been less vibrant. For any single innovation to change GDP by 5 percent is quite remarkable. Robert Fogel, for example, estimates the aggregate "social savings" of the railroad—arguably the greatest innovation of the nineteenth century—at about 5 percent of GDP in 1890.[9] While other innovations—the personal computer, for instance—might well exceed the positive economic effect of the Wal-Mart revolution, it certainly remains one of the greatest positive forces for material welfare in American economic history.

To be sure, some caveats are in order. The calculations above are literally back-of-the-envelope estimates based on reasonable interpretations of factual data. The secondary and tertiary effects of retail trade innovations are hard to fathom and quantify fully. If the Wal-Mart revolution had not occurred, perhaps other forms of innovation, such as electronic shopping, would have evolved faster and in a more robust fashion. No one knows for certain. However, the productivity enhancement in retail trade in modern times has almost unquestionably had a sizable impact on overall incomes and output, and therefore on the material standards of living of millions of Americans. Moreover, given the fact that Wal-Mart caters to relatively lower-income shoppers, this enhancement in material welfare has touched all classes of Americans, and most likely the lower-income groups more than the more affluent ones. In this sense, Wal-Mart and its imitators have constituted one of our nation's most successful, if least discussed, antipoverty innovations, as well as a powerful force for economic growth.

Conclusions

It appears to be more than coincidence that the upsurge in American productivity in the past decade or so occurred simultaneously with the sharp increase in the relative importance of big-box retail discounting. If overall annual productivity growth has risen by something on the order of 1.5 percentage points a year (from around 1.0 to around 2.5 percent), then the 0.2 percentage-point annual productivity advance that probably is attributable to the retail trade innovations discussed in this book accounts for about 13 percent of the rise in productivity growth—a pretty important factor, albeit perhaps not as important as the computer revolution. Productivity has risen by as much as 7–8 percent a year in the vibrant part of retail trade represented by the new innovators led by Wal-Mart. This has had all sorts of positive long-term effects, including higher incomes for American families. Any attack on big-box retailers such as Wal-Mart seems like an attack on sources of economic growth.

PART IV

The Future of Wal-Mart

10

Wal-Mart and the World

In an increasingly integrated world, American retailers face both more intense competition and new opportunities. As big-box chains move and expand in foreign markets, and as international chains expand in the United States, U.S. big-box stores compete not only domestically but more and more in international markets. At the same time, big-box stores, American and international, compete for goods that are produced overseas. This activity is the focus of much criticism by interests opposed to anti-big-box stores.

It is increasingly difficult to say that a firm like Wal-Mart is truly "American," despite the fact that it was founded by an American entrepreneur, is largely owned by Americans, and is headquartered in Arkansas. A growing proportion (well over 20 percent) of its sales come from overseas, and the international dimension is a major factor in the firm's current growth strategy. Moreover, an increasing portion of the merchandise sold, even in stores located in the United States, is manufactured in other nations, most often Asian.

There are challenges associated with overseas operations, however, and because of better knowledge of the local culture and customs, and perhaps better political connections, indigenously owned chains in some foreign countries sometimes have an advantage. For example, recently Wal-Mart sold its Korean operations to a local operator for $872 million, as had Carrefour previously.[1] Wal-Mart plans to exit the German market as well.

The Rise of Big-Box Stores in Europe

Although the international dimension of the pace and pattern of retail innovation is nowhere more apparent than in Western Europe, American tourists often fail to encounter the vibrant retailing market there. The historic sites, museums, and cathedrals they visit tend to be concentrated in ancient core cities, and as they travel from one city to the next, they neither stop by nor notice the swaths of more recent development that bear more similarity to American suburbs than the historical European inner cities. These suburbs have captured virtually all urban growth in recent decades as the core cities, like those in the United States, have lost population.[2] They have also captured considerable commercial growth, including huge big-box stores.

Despite tourist impressions, there is more that is similar than different about shopping in America and Europe. Visitors to the core of Madrid or Lisbon will see small convenience stores and grocery stores little larger than American convenience stores. Venturing inside, they will often find prices that are astonishingly high, much as they would also encounter in the small neighborhood markets of depressed U.S. inner cities. As in the United States, however, much of the retail activity takes place in large stores that are outside the urban core and themselves very much like American stores. While they may have had their start in Portland, Grand Rapids, or rural Arkansas, big-box stores have evolved and spread much more rapidly throughout Europe.

Retail innovation was slow to come to Western Europe, which faced a long economic recovery after World War II. In the United States, by contrast, supermarkets appeared and proliferated throughout the country in just a few years after the war was over. By 1955, large supermarkets, though not big-box stores, were to be found within convenient reach of many millions of Americans. These stores sold groceries, some variety store merchandise, and sundries, and sometimes included drugstore merchandise and pharmacy services. New services and products were added over time. With the exception of stores like Fred Meyer and Meijer's Thrifty Acres, these supermarkets and discount department stores were the rule, and the superstores remained decades away.

Europe, however, beginning its postwar retail revolution later than the United States, missed out on the proliferation of large supermarkets. As new stores eventually were built, they incorporated newer concepts of combining larger product offerings, and in 1962 the French retail chain, Carrefour, opened Europe's first "big-box" store in a Paris suburb.

Other factors contributed to the early development and proliferation of supercenters—hypermarkets, as they came to be known outside the United

States and Canada—in Western Europe. For one thing, the postwar suburbanization that began in the United States virtually upon the return of American soldiers took at least ten to fifteen years longer to develop there. As late as 1970, automobile ownership in European nations remained below the rates per household that had been achieved in the United States by 1930. This meant that even inner-ring suburbs were considerably more densely populated than in the United States. As a result, land prices were higher, and store developers tried to make the most efficient use of the more expensive available land with larger stores and larger product offerings.

Moreover, the rapid expansion of the hypermarkets provoked a political reaction. There was considerable concern about their potential to drive small companies out of business, and, as a result, some countries enacted laws to limit their expansion. Today, throughout Europe, hypermarket operators face far more regulatory hurdles than in the United States. In France, it is difficult to obtain planning permission, so that the number of hypermarket units is more limited than the market will allow. In the United Kingdom, there are limits on store size, and during the 1990s, Prime Minister John Major's Conservative government enacted strong prohibitions on new stores in suburban areas. When it became apparent that grocery prices were higher in the United Kingdom than elsewhere in Western Europe, the government commissioned a survey, in the belief that major firms were "profiteering." In fact, the report found the United Kingdom to have Europe's highest grocery prices, in part due to the land use and development controls that raise the cost structure of the industry.[3]

In the United States, Canada, Mexico, Brazil, Argentina, and other North and South American countries, supercenters are open seven days a week; some are open twenty-four hours a day. By contrast, there are significant limits on store operating hours in Europe. In France, for example, nearly all hypermarkets (and many other retail businesses) must be closed on Sundays. Many close by 8:00 p.m. on other days. Hours are even more restricted in western Germany, where stores must close by 6:00 p.m. on most weekdays and 4:00 p.m. on most Saturdays and must remain closed on Sundays. Even in Australia, which in many ways is more like North America than Europe, most stores are closed by 6:00 p.m. most weekdays.

The limited number of stores and limited store hours produce severe traffic congestion in these countries. Crowded streets often surround hypermarkets in European suburbs on Saturdays. Police and security personnel are often used to control and direct traffic at parking lots. Demand is so great that, even on the average Saturday, the European shopper can find it as difficult to find a parking place as one would in a busy American shopping center on the busiest holiday shopping day.

International Big-Box Firms

Given that the hypermarket, or superstore, was developed to its present form in Europe, it is not surprising that many of the world's large operators are headquartered there. Several of the largest international market leaders are described below.[4]

Carrefour. Paris-headquartered Carrefour is the world's second-largest retailer, behind Wal-Mart. Carrefour is well-known throughout Western Europe, where it is the largest hypermarket operator. Though generally similar in size and merchandise selection to Wal-Mart supercenters, Carrefour hypermarkets can also be much larger. Carrefour's largest European hypermarket, in Toulouse, has one hundred checkout stands and covers nearly 270,000 square feet, larger than most, if not all, U.S. supercenters. The company recently opened a hypermarket in Fuzhou, China, that covers 365,000 square feet—approximately double the size of the average Wal-Mart Supercenter.

Carrefour's business is strongly centered in Europe, with nearly 88 percent of its sales volume there. Approximately one-half of its sales volume is in France, and the company also has a strong presence in South America and China. Carrefour has recently sold underperforming hypermarket operations in Japan and Mexico, and, at this writing, was apparently considering selling its Korean operations to Tosco for nearly $1.8 billion.[5]

Carrefour operates nearly eight hundred hypermarkets around the world, as part of a portfolio of eleven thousand stores. It also is a large operator of the smaller grocery stores typical of Western Europe under the "Champion" name, and of convenience and discount stores. In 2004/2005, Carrefour's volume was $99.2 billion, while its net profit was $1.9 billion. The company has experienced strong growth, with a five-year annual revenue growth rate of

11.1 percent, slightly less than that of Wal-Mart. Its return on invested capital in 2004/2005 was 16.7 percent, which, though less than Wal-Mart's, is generally superior to that of the other largest hypermarket operators. Carrefour has approximately 430,000 employees.

Like Wal-Mart in the United States, Carrefour has suffered somewhat in recent years from competition from smaller, more nimble upstarts. Its profit margins tend to be a bit smaller than those of Wal-Mart or other leading American big-box retailers, like Home Depot or Best Buy. Major competitors in France and in some other locations include Auchan, Casino, and the cooperative, E.Leclerc.

Metro. Metro, headquartered in Germany, is Europe's second-largest retailer. Like Carrefour's, approximately one-half of Metro's sales are in its home country. However, Metro is far more concentrated than Carrefour in Europe, where 98 percent of its sales occur. Metro operates more than three hundred hypermarkets, of which 90 percent are in Germany, and has other big-box offerings in Makro, a membership discount department store, and Media Markt, a consumer electronics chain. The company also operates a large number of supermarkets and has recently opened a 325,000-square-foot membership warehouse in Tianjin, China. Recently, Metro's leadership in Germany was solidified by the purchase of money-losing Wal-Mart stores there.

Metro's 2004 sales were $77 billion, with a net profit of $1.1 billion, and its return on stockholders' equity was 17 percent. The company is growing slowly, however, with a five-year annual growth rate of 3.1 percent. It has approximately 260,000 employees.

Tesco. Tesco is headquartered in the United Kingdom and is the largest big-box chain in the country, ahead of Wal-Mart's British subsidiary, ASDA. The United Kingdom accounts for more than 70 percent of Tesco sales. Nonetheless, the company has established a strong presence in China, having purchased an interest in Hymall, which operates more than thirty hypermarkets. It also operates hypermarkets in Eastern Europe, South Korea, Thailand, Malaysia, and Taiwan and has purchased a chain of grocery stores in Japan. Tesco has a $57 billion sales volume and net profits of $2.1 billion, representing a 15 percent return on invested capital. Growth is strong, with a five-year annual rate of 12.5 percent, just slightly below that of Wal-Mart. The company has 310,000 employees.

An Asian-Based Big-Box Operator: Aeon. For all of their leadership in technological innovation in manufacturing, the Japanese have been slow in jumping on the retail trade bandwagon, in part because of onerous governmental regulations. Things are beginning to change, however. Aeon is a Japan-based company with more than four thousand stores throughout Asia and more than four hundred supercenters that operate under the name Jusco. The company also owns supermarkets and convenience stores, and, in 2005, it purchased the Carrefour stores that had been established in Japan. Total sales volume is $36 billion, with net profits of approximately $600 million. The return on invested capital is a so-so 10.7 percent. Aeon's annual growth rate over five years has been 6.9 percent—not too bad considering the relatively weak state of the Japanese economy in this period.

Chain Operations in Developing Countries. While many of the supercenters opening in developing lands are owned by American or European operators, there are some moderately successful indigenous chains. For example, in Turkey, Migros Turk is expanding rapidly, operating more than five hundred stores, including the "Ramstore" hypermarkets. The company is growing elsewhere as well, especially in Russia. Mexico has five large hypermarket chain operators. The largest is Wal-Mart, with a volume of $12.5 billion and 110,000 employees. The second-largest is Soriana, with annual revenues of $3.6 billion, but a very strong 17 percent annual growth rate over five years. Comerci (Controladora Comercial Mexicana) has a sales volume of $3.4 billion, with an annual growth rate of 8.2 percent over five years. Smaller Gigante ($2.8 billion) has opened stores in the Los Angeles area. The smallest, Chedraui, purchased all of Carrefour's Mexico stores in 2004 and has also opened stores in the Los Angeles area, under the El Super name. Chedraui's sales volume, before the Carrefour purchase, was $1.2 billion. There may be promising opportunities for some of these chains to expand into the United States, especially into areas with higher Hispanic population shares.

International Big-Box Specialty Stores

As in the United States, there has been a proliferation of category-specific big-box retailers elsewhere in the world, dealing in product lines that are also found in supermarkets or hypermarkets. These stores will often be found nearby the enclosed shopping centers anchored by hypermarkets, in a spatial arrangement similar to that found in suburban shopping areas in the United States. Just three of the largest international chains are described here.

Kingfisher. London-based Kingfisher operates the home improvement chains B&Q, Brico Depot, and Costorama. Approximately 90 percent of sales are from stores in the United Kingdom, France, and Ireland. The company has also opened twenty-one stores in China and eighteen in Taiwan, and stores in other European nations. Kingfisher does nearly $16 billion in annual volume, with a net profit of more than $400 million. Its overall performance record is fairly mediocre, with a return on invested capital of 9.5 percent, and a five-year annual sales growth rate of 3.5 percent.

Leroy Merlin. The Leroy Merlin home improvement chain, which is half-owned by the French hypermarket operator Auchan, does a volume of $8 billion. Annual growth has been 12.6 percent over five years. LeRoy Merlin stores will often be found in shopping centers alongside European hypermarkets, including Auchan stores and others, such as Carrefour.

IKEA. The furniture big-box store IKEA may have the largest stores in the world. The largest IKEA store, located in Schaumburg, Illinois, near Chicago, has approximately 430,000 square feet, which is three times the size of many hypermarkets. IKEA stores are also widely distributed, with locations in Europe, Asia, North America, and Australia. IKEA is unique among the international big-box operators in having stores in Australia, and it is developing a strong presence in China, where it recently opened a 215,000-square-foot distribution facility in the Shanghai suburbs. IKEA has an annual sales volume of $15 billion and 84,000 employees.

International Purchasing by Big-Box Operators

American and international big-box operators have established purchasing offices in China and other developing nations where goods are less expensive. This occurrence is not limited to big-box retailers, of course, and is merely another manifestation of a globalization trend that involves old-line manufacturers like General Motors and Ford, as well as high-technology firms like Dell, IBM, Intel, and Hewlett-Packard. Purchases from China have been the focus of particularly strong anti–Wal-Mart criticism. Wal-Mart is not the most China-dependent of the big-box firms, however. While a good deal of its merchandise comes from China, it is probably less than the 18 percent of goods that IKEA obtains there.[6] Further, IKEA's Internet website indicates that 30 percent of its goods overall are purchased from Asian countries. A number of the big-box store chains have established purchasing offices in China including, for example, Carrefour, whose eleven Chinese purchasing offices supply its stores around the world.

"Sweatshops." Generally, critics claim that companies in the developed world purchase goods in developing nations from firms that engage in substandard labor practices. For example, there are claims of exploitation of labor and of women, who are forced to work in "sweatshops." The critics allege that these manufacturing activities increase income inequality, both within the producing nations and in comparison with more developed nations. Moreover, they claim that the factories that produce goods for the big-box stores drive down wages in their home countries. In sum, it is often heard that the developing-world companies, including big-box retailers, are participating in a global "race to the bottom," through their international purchasing practices.[7]

The grossly inaccurate characterization of employees in low-cost countries as being paid "slave wages" and forced to work long hours is an exaggerated and emotionally loaded use of very serious terms denoting a labor condition—slavery—which the world has worked hard to eliminate.

Forced labor is illegal in virtually all nations of the world. The employees who work at low-cost manufacturing plants in China, Indonesia, India, and elsewhere are not forced to work there. They have freely taken their jobs, principally because they are the best on offer. The alternative for such an employee is not a better-paying job. It is, rather, a job that pays less or no job at all. Thus, manufacturing employees in China, Indonesia, India, and elsewhere are better off for being employed by contractors to General Motors, Carrefour, Wal-Mart, IKEA, and the like. If they were not, they would not work in the factories. It would, of course, be preferable for them to work in the safer, cleaner, and more comfortable environments typical of American or Western European factories. However, forcing such standards on weak economies would destroy the very jobs that provide the best present hope for economic advancement, simply because productivity levels are so low there.

It is instructive to compare modern-day factories in low-wage Asian countries with their American counterparts of two centuries ago. In New England textile manufacture in the early nineteenth century, a majority of the workers were women and children, often under the age of twelve. The average wage, in today's dollars, was less than thirty cents an hour.[8] Twelve-hour days were commonplace, and with poor ventilation, no air conditioning, and dismal lighting, working conditions were abysmal. Yet workers flocked to these factories, and their progeny by 1860 were making wages approaching one dollar an hour in today's money, and by the early twentieth century even more. The American "sweatshops" of the early nineteenth century created much capital formation, much innovation, and much wealth that helped propel America through its Industrial Revolution and beyond. Later on, wages got relatively high in New England, and the industry migrated to the American South, and then to Japan, then to Southeast Asia, and now to South Asia—as history repeats itself and the so-called sweatshops are incubators of prosperity.

The sweatshop issue applies to child labor as well. In societies where incomes are very low, it takes a lot of work to provide enough income for a family to live even moderately well; hence, many [most?] children work, as they did in virtually all industrialized nations in their early development. As Jagdish Bhagwati, a distinguished Columbia University economist put it, "Parents will choose to feed their children rather than schooling them if forced to make the choice."[9] Bhagwati takes the point even further, noting that efforts to outlaw child labor where it is perceived to be an economic necessity are likely to result in even more objectionable practices to circumvent the law, such as forcing daughters into prostitution. He cites a case in which the mere legislative proposal by Senator Tom Harkin to ban products of child labor drove girls into prostitution in Bangladesh.[10]

Exploitation of Women? Critics observe that the factories producing goods for big-box stores and other Western firms employ a disproportionate number of women, and they go on to suggest that women are, as a result, victims. In fact, it must be recalled that the manufacturing plants in China, Indonesia, and elsewhere have contributed to a better standard of living, rather than having retarded it.[11] Indeed, many of the factories have a disproportionate share of women working in them, but they have voluntarily chosen their employment. In many countries, developed and less developed, women have limited economic opportunities; the Chinese and Indonesian factories provide women some measure of independence that would not otherwise be possible.

Inequality. Critics claim that the factories produced by globalization increase inequality, both within and between nations. There is the potential for greater income inequality within developing nations, as more people make more money in the manufacturing plants, leaving their rural counterparts behind. This is a necessary consequence of making the transition from low to middle to high income among nations. For more than 150 years, rural residents have been leaving farms in the United States, Western Europe, and other developed nations to move to cities, where economic opportunities are concentrated. It is no different today in China and India, where rapid rates of urbanization are occurring as people seek better lives.

The inequality argument is particularly wrong in the international context. As more people work in factories, earning more than before, the nation's overall income increases. This helps close the gap (albeit only slightly) in income with more developed nations; without these factories, income inequality would have been even greater. Income convergence occurs where markets are allowed to work, property rights are protected, and the rule of law prevails. Thus, Japan's per-capita income in 1950 was only about 20 percent of the American level, but by the early twenty-first century, it had risen to 74 percent—over two-thirds of the relative differential was eliminated.[12]

Driving Down Wages. World economic and trade meetings usually attract demonstrations, sometimes violent ones, against "globalization." One of the principal claims is that the international factories supplying products to companies such as Wal-Mart and General Motors drive down the wages and standards of living in their low-income host countries. If this were so, then it should be evident in the economic data. Where there is significant manufacture of products for American and Western European markets, gross domestic product growth per capita should be falling. A review of the five low-income Asian nations with strong export growth indicates the opposite. From 1999 to 2005, world real GDP per capita rose by an average of 19 percent.[13] By comparison:

- China increased the value of its exports 229 percent. At the same time, its per-capita real GDP rose 53 percent.

- Indonesia increased the value of its exports 49 percent. At the same time, its per-capita real GDP rose 10 percent.

- India increased the value of its exports 79 percent. At the same time, its per-capita real GDP rose 56 percent.

- Bangladesh increased the value of its exports 57 percent. At the same time, its per-capita real GDP rose 22 percent.

- Vietnam increased the value of its exports 139 percent. At the same time, its per-capita real GDP rose 29 percent.

Each of the export-driven nations has experienced greater economic growth in income—significantly above the world rate. The factories provide jobs and income that would not exist if the big-box stores weren't selling their products. China, India, Indonesia, and their people would be worse off without them. Moreover, the countries that import their products, such as the United States, have been better off as well. Economic growth in the United States has not slowed with rising globalization, and lower prices from imported goods at places like Wal-Mart have brought billions of dollars of consumer surplus and welfare to ordinary Americans—a spillover effect of the internationalization of retail trade.

International Labor Standards: Better Life or More Poverty?

Critics want the United States and other developed nations to enact legislation and trade agreements that impose Western-style labor standards on developing nations. At first glance that may sound attractive; in reality, higher labor standards would reduce employment and income, leaving developing nations in even greater poverty. Why? By raising labor costs in these nations, these standards would reduce the marginal productivity of many of these workers below the marginal cost of labor, making it unprofitable to hire them. Their current factory jobs pay relatively well by Third World standards; driving those factories away would only create poverty. Imposing "international labor standards" on developing countries would be bad for them—and bad for American consumers

Wal-Mart: International Labor Policeman? Some critics want big-box retailers to take responsibility for inspecting the overseas manufacturing plants of their suppliers to ensure that they are operating in a manner consistent with labor laws in their respective countries. Making these stores the labor regulators of the world strikes us as both inappropriate and infeasible, harkening back to an imperialist era that is long past. If labor laws are being violated at a factory in Peoria, then state and federal agencies should take appropriate action. If China imports products from that plant, should the Chinese government inspect that plant to ensure that American labor laws are enforced? We have no more right to expect Wal-Mart to enforce Chinese labor laws than the Chinese have the right to enforce ours.

Wal-Mart's Role in "The Global Race to the Top." Perhaps the best hope of significant economic progress among developing world nations is expanded international trade. This cannot occur if expensive barriers are erected. Moreover, it is a mistake to view the trend toward more free international markets in terms of ideology. Rather, it is a principal factor necessary to lifting nations and their peoples out of poverty. As Jagdish Bhagwati put it, "I have always argued for free trade, not as an objective, but rather as an often powerful weapon in the arsenal of policies that we can deploy to fight poverty."[14]

Conclusions

The Wal-Mart revolution is a worldwide phenomenon in many ways. First, the big-box retailing concept has spread beyond the United States—indeed, often taking hold overseas even before it took hold in America. There are major overseas big-box operators like Carrefour that are as large or larger than all the American firms save Wal-Mart. Additionally, major U.S. retailers are rapidly expanding operations in other countries.

Globalization plays a major role in the Wal-Mart revolution in another respect, namely the fact that an increasing portion of goods sold are manufactured abroad. Despite the lament of critics, this has worked to the benefit of workers and citizens in the impoverished nations that are providing goods, as well as to that of the citizens of the United States.

In the next chapter, we turn to a broader, more comprehensive look at the rhetoric of the critics of Wal-Mart and other big-box stores.

11

Critiquing the Critics

Throughout American economic history, writers and others have sought to find villains in our capitalist economy. Sometimes the villains are individual firms, at other times, whole industries. In the late nineteenth century, many farming and other groups criticized the railroads, arguing that they were unconstrained monopolists that charged excessive rates, squeezing farmers. Out of the "farmer's revolt" came the Interstate Commerce Commission and the regulation of railroads. A generation later, Upton Sinclair complained bitterly about the meatpacking industry in *The Jungle*. Sinclair's novel was, in a sense, a forerunner of attacks on other industries, such as the munitions industry another generation further on, and the auto industry and General Motors in particular (in Ralph Nader's *Unsafe at Any Speed*), still another generation later, in the 1960s.[1] The petroleum industry has been singled out for special criticism, especially its dominant early company, the Standard Oil Company and Trust (most notably in the account of Ida Tarbell), as have, more recently, the tobacco and pharmaceutical industries.[2]

Most of these complaints have similar themes. Companies are either gouging people economically (Standard Oil in the early twentieth century or oil or drug companies generally in the past generation), or making unsafe products like the Chevrolet Corvair (Nader's claim), adulterated meat (Sinclair's mantra), or, of course, tobacco.[3]

A majority of these studies aroused public anger, and sometimes even led to remedial legislation. Yet the criticisms raised have not, in general, very well stood the test of time. Modern-day scholarship has concluded, for example, that the late nineteenth-century railroads were not as bad as they were made out to be, and the cure (regulation) may have been worse than the disease; and that the Standard Oil Company was not the embodiment of all evil and, indeed, may have brought about lower, not higher, prices for consumers of kerosene and other oil-based products.[4] Similarly, the Chevrolet Corvair, much maligned by Ralph Nader, was not a particularly dangerous car; a National Highway Traffic Safety Administration panel concluded that "the 1960–1963 Corvair compared favorably with the other contemporary vehicles used in the NHTSA Input Response Tests."[5]

Attacks on companies or industries, in short, often are biased and not based on sound empirical foundations. The Wal-Mart criticism of today follows in this historical tradition, with the empirical foundations for the charges made against the company being pretty weak.

Assessing the Criticisms of Wal-Mart and Other Big-Box Discounters

Let us review some of the charges made against big-box discounters in general, and Wal-Mart in particular.

"Wal-Mart Costs Jobs." According to one of the biggest anti–Wal-Mart polemicists, Bill Quinn, "At least three jobs are lost for every two jobs created by a Wal-Mart."[6] The somewhat less hysterically subjective Charles Fishman concludes that "Wal-Mart . . . created new retail jobs for itself, while its scale and efficiency were sucking the oxygen away from job creation in the rest of the retail trade industry."[7] Fishman also notes that while Wal-Mart was adding hundreds of thousands of jobs, manufacturing was losing millions, in part because of the importation by Wal-Mart of cheap foreign goods.[8] So the allegation is that there has been a direct loss from driving competitors out of business and an indirect loss from Wal-Mart providing a haven for inexpensive foreign-made goods.

Speaking mainly of the direct job-loss effects, for every serious, high-quality scientific study that shows job loss, there are perhaps three showing the opposite.[9] The preponderance of evidence rejects the claims of Wal-Mart's detractors, recognizing, of course, that there are some persons who are displaced because of Wal-Mart, but arguing that number is typically less than the number of jobs that Wal-Mart creates.

Other statistical analysis we have done, not reported earlier, is also completely inconsistent with the "Wal-Mart destroys jobs" hypothesis. Using data from 2004, we applied regression analysis to explain interstate variations in unemployment rates in terms of the intensity of Wal-Mart's presence (as measured by stores per million inhabitants), as well as a number of other control factors. We tried several alternative models using different variables unrelated to Wal-Mart. In no case was there a statistically significant relationship between Wal-Mart's presence and the unemployment rate, and the strongest observed relationship in any of the regressions was actually negative (more Wal-Mart, lower unemployment). By contrast, several variables unrelated to Wal-Mart had a significant impact on unemployment.

Of course, many believe that Wal-Mart destroys jobs by promoting foreign imports to the United States. The Wake-Up Wal-Mart website of the United Food and Commercial Workers Union asks visitors to sign their "six demands for change" at Wal-Mart, one of which is a plea for Wal-Mart to "Buy American. Establish a 'Buy America' program that annually increases the percentage of 'Made in America' goods purchased by Wal-Mart so as to help protect American jobs."[10]

Almost every economics textbook shows the fallacy of the argument "foreign imports cost American jobs." We will quote from two popular ones, written by well-known economists of opposite political persuasions. Joseph Stiglitz (a Nobel laureate in economics who chaired President Clinton's Council of Economic Advisers) says that "while trade costs some workers their jobs, it creates jobs for others. Beyond that, consumers benefit because trade enables them to buy those goods that foreigners can make less expensively and better than Americans can."[11] Note how similar these comments are to the words of Gregory Mankiw (who chaired the CEA during George W. Bush's presidency): "Opponents of free trade often argue that trade with other countries destroys domestic jobs. . . . Yet free trade creates jobs at the same time that it destroys them."[12]

Figure 11-1 looks at two periods in American history, 1970–80, when imports were relatively modest in relation to the national output and Wal-Mart was still a relatively small force in American retailing, and 1994–2004, when imports had grown a great deal relatively, and Wal-Mart had assumed much greater importance. Note that as exports grew in relative importance, the average unemployment rate actually fell fairly markedly.[13]

FIGURE 11-1

IMPORTS AND UNEMPLOYMENT, 1970–1980 VS. 1994–2004

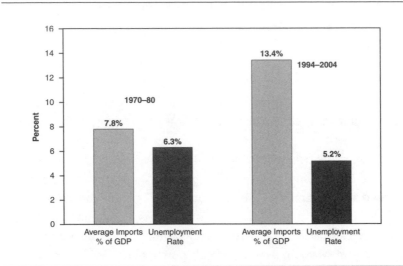

SOURCE: *Economic Report of the President* (Washington, D.C.: Government Printing Office, 2005).

While this "proves" nothing (since there are other factors also involved in unemployment determination), it fits in very well with the conventional economic wisdom: international trade does not reduce job opportunities. We cannot know precisely how much of the increased importation reflects the influence of Wal-Mart, but it actually is quantitatively fairly small given the composition and magnitudes of imports. For example, calendar year 2004 almost coincides with Wal-Mart's 2005 fiscal year. Even if 60 percent of the goods sold at Wal-Mart were imported, it is hard to conceive that much more than 7 or 8 percent of goods imported into the United States were sold by Wal-Mart; and in the absence of Wal-Mart, a large proportion of those (probably a majority) would have been sold by other retailers.[14] But even if Wal-Mart's role were large, the loss of jobs in American manufacturing to workers in, say, China, who make goods sold at Wal-Mart, is compensated by less obviously visible jobs created elsewhere as a consequence of increased exports (financed in part from earnings from imports), increased foreign investment in the United States, and higher economic growth arising from greater gains from trade.

Wal-Mart Pays Low Wages and Thus Lowers Incomes. Three important considerations regarding wages are largely ignored by Wal-Mart's critics. The first is that workers in retail trade are relatively lowly paid for the simple reason that most retail jobs require relatively low levels of entering skills. Within hours of beginning employment, the typical worker at Wal-Mart or another big-box store like Home Depot or Costco can learn the rudiments of the job—how to work the cash registers, how to get goods to the shelves, how to greet customers, and so forth.

The second important thing typically ignored by critics is the question of what Wal-Mart workers would do if not employed by Wal-Mart. Would they work at the average pay level for all American workers (which is higher than typical Wal-Mart wages)? The reality is that in the absence of Wal-Mart, most workers would be doing similar work for other employers, for similar wages and benefits. Some workers would be unemployed, "earning" distinctly less. While a few lucky ones would be faring better with alternative employers it is very unlikely, given the empirical evidence, that that would be true of more than a minority.

Finally, if Wal-Mart workers are so unhappy with their conditions, why haven't they unionized? Why are there not lots of disenchanted Wal-Mart workers demanding collective bargaining? Why doesn't Wal-Mart have dramatically higher turnover rates than the rest of the industry, reflecting employees dissatisfaction with low wages?[15] Why has relatively little criticism come from Wal-Mart workers themselves? Most of it has come from workers at competing firms, many of them members of a labor union that Wal-Mart members have shown little interest in joining.

Critics often note that average wages of all workers in retail trade are fairly substantially above the average wage of Wal-Mart employees of roughly $10 an hour. Again, this reflects several phenomena: Wal-Mart stores are concentrated in lower-income areas where market wage rates tend to be relatively low. And many retail workers are in more lucrative markets; it is inappropriate to compare the wages of a salesperson at an upscale store like Tiffany's or Neiman Marcus with Wal-Mart. Finally, the published data on Wal-Mart employees excludes salaried employees, who tend to be more skilled, more educated, and more experienced—and, naturally, higher paid.

It is also worth remembering that Wal-Mart has lowered prices and increased productivity levels in the American economy as a whole, which has increased the purchasing power of all Americans, including Wal-Mart employees. As indicated earlier, most researchers believe that Wal-Mart's presence has led to some measurable general decline in prices from what otherwise would exist. This gives workers the opportunity to buy more goods—in effect, raising their real incomes. The dramatic increase in worker productivity in the big-box retail trade has lowered the amount of the nation's resources needed to get goods from manufacturers to consumers and has raised average wages, since wage levels are clearly closely linked to productivity advance.[16]

By the way, the notion that a retail innovator pays lower wages than its competition is hardly new. In a 1931 Federal Trade Commission study, it was argued that weekly wages of workers in independent groceries and drugstores were about 20 percent higher than for workers in chain operations.[17] This is actually a greater differential than most critics claim exists today with respect to Wal-Mart and its workers.

Wal-Mart Rips Apart Communities and Causes Urban Sprawl. Critics like Americans to believe that hundreds of idyllic American communities existed until Wal-Mart came in and destroyed the downtown, reducing the cohesion and financial support of people who are the glue that holds communities together and helps serve the communal good. For example, here is how one Wal-Mart arch-critic put it:

> When a dollar is spent at Wal-Mart instead of the local hardware store, it's not just the hardware store losing that dollar in revenue. Also losing might be the local hauling company that delivers to the store or the café where the store manager has dinner. Instead, that dollar goes directly to the Walton family's private Fort Knox in Bentonville, where it rafts up against billions of other bucks from around the world.[18]

This makes no sense. Is there any evidence that managers at Wal-Mart are less likely to frequent local restaurants than managers of local businesses—particularly if there are more Wal-Mart managers, since it is a larger store?

New ways of doing things have often seemed to threaten the "way of life" in rural and small-town America. A century ago, the Sears, Roebuck and Montgomery Ward catalogues posed a threat to small downtown general stores and specialty shops. The chain stores—Woolworth's and W. T. Grant, and, in food retailing, stores like A&P, Winn-Dixie, Safeway, and Kroger—were also said to disrupt the delicate equilibrium of the small town with their allegedly discriminatory or predatory pricing practices. In the 1950s, '60s, and '70s, the emergence of malls on the edges of towns was said to be the death knell of downtowns. In some small communities, even governmental innovation was said to threaten community spirit, especially via the merger of school districts in the consolidation movement of the mid-twentieth century, the disappearance of some small-town post offices, and the building of the interstate highway system.

Thus, the perception that Wal-Mart and other big-box stores pose a threat is just the latest in a series of complaints over change that has continued for many generations. In most communities, downtowns started declining long before Wal-Mart came along, victims of the shortage of parking that is so fatal in an automobile age. While Wal-Mart might have accelerated the trend in some instances, it is a gross exaggeration to say, "Wal-Mart has destroyed small downtown America."

A somewhat related but different claim is that Wal-Mart and other big-box stores, located on the fringes of towns, promote urban sprawl and all its attendant problems—greater traffic congestion, deteriorating inner cities, environmental destruction, bland, visually affronting architecture, and so on. These arguments are particularly questionable. The overwhelming majority of Wal-Mart stores are located in smaller communities, typically with fewer than twenty thousand persons in the town and fifty thousand or so in the county. To speak of "urban sprawl" in such towns is almost laughable, as the maximum commuting time from one side of town to the other is, at most, twenty minutes or so.

Indeed, there is evidence that Wal-Mart benefits small communities by bringing them retail opportunities that used to be available only in larger, more congested, and sprawling urban areas. This has reduced the need to drive long distances just to buy competitively priced goods, reducing the need for massive shopping complexes in large urban centers. Michael Hicks, who has studied Wal-Mart as intensively as anyone, reaches similar conclusions.[19]

Wal-Mart Does Not Provide Health Benefits for Its Employees. An ancillary argument to the "Wal-Mart treats its employees badly" criticism is the claim that the company does not provide health insurance for its workers. As discussed earlier, this is simply false: more than six hundred thousand workers receive Wal-Mart-subsidized health benefits. Related to this argument is the claim that Wal-Mart has an unfair market advantage, in that its employees get taxpayer-provided health insurance through Medicaid. But most Wal-Mart employees do not get Medicaid—far more are on a company-sponsored health insurance policy than on Medicaid. And the incidence of Medicaid recipients among Wal-Mart employees appears similar to that of the general population, or among employees of competing retail firms.

This last point became somewhat embarrassingly obvious recently in the state of Washington. The state legislature was considering a bill proposed by organized labor which, in effect, would have required Wal-Mart to provide more health insurance. It was pointed out that 3,180 Wal-Mart workers or their dependents received Medicaid. However, it later became known that 3,127 state government workers *also* received Medicaid—nearly the same number, albeit a somewhat smaller fraction of the state workforce.[20] Even relatively well-paid government workers sometimes receive Medicaid benefits.

Within the last year, Wal-Mart has responded to criticism of its health insurance benefits program by significantly improving coverage for its workers, shortening the period employees are required to work before becoming eligible for benefits. A significant number are eligible for a previously unavailable no-frills policy costing only $11 a month.[21]

"Wal-Mart Is a Burden on Governments." An extension of the Medicaid issue relates to the total burden that Wal-Mart and other big-box retailers impose on governments. Probably the best way to frame the question is to ask what the level of governmental services and taxes would be in the absence of Wal-Mart (or other big-box discounters). Wal-Mart can impose new costs on governments—in addition to alleged higher welfare spending, a good example is expenditures for widening roads to deal with traffic congestion in the area of a new Wal-Mart store.

But Wal-Mart brings in new revenues as well. On balance, the number of jobs typically increases after Wal-Mart enters a community. The company pays property taxes on the new store; sales tax revenues typically increase; and Wal-Mart employees also pay property taxes. The question is whether the new tax revenues cover the marginal costs to governments arising from the new store. Michael Hicks, who has studied this issue extensively, says the answer is "yes," and we find it intuitively difficult to believe that major new business would be a net burden on a community.[22]

Other Criticisms. Critics of Wal-Mart have seized on other issues as well. They claim the company commits significant violations of labor laws. One particular concern is the hiring of child labor. This problem allegedly has two dimensions to it, one relating to its American and overseas stores, but the more important is the second one relating to the employees in plants of overseas suppliers, many of which, no doubt, have workers who are thirteen or fourteen years old or even younger.

To us, the appropriate question is, has Wal-Mart demonstrated a corporate contempt or violation of domestic labor laws that is out of line with industry standards or with what its sheer size would lead one to expect? Any company with literally more employees than the U.S. Army might be expected to experience some incidents of rogue, illegal actions that are highly inappropriate and unethical—as does the U.S. Army which, nonetheless, is regarded generally as a highly professional organization deserving of respect.

Regarding foreign workers, other nations very appropriately have less exacting labor laws than the U.S. does. As indicated earlier, in the 1820s, children, many of them preteens, were working, quite legally, in New England textile mills for long hours in poorly ventilated conditions and making less than 30 cents an hour in current dollars.[23] The United Food and Commercial Workers Union has complained that workers in Honduran shirt factories make only $35 a week—at least double the typical wage in an inflation-adjusted sense prevailing in those early New England textile mills.[24] Yet those early New England families, like those in Honduras today, were delighted at the income provided by such employment, which helped materially increase family incomes and the standard of living. As families grew wealthier and wages increased as a result of advances in productivity financed, in part, by savings of companies and their workers, child labor participation in early America declined, and labor laws ratified this trend, as a more affluent country decided children should not work. Wal-Mart's suppliers today are very similar to these early textile manufacturers, providing job opportunities and an improved quality of life for many very poor and sometimes economically desperate people.

A similar claim relates to alleged sex discrimination. We do not have any gender-specific wage data, but it is probably true that, on average, men make more than women at Wal-Mart. That, however, does not prove anything, as the same thing could be said of virtually all major American corporations. Certainly as a matter of company policy, there is no evidence that Wal-Mart deliberately discriminates against women routinely, class action lawsuits notwithstanding (again, in a company with thousands of stores, it is conceivable that a few rogue store managers might show prejudicial actions against women). In the United States as a whole, median weekly pay for women over the age of twenty-five in the aggregate is 21.4 percent less than for men of comparable age, in large part because men have more managerial and professional jobs, greater experience, and so on.[25] Our guess is that the gender-based wage differential at Wal-Mart is no greater, and probably less, than that national norm.

Conclusions

In our judgment, the criticisms directed against Wal-Mart are generally weak and/or erroneous. Wal-Mart does not hurt workers, either in terms of employment opportunities or in terms of compensation. Wal-Mart is not the primary cause of the death of downtowns or the increase in urban sprawl. It is not a major reason American imports have increased in recent decades. While a company Wal-Mart's size will always have a few rogue employees who will behave unethically or illegally, their numbers are relatively few. Wal-Mart is perhaps no saint, but it is not a major sinner, either.

12

What Should We Do About Wal-Mart?

There have been increasingly strong calls for legislative and other actions to alter the behavior of Wal-Mart and other big-box retail stores. At the local level, these calls include such pleas as imposing zoning restrictions and limits on store size. At the state level, many are promoting legislation designed to force Wal-Mart (and in some cases other retailers) to provide health care benefits for employees. At the national level, some groups are advocating higher minimum wages, restrictions on immigrant labor, and other legislative initiatives potentially affecting Wal-Mart and other retail stores.

Not all the proposed initiatives are what might be termed "anti–Wal-Mart." There are some communities that want Wal-Mart (or Target or Home Depot) stores, and are willing to bribe Wal-Mart (or other stores) to get them, usually by offering tax incentives, assistance in improving transportation access, and so forth. Those who dislike Wal-Mart want to tax or regulate it, while Wal-Mart supporters often favor granting it subsidies and tax abatements.

In this chapter we reject both of these positions. We believe the optimal thing for most communities to do is to treat Wal-Mart exactly like competing retailers and other businesses. As a general proposition, that means *doing nothing*, except giving Wal-Mart the same government services and the same tax and regulatory burden that is imposed on competing enterprises.[1] To do otherwise would be to distort the allocation of resources from what the forces of the market dictate, inevitably reducing the economic welfare of the populace.

Policies Relating to Employee Relations

The Wal-Mart critics have probably stressed the most what they perceive to be the inadequate pay and insurance and other benefits of its employees.

This is not surprising, since a large part of the anti–Wal-Mart criticism is led by labor union members for whom Wal-Mart is a particular nemesis, since it has taken sales away from unionized stores, reducing unionized employment and union power. If one accepts (which we do not) that Wal-Mart provides inadequate pay and benefits for its workers, what are the policy options? Four types of policies might be advocated:

- Minimum-wage increases, directed either to all workers or to employees of big-box retail stores;

- Mandated benefits coverage at some level, particularly health insurance, either directed to all businesses or to large retail stores;

- Tax and expenditure policies designed to provide incentives to adopt higher wages or benefits;

- Changes in the National Labor Relations Act that would make it easier for unions to force collective bargaining on large employers.

It would be possible to achieve the objectives of the critics by adopting one, some, or all of these policies. But would that be wise?

At the outset we repeat that the underlying factual premises used to support such policies are, in our judgment, incorrect. Wal-Mart employees, for example, are not particularly underpaid. Relatively few employees face serious problems getting medical care. Thus, in our view, the types of policies enumerated above are essentially solutions in search of a problem.

Minimum-Wage Legislation. Having said that, however, does it really matter if public policymakers come up with a solution to a nonproblem? If the proposed legislation is relatively innocuous, perhaps no great harm would come from it. Unfortunately, however, the evidence is fairly clear that likely remedial legislation would have significantly detrimental economic effects.

Take the minimum wage. Any increase in the general minimum wage of, say, 20 or even 25 percent will have only the most minimal impact on Wal-Mart, since relatively few employees make less than $6.50 an hour, and the average hourly wage exceeds $10.00. A 25 percent increase in the federal minimum wage standard would raise it to $6.44 an hour, affecting few

Wal-Mart employees. Any increase that significantly affected Wal-Mart would have to be very large—at least 40 percent, bringing the wage up to perhaps $7.25 an hour—and even an increase of that magnitude would affect only a minority of workers.[2]

A mammoth body of literature argues that governmentally mandated minimum wages have several undesirable economic effects: They reduce employment and increase unemployment; they can reduce fringe benefits such as health insurance; they have particularly adverse effects on minorities; and they do not do what they were originally intended to do— reduce poverty.[3]

With reference to the last point, the conclusion of a recent study is a particularly strong indictment of these laws: "Although minimum wages increase the incomes of some poor families, the evidence indicates that their overall net effect is, if anything, to increase the proportions of families with incomes below or near the poverty line."[4] Nobel laureate Joseph Stiglitz perhaps put it best when he wrote in 1993 that "a higher minimum wage does not seem a particularly useful way to help the poor. Most poor people earn more than the minimum wage *when they are working*: their problem is not low wages. . . . The minimum wage is a not a good way of trying to deal with the problem of poverty."[5] The laws may have still other unintended adverse consequences, such as lowering school enrollments.[6]

Looking at Wal-Mart and other big-box discounters more specifically, two other problems with the minimum wage emerge. First, there is ample evidence from another low-wage industry, restaurants, that minimum wages have very significant unemployment effects.[7] But probably more important, and often neglected in this debate, is that minimum wage levels almost certainly have very significant adverse effects on consumers and/or stockholders, many of whom in Wal-Mart's case are also employees. Higher minimum wages either squeeze profit margins, lowering the value of Wal-Mart stock and leading to a reduction in the net worth of thousands of stockholders, or, more likely, lead to higher prices for consumers, which significantly reduce the welfare gains from consumer surplus discussed earlier.

Thus, minimum wage laws are, put bluntly, a bad way to deal with the alleged problem of low wages in the big-box discount industry. For them to have any impact, they would have to be increased by very large amounts.

This almost certainly would have significant unemployment effects on workers and lead to massive welfare losses to consumers.

Mandated Health Benefits. In very large part, the arguments made above apply to attempts to require Wal-Mart, and perhaps other big-box retailers, to extend to their employees a certain level of health care benefits. Again, government is forcing firms to pay in total compensation (in this case, the fringe-benefit component of total compensation) more than what market forces dictate. This has the same predictable impact on unemployment, product prices, and so forth as do minimum wage laws.

Yet, in many ways, mandated health benefits pose a more serious threat to the economic welfare of Americans, for several reasons:

- Whereas efforts to raise the minimum wage have had only limited success, the movement to mandate health insurance benefits is very strong and sometimes successful at the state level.

- Some of these laws are targeted only at Wal-Mart rather than the general population of employers.

- Laws of this kind aggravate one of America's leading economic problems, the high and soaring cost of health care.

- Legislation such as this tends to reduce worker choice and thus hurts their economic welfare.

On January 12, 2006, the Maryland legislature overrode a veto by Governor Robert Ehrlich and enacted the first state law mandating Wal-Mart to increase health insurance spending.[8] The law required employers with ten thousand or more workers in the state of Maryland to spend a minimum of 8 percent of payrolls on health insurance, or else pay into the state Medicaid fund. The ten-thousand-employee threshold meant the legislation applied to only a handful of employers, only one other of which, Giant Foods, was in retail trade.

The Maryland legislation (and similar legislation in Suffolk County, New York) sent shock waves around the country, and even galvanized some business groups that heretofore had been largely indifferent to the

Wal-Mart-bashing. The Retail Industry Leaders Association filed lawsuits arguing that the laws violate the Employee Retirement Security Act of 1974 (ERISA). ERISA was designed to allow employers to offer uniform benefit packages nationwide, free of state restrictions. Some legislative supporters of the law in Maryland also came under attack when it was revealed that they had accepted campaign contributions from the United Food and Commercial Workers Union shortly before the vote.[9]

Emboldened by the Maryland success, the union groups pushing the legislation moved forward with similar bills in over thirty states. In some cases, they were joined as allies by business competitors of Wal-Mart who saw this as a way of gaining market share or profitability.[10] While the legal challenges to these laws under ERISA at this writing have been successful, the move to mandate benefits is far from dead.

These laws are particularly pernicious because they apply only to Wal-Mart, or to a select small group of large employers. The smaller discount big-box operations, including Target or Home Depot in some cases (not so small in any absolute sense), do not have to face the mandates Wal-Mart faces. This patently violates basic concepts of economic neutrality that should govern any public policy. The government is trying to burden Wal-Mart because it is big, and it is big because it has been successful in giving people what they want. Laws that are not neutral lead to a distortion in the allocation of resources, artificially reducing a competitive advantage that largely has resulted from the company's lauded economic efficiency.

Additionally, health care prices have been the fastest-rising major component of the Consumer Price Index for decades. Whereas in the middle of the last century we devoted 5 percent or so of our national output to health care, that has now tripled to over 15 percent, above that of any other major nation in the world.[11] Part of this growth reflects the impact on rising demand for health care services from a growing population, rising life expectancy, higher incomes, and new technologies that permit longer life but are expensive. Another part, however, reflects the huge rise in third-party payments that have partly arisen because of various tax policies of the federal government (for example, the tax deductibility of some health care costs), not to mention the Medicare and Medicaid programs. When third parties pay most of the bills, the customer is insensitive to costs and demands expensive treatments for which other citizens pay. The attempt to mandate employers to give generous health insurance packages merely aggravates the third-party problem and increases the rise in health care costs.

The mandating of insurance benefits presumes that the government has a better sense of how employees should allocate their earnings among various alternative uses than do the employees. If Wal-Mart is forced to subsidize health care insurance to the extent of, say, one dollar an hour when previously it was spending, say, fifty cents, the company either faces fifty cents more in total labor costs, or it reduces its wage payments to offset the mandatory insurance. If it does the latter, it is forcing employees to take part of their total compensation in health care benefits, benefits that some of them might prefer to forgo, perhaps because they can receive them through their spouses' insurance. A government mandate would actually reduce the welfare of the worker, who gives up cash income for an unneeded benefit. If the higher insurance cost leads to higher overall labor costs, Wal-Mart may be forced to hire fewer workers, or move some operations (such as distribution centers) to other states, reducing the welfare of workers in the state with the insurance mandate.

This health care debate may have far broader implications than merely the provision of insurance benefits to the less than one million employees not insured by Wal-Mart (some of whom are otherwise insured). Wal-Mart, in order to fend off criticism and try to level the playing field in a way advantageous to it, could at some date endorse a national health care plan. Andy Stern of the Service Employees International Union, a major critic of Wal-Mart (and financier of Wal-Mart Watch), has said, "If Wal-Mart's CEO, Lee Scott, were to come out and say, 'We need a national health-care system that works for everyone,' then it's a whole new ball game."[12]

Such a solution, in our judgment, would have far-reaching negative consequences for the nation, reducing the limited market incentives in the current health care system, breeding inefficiencies, and reducing choices and ultimately the quality of health care for American citizens. We doubt very much whether Sam Walton, with his distrust of big government, would have considered supporting such a scheme. But the new Wal-Mart, discussed below, might seize on such an approach as being good for the company, if not the country.

Tax Subsidy Schemes. An alternative approach to raising wages and benefits that uses a carrot as well as a stick would be for government to provide matching monies or employee subsidies to cover some health care costs or even higher wages. This would be a variant on the Earned Income Tax Credit idea. Workers earning less than a threshold income could, for example, receive a tax credit usable in a Health Savings Account tied to health insurance. While this approach less clearly distorts the allocation of resources and so is less objectionable than mandates that artificially raise input costs to employers, it is nonetheless a costly subsidy, and one that almost certainly would have to be provided to all low-income workers, not just those working for big box discounters. The disincentive effects of raising taxes to fund such a program, for example, could be very large.[13]

Wal-Mart's Impact on Communities and the Environment

While labor unions have charged Wal-Mart with paying substandard wages and benefits, other groups have been at the forefront of attacking the company and other big-box discounters for their allegedly deleterious impact on communities and their environment. We are told that Wal-Mart destroys downtown and other businesses, thus hurting local economies while promoting congestion, environmental degradation, and urban sprawl.

It is important to remember that Wal-Mart provides goods, but customers must buy them. If traffic on the road to Wal-Mart is pretty congested, it is because local citizens like the store and want to shop there. If customers who used to buy their tools at the local hardware store now go to Home Depot, Lowe's, or Wal-Mart, it is because they perceive that they are better off at the new big-box alternatives, with more choice of goods, lower prices, better parking, and so forth. The "villains" are not the new stores but rather the large number of citizens who like them.

And the critics are not all wrong. It is no doubt true that some local businesses suffer because of a Wal-Mart's (or a Home Depot's or a Costco's) opening. Some prominent local citizens may see declining incomes and may even go out of business. And some streets will be more congested than previously. Some older buildings may be razed to make way for the new store. All of these things happen—but they have always happened. The history of

American retailing is a story of constant change—indeed, the history of the entire economy is one where things are seldom done exactly the same way in any field from one generation to the next. On this question, at least, the French are right: The more things change, the more they remain the same.

And the changes are basically for the good. The new methods of retailing are superior to the older ones. Wal-Mart offers a bigger selection of goods at lower prices than the variety stores like Woolworth's and Kresge ever did, stores that were its early competitors in some towns. Wal-Mart's prices on clothing items tend to be lower than those at Sears, Roebuck and the local department store. The grocery department at the Wal-Mart Supercenter typically offers lower prices and often more choice than the traditional chains like A&P, Kroger, and Safeway.

A little historical perspective is often useful in evaluating arguments. Earlier in history, chain stores like A&P, Kroger, and Woolworth's were highly successful—they had their generation or more of retail supremacy as did the mail-order houses like Sears, Roebuck and Montgomery Ward, or the mainline department stores that began supplanting the smaller specialty shops in the late nineteenth and early twentieth centuries in American cities.

Retail is constantly evolving. For example, in 1900, nearly all persons buying tobacco went to very small, individual cigar stores to buy from a limited selection of merchandise sold at rather high markups from wholesale prices. A chain evolved after 1901 that went from $93,374 in sales to $78,918,582 by 1920 by offering a good selection of cigars at lower prices.[14] As one of the founders said of those two decades,

> We had plenty of opposition. . . . The independents fought us
> tooth and nail—not because we were a chain but because we
> were supposed to be the outlet for the "tobacco trust." In those
> trust-busting days, it was the easiest thing . . . to raise a hue
> and cry against anything connected with "the interests" and
> the "tobacco trust" was regarded as one of the wickedest of
> them all.[15]

The independents decried the loss of the local cigar store to the impersonal chains. The same thing happened in other forms of retailing, such as drugstores, and led to generally successful cries for state "fair trade" laws designed to restrict price-cutting, and ultimately to federal legislation such as the Miller-Tydings Act (see chapter 3).

Thus the assault on Wal-Mart is, in a sense, a continuation of an American tradition, in which the traditional form of retailing tries through legislative mandate to restrict the new, generally more efficient, competitor. Small businesses did this in the 1920s and '30s in the push for fair trade laws. The United Food and Commercial Workers Union and some grocery chains are doing it today, at the state level by trying to force mandatory insurance coverage on Wal-Mart, and at the local level by using zoning or even minimum wage regulations to keep Wal-Mart out of town.

Urban Sprawl and Congestion. In our judgment, one of the sillier arguments used against the big-box discount stores is that they promote urban sprawl. Before explaining why, we would note that concern over urban sprawl is not universal in nature. In surveys among ordinary citizens asking them what they think are the greatest problems confronting America today, you often will hear mentioned unemployment, the threat of terrorists, excessive crime, or deficiencies in the educational system, but far less often is urban sprawl suggested. In the decades after World War II, people voted with their feet to move away from relatively densely populated urban centers to suburban areas where population densities were somewhat lower, in the process creating urban sprawl. Urban sprawl came into being because Americans wanted it, and came long before Wal-Mart was a major feature of American life.

However, even if urban sprawl is a problem, Wal-Mart is almost certainly not a significant cause of it. A much more compelling case can be made that Wal-Mart is reducing urban sprawl, since its stores are predominantly located in smaller counties that are not truly very urban. By bringing customers low prices and lots of choice, Wal-Mart has reduced the need for small-town Americans to drive to big urban centers to buy their goods; in that sense, it has helped support the vitality of small-town economies, not undermined them. Consequently, the growth of big-box discount stores can be said to have contributed to a spatial decentralization of retailing in America, much as has the modern online shopping outlets, or mail-order houses like Land's End.[16]

Suppose you say to people, "Wal-Mart wants to come to our small town but that is going to increase traffic congestion on the street in front of the

store. How should we deal with this problem: prohibit Wal-Mart from coming to town or widen the street in front of the store?" While the answer will
vary from community to community, we would suspect that a sizable majority of those queried would favor widening the street. Incremental property,
sales, and, in some instances, income-tax revenues derived from the new
store can finance the improvements to the roadway, easing the congestion.

Declining Downtowns. It is no doubt true that Wal-Mart sometimes reduces
the vibrancy of downtown business districts. Yet the demise of the downtown
usually long predated Wal-Mart. Because Americans overwhelmingly prefer
the automobile as a mode of transportation, new strip malls and shopping
centers with plenty of free parking on the outskirts of all but the smallest
communities brought about a decline in the downtown shopping district
before Wal-Mart arrived and became a dominant force in American retailing.

Policies Regarding Globalization and Overseas Worker Standards

Earlier, we dealt extensively with the international issues relating to big-box
stores. Critics might advocate higher tariffs or quotas on imports as one way
to deal with the issue that "Wal-Mart has cost America many manufacturing jobs." They might advocate international labor standards, setting minimum wages, maximum hours, limits on child labor, or certain mandated
fringe benefits.

Both of these approaches would lower the standard of living globally.
The one thing that virtually all economists agree on is that trade restrictions
have negative effects on economic growth. The era of America's preemi-
nence as a world economic power, since World War II, is one of generally
declining barriers to trade globally, a phenomenon that has enormously
contributed to the "take-off" into economic growth of nations such as
Japan, Korea, Malaysia, Brazil, and, increasingly, China and India.

International labor standards are a "one-size-fits-all" approach to labor
markets that are quite disparate. Poor countries cannot afford to prohibit
child labor, long work weeks, and so forth. Such rules would destroy the
advantages these nations have and retard the export-driven economic
growth that has occurred. It would be a cruel and inhumane policy toward

some of the poorest people on our planet. It is immoral as well as inadvisable economically. Moreover, such international labor standards would severely compromise American sovereignty.

Should Wal-Mart Enter Banking?

For several years, Wal-Mart has sought to expand its franchise horizontally by introducing banking services into its stores, via a Wal-Mart-owned bank. Its efforts to obtain a bank charter have been consistently rebuffed, in part by an opposition led by the usual critics, but also by banking interests who do not want competition. What should public policy be?

In our judgment, Wal-Mart should be allowed to enter the banking business and to have banking services in its stores. It is a natural expansion of the one-stop shopping concept that has the company selling services (such as hairstyling and car repair) in some of its supercenters, as well as merchandise. It would be handy to be able to bank at Wal-Mart. Whether the company is making the right business decision by wanting to enter banking, we are uncertain, although it intuitively sounds like a good move. In any case, Wal-Mart should have the *right* to make mistakes, if the bank initiative is that.

There are legitimate issues to be raised when anyone enters the banking business, and Depression-era banking laws designed to protect depositors may serve some useful purpose, although that is a debatable proposition best discussed elsewhere. Certainly, it is not unreasonable to prevent Wal-Mart from excessively commingling bank assets and operations with corporate funds derived from retailing. Yet subject to some conditions like this, it strikes us as anticonsumer to deny customers the opportunity to bank at the same place as they shop, and it also seems to us that most of the opposition reflects the anticompetitive urges of critics rather than a legitimate concern for the welfare of potential bank customers.

The Other Side of the Coin: Subsidizing Wal-Mart or Other Stores

This book has argued that, on the whole, Wal-Mart has been a force for good in our society, doing far more to help Americans than to hurt them. While there have been losers from the innovations fostered by Wal-Mart and its imitators, they are vastly outnumbered by winners, mostly consumers who receive literally tens of billions of dollars of consumer welfare annually because of their presence. If that is so, cannot a case be made that these stores promote a community good beyond what they capture in their own profits, so that we should encourage them, luring them to town with tax incentives, guarantees of improved roads, and the like? At the national level, is there not a decent case to be made to give them special tax benefits?

While the case for giving special subsidies to Wal-Mart is probably more compelling than the case for imposing special tax or regulatory requirements on it, it is our position that special subsidies are, in general, inappropriate. They serve to distort the allocation of resources from what the interactions of consumers and suppliers in a free market would dictate. These distortions influence the shape of retailing in ways that differ, at least to some degree, from what consumers would truly prefer.

Some states, in their eagerness to attract new businesses, give tax abatements or other subsidies to practically all those of reasonable size (say, with twenty-five or more employees). We view such policies as inappropriate, a form of corporate welfare that discriminates against smaller, established local businesses and distorts resource allocation. Having said that, however, it would be wrong to deny Wal-Mart (or Target, Home Depot, Costco, or other big-box retailer) the same tax breaks afforded other new retailers. To do so would be to impose a distortion on top of a distortion. While not an optimal policy, subsidizing Wal-Mart with tax breaks as part of a *generalized* subsidization of new businesses is probably preferable to denying it that subsidy. But, we reiterate, the optimal policy would be to subsidize no one—let everyone compete on a level playing field.

Leveling the Playing Field: Stop Subsidizing Wal-Mart's Critics

A large portion of the opposition to Wal-Mart is led by unions representing workers in old forms of retailing with stagnant productivity growth that are losing out to more efficient big-box stores. Union power is dwindling, and this campaign may be less about protecting workers and saving the environment and more about using public policy to stifle welfare-enhancing competition from big-box discounters. By trying to stop Wal-Mart, groups like the United Food and Commercial Workers are trying to deny welfare-enhancing savings that help millions of low-income people every year. The fight against Wal-Mart is arguably a fight led by self-interested individuals who are willing to hurt the poor and disadvantaged in pursuit of their own welfare.

The funds used by labor unions to finance the majority of the anti–Wal-Mart campaign have come from compulsory union dues. In many states, in order to work at the local grocery store, you have to join a union such as the United Food and Commercial Workers. Once in the union, you must pay dues that are used extensively for political purposes such as trying to pass laws that would mandate health insurance benefits for Wal-Mart. The power of government, through the National Labor Relations Act and other legislation, is used to force some workers to pay into a union anti–Wal-Mart campaign to which they personally might not subscribe. This practice is a dubious use of the coercive power of government to reduce the freedom of action of employees, and helps finance the anti–Wal-Mart effort. Public policy neutrality would require that union membership be voluntary, and would prohibit use of union dues for political purposes without explicit worker consent.

Appeasing the Unappeasable: Wal-Mart's Public Relations Campaign

The enormous growth in anti–Wal-Mart sentiment was at first largely ignored by the company. The late Sam Walton seemed to have an attitude similar to that of John D. Rockefeller of the Standard Oil Company around 1900. He felt that if he did his job well and offered everyday low prices to his customers, the malcontents who disparaged his business practices would be largely ignored. For more than a decade after Sam's death, Wal-Mart officials seemed to follow a similar policy, spending next to nothing on public relations and lobbyists.

In recent years, all that has changed. Wal-Mart has retained a small army of lobbyists and public relations specialists. It appears to us that a major Wal-Mart strategy now seems to be to try to appease the opposition, while still opposing anti–Wal-Mart legislation more directly as it is

proposed at the state level. The strategy includes offering some improvements in the health insurance program for employees and even advocating raising the minimum wage, a goal dear to the hearts of labor union
leaders.[17] It involves starting to sell organic shrimp, biodegradable goods,
and other "green" products to appease the environmentalists. Wal-Mart
hired a top Democratic Party insider, Leslie Dach (communications director during the Michael Dukakis 1988 campaign against George H. W.
Bush for president, and later adviser to both President Clinton and the
Democratic National Committee in the 2004 campaign) to become executive vice president of corporate affairs and government relations and a
member of the Wal-Mart Executive Committee.[18] Wal-Mart has even
hired a former nun who once ran the League of Women Voters to "lead
the company's sustainability efforts."[19]

Three examples from speeches or press releases by Wal-Mart and/or its
chief executive officer Lee Scott demonstrate the company's new stance:

> The factories in China are going to end up having to be held
> up to the same standards as the factories in the U.S. There will
> be a day of reckoning for retailers. If somebody wakes up and
> finds out that children that are down the river from that factory
> where you save three cents a foot in the cost of garden hose
> are developing cancers at significant rates—so that the Ameri-
> can public can save three cents a foot—those things won't
> be tolerated.[20]

> Wal-Mart today announced plans to purchase all of its wild-
> caught and frozen fish for the North American market from
> Marine Stewardship Council (MSC) certified fisheries within the
> next three to five years. The first step toward this goal will be to
> have product that comes from MSC-certified fisheries carry the
> MSC eco-label starting later this year.[21]

> In a keynote speech today at the National Governors Association
> Winter meeting, Wal-Mart Stores, Inc. CEO Lee Scott called for
> a "new commitment" between government and businesses to
> solve health care challenges facing America's working families.[22]

Is this talk simply rhetoric, or a call for action? It is far too early to say definitely, but already there are signs that Wal-Mart is moving aggressively on promoting organic foods and fibers—for example, buying an entire farm crop of organic cotton.[23] This might be done mainly because of a business decision that consumer tastes are moving in this direction, and that Wal-Mart is moving to lure higher-income customers who tend to be the biggest purchasers of organic products into its stores. It may be a brilliant marketing strategy. But it may also be done mainly to appease environmental critics. Similarly, in the summer of 2006, Wal-Mart announced an average 6 percent increase in starting pay at a large number of stores, plus increases in performance-based pay.[24]

There are two potential problems with Wal-Mart's new "kinder and gentler" approach. First, if it is a genuine attempt to convince Wal-Mart critics that Wal-Mart shares their concerns and really wants to be allies in their causes (equitable working conditions, a sustainable environment, and so on), we are highly skeptical that it will work. A large part of the opposition to Wal-Mart is funded by labor unions that have one overriding goal—either to unionize Wal-Mart or greatly reduce its scope and market share. It is unlikely they will be appeased by any moves to, say, raise wages or benefits that do not involve union membership. Moreover, little that Wal-Mart has done addresses the concerns of the antiglobalization opposition.

Second, in its attempt to appease critics, Wal-Mart may be risking abandoning the strategy that made it strong and successful: everyday low prices. If Wal-Mart is suggesting it will require its suppliers to pay overseas workers higher wages, or if it offers expensive benefits to workers heretofore not provided, it will raise the costs of products, lowering the great benefit to Americans, especially lower-income ones, of having access to low-priced goods. In one of the quotes above, Lee Scott seems to be saying, "Let Americans pay more for garden hose." There seems to be a tradeoff here—a willingness to sacrifice some of Sam Walton's vision for the company in order to try to placate some critics. It may be too high of a price to pay.

To be sure, not all Wal-Mart's belated public relations offensive has been directed to promoting such concepts as sustainable economic development or organic goods. An interesting approach takes a leaf from the book of the unions opposing Wal-Mart: establishing a website, Working Families for Wal-Mart, financed by Wal-Mart but run largely by volunteers. Led originally by former chief spokesman (and former paid Wal-Mart consultant) Andrew Young, former UN ambassador, the site seems to emphasize Wal-Mart's greatest strength: the great benefits it provides to poorer Americans. As Ambassador Young has put it in an op-ed in the *Atlanta Journal Constitution*:

> Those who have committed their lives to helping the poor believe that if more companies followed Wal-Mart's lead, and provided opportunity and savings to those who need it most, more Americans who are battling poverty would be able to ascend the rungs of the ladder that leads to the American dream.[25]

Another area in which Wal-Mart showed early on that it was relatively naïve in fighting political battles relates to campaign contributions. In the fight over mandatory health insurance in Maryland, the Service Employees International Union (SEIU) and the United Food and Commercial Workers International Union (UFCW) spent over $36,000 in donations to forty-eight Maryland legislators (over one-fourth the total legislature), vastly more than spent by Wal-Mart in its donations to a mere seven legislators.[26] While Wal-Mart did spend money on a public campaign explaining the evils of the Maryland vote, it did not put much money where it counts—in the pockets of legislators (or, strictly speaking, their campaign operations). It is sad but apparently true that to pass legislation, you increasingly have to "pay to play," a form of legalized corruption that, unfortunately, Wal-Mart probably must indulge in if it is going to ward off regulatory efforts.

The Future of Wal-Mart and Other Big-Box Discounters

It has been our historical observation that public protest movements against companies often come after the target firm has actually started to show signs of weakness and decline. The classic example is the Standard Oil Trust, opposition to which intensified after 1900 even though the company's invincibility and market share had started to erode, in part because of the discovery of new oil fields overseas and in Texas. So it may be with Wal-Mart. There are signs that although the company continues to grow in an absolute sense, with rising sales and profits, its period of retail ascendancy has peaked.

FIGURE 12-1

INFLATION-ADJUSTED CHANGING STOCK PRICE,
WAL-MART AND COMPETITORS, MARCH 2001–MARCH 2006 (PERCENT)

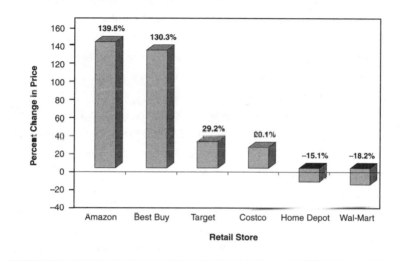

SOURCE: Yahoo Finance, "Historical Prices," http://finance.yahoo.com/q/hp?s=WMT (accessed June 29, 2006).

Figure 12-1 shows the five-year change in stock prices from March 9, 2001, to March 10, 2006, for Wal-Mart and five retail competitors: Amazon.com, Best Buy, Costco, Home Depot, and Target. Wal-Mart had the worst performance of the group, with a fairly significant decline in inflation-adjusted stock price, performing only slightly worse than Home Depot, well below competitors Target and Costco, and horribly compared to the extraordinary gains registered by Best Buy and by Internet competitor Amazon.com.

Why is Wal-Mart stock in the doldrums? Not because earnings are declining—they actually rose handsomely over the period, from $6.2 billion in fiscal year 2001 to over $11.2 billion in fiscal year 2006, with a return on stockholder equity in excess of 20 percent at the end of the period. Partly, the answer relates to the fact that Wal-Mart's torrid growth rate has slowed considerably, and some rivals are starting to show faster sales increases. Wal-Mart has gone from being a growth stock bought for anticipated capital gains to being an almost stodgy mainstream stock whose valuation is now relatively low in relation to earnings. A similar reasoning is behind the relatively poor performance of Home Depot stores, another company with rising earnings, that is losing some market share to competitors such as Lowe's.

A second factor in Wal-Mart's stock decline, of course, is investor wariness over potential adverse public-policy impacts of the anti–Wal-Mart campaign. If the unions and other anti–Wal-Mart critics are successful in forcing the company to raise its costs, its high profit margins and competitive advantage will erode. Uncertainty over that prospect has no doubt contributed to the stock's relatively poor performance.

Market leaders in any given industry typically find their commanding lead erode over time. At the time it was formed in 1901, the U.S. Steel Corporation had over 40 percent of the steel market and was America's leading corporation in terms of capitalization. Over time, its power waned. The same happened to General Motors, the American Tobacco Company, AT&T, and IBM, to mention just a few, and is probably happening now to Microsoft as well. In a dynamic society, tastes and methods of production change, and the market leader usually finds other entrepreneurs becoming more competitive as they grasp these changes as quickly as or more quickly than the leader. Wal-Mart's losing some of its dominance is not only likely; it is natural and expected, given past historical trends.

Sam Walton had a keen appreciation of the role of change. He exploited change in challenging the variety stores and conventional apparel chain stores like J. C. Penney and Sears, Roebuck. He found ways to cut costs dramatically through such high-tech innovations as his computer-based system of having very tight inventory controls and such old-fashioned penny-pinching as having executives share hotel rooms. (His penny-pinching was no doubt a factor in his firm's long-term disdain for hiring specialists in public relations.) He understood the importance of parking and offering customers lots of choices, and the possibilities of economies of scale. He foresaw the largely untapped market for large stores in smaller communities where competition was weak. His vision, his foresight, his boldness, and his hard work made him and his company successful. In his autobiography written at the very end of his life, he wondered whether his company was becoming too big: "Can a $100 billion retailer really function as efficiently and productively as it should? Or would maybe five $20 billion companies work better?"[27] Maybe bigness breeds complacency, bureaucracy, and vulnerability to public attack, and Sam's musing about some reorganization of his firm through spinoffs of operations may have been a sound one.

One of Sam's ten rules for running a successful company was "Swim upstream. Go the other way. Ignore the conventional wisdom. If everyone else is doing it one way, there's a good chance you can find your niche by going exactly in the opposite direction."[28] Wal-Mart has been relatively slow in changing its basic model. As it sees competitors like Target and Costco grab sales away from it, it has started to cater more to somewhat more upscale customers, reflecting the rise in income in America over time. To be sure, there are dangers in this—if it becomes too upscale, it loses its "everyday low price" appeal to the less affluent but highly loyal customers who have been its bread and butter. Perhaps that is an argument for Wal-Mart to open a new type of slightly more upscale store, separate from the supercenters that appeal to the less affluent (similarly, following Sam's thought, it might be wise to spin off Sam's Clubs as a separate company).

Wal-Mart is participating in the Internet sales boom, but not as a dominant player. eBay made over a billion dollars in 2005, more than double two years earlier, and has a market valuation approaching one-third that of Wal-Mart, even though it has only 1 percent as many employees. It is performing as a company much like Wal-Mart did in its early days, and Wall Street has given it and other Internet discounters like Amazon relatively higher stock prices in relation to earnings. This reflects the view that the financial community thinks Wal-Mart's moment of glory has largely passed, and it has gone from being a growth company to being part of the old-time retail tradition. A new computer-driven technology may soon do to Wal-Mart what Wal-Mart did to Woolworth's and Sears. The more things change, the more they remain the same.

Conclusions

Wal-Mart is a quintessential American success story, almost a perfect example of Yankee ingenuity and risk-taking at its best. "Everyday low prices" made Sam Walton rich, but they also enriched millions of consumers, many of them persons of modest means. No one has done more for the common man and woman than Sam Walton. Wal-Mart provided job opportunities to many, and made thousands of employees into capitalists through their stock ownership. Its innovative, efficient ways of doing business transformed American retailing, dramatically raising productivity to such an extent that it materially affected the growth of the entire nation in a positive direction.

Change comes at a price, however, and for every score of winners who benefited from Wal-Mart, there was a loser or two, especially competitors who lost market share and income, and their workers. No doubt some traditionalists genuinely bemoan the passing of older stores, and environmentalists cringe at the traffic congestion of cars traveling to Wal-Mart. Yet these people are greatly outnumbered by those who embrace change, who want more goods at lower prices, and who accept retail innovation as earlier generations of Americans accepted it.

Regarding public policy, the evidence supports having a policy of benign neutrality towards Wal-Mart and other big-box discount retailers. On the whole, they are improving the welfare of the American people. Subsidizing them through government policy, however, would be inadvisable, putting the government in the position, for which it is ill-equipped, of picking winners and losers in a market economy. Roughly speaking, the optimal policy toward Wal-Mart is: Do nothing. From a narrow policy sense, then, this book is much ado about nothing. But it is far from nothing in a broader sense: the story of modern retail innovation in America is a story about risk-taking entrepreneurs doing bold things to enrich themselves, all the while improving people's lives, reducing poverty, and expanding choices and human horizons.

Notes

Chapter 1: The Importance of Retail Innovations

1. Adam Smith, *An Inquiry into the Nature and Causes of the Wealth of Nations* (Oxford: Oxford University Press, 1976).

2. Jules Dupuit, "De la mesure de l'utilité des travaux publics," *Annales des Ponts et Chaussees*, 1844, reprinted in Kenneth J. Arrow and Tibor Scitovsky, eds., *American Economic Association Readings in Welfare Economics* (Homewood, Ill.: Richard D. Irwin, 1969).

3. Alfred Marshall, *Principles of Economics* (London: Macmillan, 1890). The Marshall textbook dominated the English-speaking world for many decades and went through eight editions.

4. For readers for whom the graphical analysis is difficult, skipping the graphs should not greatly reduce understanding of the overall point being made here.

5. J. R. Hicks, "The Rehabilitation of Consumers' Surplus," *Review of Economic Studies* 8 (February 1941): 106–16, reprinted in Arrow and Scitovsky, eds., *American Economic Association Readings*; Arnold C. Harberger, "Three Basic Postulates for Applied Welfare Economics: An Interpretive Essay," *Journal of Economic Literature* 9 (September 1971): 785–97; and Jerry A. Hausman, "Exact Consumer's Surplus and Deadweight Loss," *American Economic Review* 71 (September 1981): 662–76.

6. Citing a number of technical difficulties, Daniel T. Slesnick argued in a survey article on welfare measurement that "consumer's surplus should not be used as a welfare measure." See his "Empirical Approaches to the Measurement of Welfare," *Journal of Economic Literature* 36 (December 1998): 2108. For a representative highly technical piece on this topic, see Claude Hillinger, "Money Metric, Consumer Surplus and Welfare Measurement," *German Economic Review* 2 (May 2001): 177–93.

7. Erik Brynjolfsson, Yu Hu, and Michael D. Smith, "Consumer Surplus in the Digital Economy: Estimating the Value of Increased Product Variety at Online Booksellers," *Management Science* 49 (November 2003): 1580–96.

8. Emek Basker, "Selling a Cheaper Mousetrap: Wal-Mart's Effect on Retail Prices," *Journal of Urban Economics* 58, no. 2 (September 2005): 203–29.

9. Jerry Hausman and Ephraim Leibtag, "Consumer Benefits from Increased Competition in Shopping Outlets: Measuring the Effect of Wal-Mart" (paper, EC conference, Marseilles, France, December 2004).

10. The argument is usually discussed with regard to the economics of tariffs—the gains to producers from enhanced producer surplus from tariffs are more than offset by the loss to consumers from lower consumer surplus. For one textbook example of the graphics of this, see James D. Gwartney, Richard L. Stroup, and Russell S. Sobel, *Macroeconomics: Private and Public Choice*, 9th ed. (Fort Worth, Tex.: Dryden Press, 2000), 446.

11. For information about Wal-Mart giving, go to www.walmartfoundation.org (accessed June 26, 2006).

12. John Tierney, "From FEMA to WEMA," *New York Times,* September 20, 2005.

13. The information in this section depends heavily on Gallup Poll News Service, *Gallup Poll Social Series: Work & Education*, August 8–11, 2005.

Chapter 2: Wal-Mart and Its Critics

1. Examples of other anti–Wal-Mart sites are www.wakeupwalmart.com and www.hel-mart.com/.

2. Al Norman, *Slam-Dunking Wal-Mart* (Atlantic City, N.J.: Raphel Marketing, 1999) and his *The Case Against Wal-Mart* (Atlantic City, N.J.: Raphel Marketing, 2004); John Dicker, *The United States of Wal-Mart* (New York: Jeremy T. Tarchell/Penguin, 2005); Bill Quinn, *How Wal-Mart Is Destroying America* (Berkeley, Calif.: Ten Speed Press, 2005); and Anthony Bianco, *The Bully of Bentonville: How the High Cost of Wal-Mart's Everyday Low Prices Is Hurting America* (New York: Doubleday, 2006). A book that purports to be evenhanded but which, in fact, is rather critical of Wal-Mart is Charles Fishman's *The Wal-Mart Effect* (New York: Penguin Press, 2006).

3. Examples of pro–Wal-Mart books: Sam Walton, *Made in America* (New York: Doubleday, 1992); Don Soderquist, *The Wal-Mart Way: The Inside Story of the Success of the World's Largest Company* (Nashville, Tenn.: Nelson Business, 2005); Robert Slater, *The Wal-Mart Triumph* (New York: Penguin, 2003); and Michael Bergdahl, *What I Learned from Sam Walton* (Hoboken, N.J.: John Wiley & Sons, 2004).

4. Jason Furman, "Wal-Mart: A Progressive Success Story," paper, November 28, 2005, available at www.americanprogress.org/kf/walmart_progressive.pdf.

5. Wal-Mart Watch, "Forward This to a Friend," various pages on website, www.walmartwatch.com (accessed September 7, 2006).

6. Quoted in Larry Elliott, "Brown's Globalisation Panel of 'Wise Men' Attacked from All Sides," *Guardian*, March 22, 2006.

7. Wal-Mart Watch, "Meet the Waltons: More Wealth Amassed Off American Taxpayers," press release, March 10, 2006, http://walmartwatch.com/press/releases/meet_the_waltons_more_wealth_amassed_off_american_taxpayers/ (accessed September 7, 2006).

8. Mark Gruenberg, "Anti Wal-Mart Campaign Unites Unionists with Other Activists," International Labor Communications Association, November 21, 2005, www.ilcaonline.org/modules.php?op=modload&name=News&file=article&sid=2680 (accessed March 27, 2006).

9. Quinn, *How Wal-Mart Is Destroying America*, 72.

10. As quoted in Gwartney, Stroup, and Sobel, *Macroeconomics*, 451.

11. See Wal-Mart Watch, "About Wal-Mart Watch," http://walmartwatch.com/home/pages/about (accessed September 7, 2006).

12. *Everyday Low Wages: The Hidden Price We All Pay For Wal-Mart*, Democratic Staff, Committee on Education and the Work Force, U.S. House of Representatives, February 16, 2004, available at http://mindfully.org/industry/2004/Wal-Mart-Labor-Record16beb04.htm

13. Philip Mattera and Anne Purinton, *Shopping for Subsidies: How Wal-Mart Uses Taxpayer Money to Finance Its Never-Ending Growth*, Good Jobs First, 2004, www.goodjobsfirst.org/pdf/wmtstudy.pdf (accessed June 26, 2006).

Chapter 3: A History of Retail Innovation
in America before Wal-Mart

1. The authors consulted a number of historical surveys in preparing this chapter. Of particular use was Donald L. Kemmerer and C. Clyde Jones, *American Economic History* (New York: McGraw-Hill, 1959), especially chapters 13, 20, and 28.

2. Angus Maddison, *The World Economy: A Millennial Perspective* (Paris: Organisation for Economic Co-operation and Development, 2001), 264.

3. On early peddling, see Richardson Wright, *Hawkers and Walkers in Early America* (Philadelphia: Lippincott, 1927).

4. An old but classic study on the rise of general stores is Lewis Atherton, *The Pioneer Merchants in Mid-America* (Columbia, Mo.: University of Missouri Press, 1939).

5. Ibid.

6. See Ralph Hower, *History of Macy's, 1858–1919* (Cambridge, Mass.: Harvard University Press, 1943) for the most encyclopedic account of the development of this famous department store. For a more recent book that argues that modern-day leveraged buyout techniques mortally wounded the company, see Jeffrey A.

Trachtenberg, *The Rain on Macy's Parade: How Greed, Ambitions and Folly Ruined America's Greatest Store* (New York: Times Books, 1996). See also Robert W. Twyman, *History of Marshall Field & Company* (Philadelphia: University of Pennsylvania Press, 1954) and Joseph Appel, *The Business Biography of John Wanamaker*, 2 vols. (New York: Macmillan, 1930).

7. Authors' calculations based on the Consumer Price Index for All Urban Consumers. For data, see U.S. Bureau of the Census, *Historical Statistics of the United States, Colonial Times to 1970* (Washington, D.C.: Government Printing Office, 1975), 211, and the *Economic Report of the President* (Washington, D.C.: Government Printing Office, 2005), 282.

8. Modern biographies of Woolworth and his company include John P. Nichols, *Skyline Queen and the Merchant Prince: The Woolworth Story* (New York: Trident Press, 1973), and Karen Plunkett-Powell, *Remembering Woolworth's: A Nostalgic History of the World's Most Famous Five-and-Dime* (New York: St. Martin's Press, 1999). The older John Winkler's *Five and Ten* (New York: McBride, 1940) is also highly readable.

9. An excellent history of chain stores is Godfrey M. Lebhar, *Chain Stores in America, 1859–1959* (New York: Chain Store Publishing Corporation, 1959).

10. The standard history on Sears in the early twentieth century is Boris Emmet and John Jeuck, *Catalogues and Counters: A History of Sears, Roebuck and Company* (Chicago: University of Chicago Press, 1950). For a more recent account, see James Worthy, *Shaping an American Institution: Robert E. Wood and Sears, Roebuck* (Urbana: University of Illinois Press, 1984). For an interesting comparison of Sears's success in the 1920s with its failure in the 1980s, see Daniel Raff and Peter Temin, "Sears Roebuck in the Twentieth Century: Competition, Complementarities and the Problem of Wasting Assets," in *Learning by Doing in Markets, Films and Nations*, ed. Naomi R. Lamoreaux, Daniel Raff, and Peter Temin (Chicago: University of Chicago Press, 1999).

11. See Raff and Temin, 49, for interesting sales data for the 1980s, the decade in which Sears lost its sales superiority.

12. Some stores, such as Marshall Field's and Filene's, have actually been owned by more than one chain over time. Both Allied Department Stores and Federated Department Stores were purchased in the 1980s by the Canadian developer, Robert Campeau, who drove both of them into bankruptcy, although they emerged in somewhat altered forms with new leadership in the early 1990s.

13. Zachary Courser, *Wal-Mart and the Politics of American Retail* (Washington, D.C.: Competitive Enterprise Institute, November 18, 2005), 5.

14. Ibid., 7.

15. Ibid., 8. For a more extended treatment of legislation directed against chain stores, see Lebhar, *Chain Stores in America*.

16. *Schwegmann Bros. v. Calvert Corp.*, 341 U.S. 384 (1951).

17. For another, slightly fuller account, see Paul A. London, *The Competition Solution* (Washington, D.C.: AEI Press, 2004), especially chapter 6.

18. Most scholars believe the Consumer Price Index overstates the inflation rate; the true inflation-adjusted value of $1 billion in 1965 may be closer to $5 billion or even less. See David E. Lebow and Jeremy B. Rudd, "Measurement Error in the Consumer Price Index: Where Do We Stand?" *Journal of Economic Literature* 41, no. 1 (March 2003): 159–201.

19. Industry-specific national income data are generally unavailable until after World War II, late in the period studied. Relative employment in retailing from 1948 to 1965 grew, whereas the national income data show no corresponding growth in the relative importance of retailing. This is consistent with the thesis that labor productivity was rising slower in retailing than elsewhere. The productivity issue is addressed more extensively later in the book.

Chapter 4: The Wal-Mart Story

1. This account is largely derived from *Wikipedia*, s.v., "Ann & Hope Department Stores," http://cn.wikipedia.org/wiki/Ann_&_Hope_Department_Stores (accessed June 26, 2006).

2. There are several short but useful Internet sources on Cunningham and Kmart. See, for example, Harvard Business School, "Harry B. Cunningham," *20th Century Great American Business Leaders*, www.hbs.edu/leadership/database/leaders/192/ (accessed August 12, 2006), and Everything2.com, "Kmart," http://everything2.com/index.pl?node=Kmart (accessed June 26, 2006).

3. Walton, *Made in America*, viii.

4. This account is necessarily abbreviated, and excludes mention of some important names, such as John Geisse, who was involved in the founding of Venture and Target Stores, and other companies, such as the E. J. Korvette chain in the eastern states.

5. Walton, *Made in America*, back dust jacket.

6. Ibid., 156.

7. On Rockefeller's life, see the magnificent biography by Ron Chernow, *Titan: The Life of John D. Rockefeller, Sr.* (New York: Random House, 1998). An older and more exhaustive (two-volume) biography is Allan Nevins, *John D. Rockefeller: The Heroic Age of American Enterprise* (New York: Charles Scribner's Sons, 1940); a one-volume abridgement of the Nevins biography by William Greenleaf appeared as *Study in Power* (New York: Scribner, 1959). On Sam Walton, read *Made in America*.

8. Walton, *Made in America*, 189.

9. Ibid., 132.

10. Profits for 1975 were reduced substantially because of the adoption of the LIFO (last in, first out) method of evaluating inventories (as opposed to the FIFO— first in, first out—method used previously). The 1975 profit margin in table 4-2

reflects the new accounting method (used in subsequent years), while the profit margin for the same year in table 4-1 is based on the older FIFO method. In periods of high inflation, as this era was, the evaluation of inventories becomes more difficult, and the inventory accounting method used materially affects reported earnings.

11. Most of the information in this section comes from various annual reports for Wal-Mart, as posted at Wal-Mart, "Shareholder Information: Annual Reports," http://walmartstores.com/GlobalWMStoresWeb/navigate.do?catg=453& contId=5700 (accessed June 26, 2006).

12. Walton, *Made in America,* 195.

13. Based on the 2005 Fortune 500 rankings, available at http://money.cnn.com/magazines/fortune/fortune500/full_list/ (accessed August 14, 2006).

14. Authors' calculations based on data in Wal-Mart, *Wal-Mart Annual Report 2005,* 17, 22–23, www.walmartstores.com/Files/2005AnnualReport.pdf (accessed August 11, 2006).

15. Ann Zimmerman and Kris Hudson, "Looking Upscale, Wal-Mart Begins A Big Makeover," *Wall Street Journal,* September 17–18, 2005, A1.

16. Walton, *Made in America,* 217, 233.

17. Ibid., 253.

18. See Wal-Mart, *Wal-Mart Annual Report 1995,* 12–13, www.walmartstores.com/Files/1995AnnualReport.pdf, and *Wal-Mart Annual Report 2005,* 22–23, www.walmartstores.com/Files/2005AnnualReport.pdf (both accessed August 11, 2006).

Chapter 5: Imitators and Innovators

1. Financial and operating data are from corporate annual reports, Hoover's (www.hoovers.com/) and Deloitte, "2005 Global Powers of Retailing," www.deloitte.com/dtt/cda/doc/content/US_CB_GlobalPowers2005.pdf (accessed June 26, 2006), and company 10-K reports.

2. Newmarketbuilders, "Wal-Mart Store #5260—Target, Come See the (Near) Future," *newmarketbuilders' retail blog,* February 12, 2006, http://newmarketblog.blogspot.com/2006/02/wal-mart-store-5260-target-come-see.html (accessed June 26, 2006).

3. Kmart Corporation, "Kmart Annual Report 1995," www.kmartcorp.com/corp/investor/annual/annual_1995/d4_ct.stm (accessed August 11, 2006).

4. This paragraph relies highly on Brian Grow, Diane Brady, and Michael Arndt, "Renovating Home Depot," *Business Week,* March 6, 2006, www.businessweek.com/magazine/content/06_10/b3974001.htm (accessed August 11, 2006).

5. Robert Berner, "Watch Out Best Buy and Circuit City," *Business Week Online,* November 21, 2005, www.businessweek.com/magazine/content/05_47/b3960082.htm (accessed June 26, 2006).

6. Ellen P. Gabler, "Success Means Best Buy's Eq-life Stores Multiply," *Minneapolis St. Paul Business Journal*, April 21, 2005, www.bizjournals.com/twincities/stories/2005/04/25/story6.html (accessed August 11, 2006).

7. Ellen P. Gabler, "Best Buy Opening Small-Biz Centers," *Minneapolis St. Paul Business Journal*, June 10, 2005, http://twincities.bizjournals.com/twincities/stories/2005/06/13/story1.html (accessed August 11, 2006).

8. Earlier comparable data are not available due to a major divestiture.

9. Joseph A. Schumpeter, *Capitalism, Socialism, and Democracy* (New York: Harper, 1975), 82–85.

10. Kate DuBose Tomassi, "Circuit City Makes Progress But Margin Issues Persist," *Forbes.com*, March 17, 2006, www.forbes.com/2006/03/17/circuit-city-0317markets04_print.html (accessed June 26, 2006).

11. Deloitte, *2005 Global Powers of Retailing*, G15, www.deloitte.com/dtt/cda/doc/content/US_CB_GlobalPowers2005.pdf (accessed August 11, 2006).

Chapter 6: Employment and Wage Effects of Discount Stores

1. Previously, businesses were classified according to the Standard Industrial Classification (SIC) system. Beginning with the 1998 data, the North American Industry Classification System (NAICS) has been used. The stores operated by Wal-Mart, including Sam's Club, fit into the general merchandise category. For more details, see Office of Management and Budget, *North American Industry Classification System: United States, 1997* (Lanham, Md.: Bernan Press, 1998), 445–47.

2. See Erich H. Strassner and Thomas F. Howells III, "Annual Industry Accounts," in the U.S. Department of Commerce's *Survey of Current Business*, May 2005, especially p. 9 for more details.

3. Data used in estimation come from U.S. Department of Commerce, Bureau of Economic Analysis, table 6.4D, "National Income and Products Table: Full-Time and Part-Time Employees by Industry," www.bea.gov/bea/dn/nipaweb/TableView.asp?SelectedTable=182&FirstYear=2004&LastYear=2005&Freq=Year (accessed August 11, 2006). Data were also obtained from Wal-Mart, *Wal-Mart Annual Report 1999*, 18, www.walmartstores.com/Files/1999_annualreport.pdf, and *Wal-Mart Annual Report 2002*, 14–15, www.walmartstores.com/Files/2002_annualreport.pdf (both accessed August 14, 2006).

4. The major work is Richard Vedder and Lowell Gallaway, *Out of Work: Unemployment and Government in Twentieth-Century America* (New York: New York University Press, 1997). The adjusted real wage is the inflation-corrected wage rate (money wages divided by the price level), adjusted by an index measuring labor productivity. The adjusted real wage is about equal to labor's share of the national

income. When labor's share rises, profits are relatively squeezed, and the quantity of labor demanded falls, creating unemployment.

5. Still another approach is to look at state unemployment rates as they relate to Wal-Mart's presence. Some preliminary examination using this approach showed no statistically significant relationship between Wal-Mart's presence and unemployment. While the evidence did not support the hypothesis that "Wal-Mart on balance creates new jobs," it also did not support the opposite hypothesis suggested by some critics that Wal-Mart, on net, destroys jobs.

6. The Wal-Mart and employment data are not stationary in nature over time, tending to rise fairly consistently. This violates basic classical statistical assumptions and creates the potential for spurious correlation. Also, there is the possibility that there is some omitted error bias—that factors excluded from the analysis provide the true major explanations of falling unemployment over time.

7. On this point, see chapter 7 and Emek Basker, "Job Creation or Destruction: Labor Market Effects of Wal-Mart Expansion," *Review of Economics and Statistics* 87 (February 2005): 174–83.

8. Even in early times when travel and communication costs were high, the amount of monopsonistic exploitation in local labor markets, while real, was far less than some accounts would suggest. On this point, see Richard K. Vedder, Lowell E. Gallaway, and David Klingaman, "Discrimination and Exploitation in Antebellum American Cotton Textile Manufacturing," in Paul Uselding, ed., *Research in Economic History*, vol. 3 (Greenwich, Conn.: JAI Press, 1978).

9. The last two votes on unionization at Wal-Mart stores occurred in 2005 in New Castle, Pennsylvania and Loveland, Colorado, where the votes went against unionization by lopsided margins. See "Wal-Mart Workers Reject Plan to Unionize," The DenverChannel.com, February 25, 2005, available at www.thedenverchannel.com/money/4231767/detail.html, accessed on October 13, 2006.

10. The most striking evidence here is the fact that there have been very few unionization elections in Wal-Mart's history. In 2000, the meat cutters at Wal-Mart stores did vote to unionize, but the company decided to outsource that function, a decision it claimed to have made independent of the union vote. A vote in Quebec to unionize was followed by Wal-Mart's decision to exit the business there.

11. Walmartfacts.com, "Wal-Mart Associate Center," www.walmartfacts.com/associates/defacult.aspx#a41 (accessed September 12, 2005).

12. See U.S. Department of Labor, Bureau of Labor Statistics, "Table 5. Private Industry, By Major Occupational Groups and Bargaining Status," news release, www.bls.gov/news.release/ecec.t05.htm (accessed June 26, 2006).

13. U.S. Department of Labor, Bureau of Labor Statistics, "Earnings of Production or Nonsupervisory Workers on Private Nonfarm Payrolls in Current and Constant Dollars By Industry," news release, www.bls.gov/news.release/realer.t02thm (accessed September 12, 2005).

14. Data are as reported before, from Wal-Mart, *Wal-Mart Annual Report 2005*; U.S. Census Bureau, "State and County QuickFacts," http://quickfacts.census.gov/qfd/index.html (accessed August 13, 2006); and U.S. Department of Commerce, Bureau of Economic Analysis, *Regional Economic Profiles*, www.bea.gov/bea/regional/reis/default.cfm?catable=CA30 (accessed August 13, 2006).

15. If anything, this statement is conservative. For example, looking at the state of Georgia, the average wage in all occupations in early 2005 was over 30 percent higher in the Atlanta metro area than in all other areas of the state. See www.bls.gov/oes.current/oes_12060.htm, and www.bls.gov./oes/current/oes_ga.htm#b00-0000, last accessed October 12, 2006. We subtracted the Atlanta figures from the state averages to calculate a non-Atlanta metro area wage.

16. Wal-Mart, "State By State," www.walmartfacts.com/StateByState/ (accessed August 13, 2006).

17. Data are for the fourth quarter of 2004, and obtained from U.S. Department of Labor, Bureau of Labor Statistics, "Table 4. Covered (1) Establishments, Employment, and Wages by State, third quarter 2005 (2)," news release, www.bls.gov/news.release/cewqtr.t04.htm (accessed June 26, 2006).

18. U.S. Department of Labor, Bureau of Labor Statistics, *National Compensation Survey*, http://data.bls.gov/cgi-bin/dsrv (accessed September 12, 2005).

19. Stacy J. Willis, "Picketers for Hire: The Strange Business of Protesting Jobs That May Be Better Than Yours," *Las Vegas Weekly*, September 8–14, 2005.

20. Walmartfacts.com, "Wal-Mart Associate Center."

21. Data in this paragraph are from the U.S. Department of Labor, Bureau of Labor Statistics, *National Compensation Survey: Employee Benefits in Private Industry in the United States, March 2005*, August 2005, especially table 2, page 6, www.bls.gov/ncs/ebs/sp/ebsm0003.pdf, last accessed September 12, 2005.

22. Gregory Freeman, *Wal-Mart Supercenters: What's in Store for Southern California?* (Los Angeles: Los Angeles County Economic Development Corporation, January 2004), especially section 2.

23. In 2002, for example, there were 49,755,000 Medicaid recipients, less than 18 percent of the total population. See U.S. Bureau of the Census, *Statistical Abstract of the United States,* 126th edition (Washington, D.C.: Government Printing Office, 2006), 106, available at www.census.gov/compendia/stabab/health_nutrition/health.pdf, accessed on October 13, 2006.

24. Walton, *Made in America,* 132.

25. Some Bureau of Labor Statistics data estimate total employer nonwage costs at closer to 30 percent per employee in service industries, but these estimates include items that Wal-Mart is almost certainly not including in its statement of fringe benefits costs, including the employer share of Social Security, a major item. For example, in a September 22, 2006 press release of the Bureau of Labor Statistics, private sector service industry total fringe benefits were estimated to equal

32.8 percent of wages; excluding mandated benefits, fringe benefits fall to about 20 percent of wage compensation. See www.bls.gov/mews/release/ecec/toc.htm, accessed on October 13, 2006.

Chapter 7: Competition and Communities

1. A representative critique making this claim is Quinn, *How Wal-Mart Is Destroying America*, chapter 1.

2. Data on store openings were obtained from the Wal-Mart website, www.walmartfacts.com/FeaturedTopics/?id=8 (accessed August 11, 2006). The CA30, regional economic profiles, data were used for the twenty-five counties, obtained at the website of the U.S. Department of Commerce, Bureau of Economic Analysis, *Regional Economic Accounts*, www.bea.gov/bea/regional/reis/default.cfm?catable=CA30 (accessed September 7, 2006).

3. *Economic Report of the President* (2005), table B-35, 253.

4. Basker, "Selling a Cheaper Mousetrap."

5. Hausman and Leibtag, "Consumer Benefits from Increased Competition."

6. Ibid., 29–30.

7. Global Insight is the successor company to Data Resources Inc. and Wharton Econometric Forecasting Associates, generally acknowledged to be two of the leading economic consulting and forecasting firms. Both were formed by faculty from prestigious universities such as Harvard and the University of Pennsylvania.

8. Global Insight, "The Economic Impact of Wal-Mart" (paper, Economic Impact Research Conference: An In-Depth Look at Wal-Mart and Society, Washington, D.C., November 4, 2005), appendix A, 39–58.

9. Mike Troy, "Study Says Wal-Mart Is Positive Factor in Economy," *DSN Retailing Today*, November 21, 2005, available at www.findarticles.com/p/article/mi_mOTNP/is_22_44/ai_n155893514, last accessed October 13, 2006.

10. Pew Research Center, *Wal-Mart a Good Place to Shop But Some Critics Too*, December 15, 2005, http://people-press.org/reports/display.php3?ReportID=265 (accessed December 15, 2005).

11. Ibid., 8.

12. See "The Economic Impact of Wal-Mart," 1–2, for a summary of the entire study.

13. Michael J. Hicks, "What Do Quarterly Workforce Dynamics Tell Us About Wal-Mart? Evidence from New Stores in Pennsylvania" (paper, Economic Impact Research Conference: An In-Depth Look at Wal-Mart and Society, Washington, D.C., November 4, 2005).

14. Russell S. Sobel and Andrea M. Dean, "Has Wal-Mart Buried Mom and Pop? The Impact of Wal-Mart on Self-Employment and Small Establishments in the

United States," unpublished manuscript, Department of Economics, West Virginia University, 2006.

15. Kenneth E. Stone is the author of several studies, including his *Competing With the Retail Giants* (New York: John Wiley and Sons, 1995).

16. Basker, "Job Creation or Destruction?"

17. David Neumark, Junfu Zhang, and Stephen Ciccarella, "The Effects of Wal-Mart on Local Labor Markets" (paper, Economic Impact Research Conference: An In-Depth Look at Wal-Mart and Society, Washington, D.C., November 4, 2005).

18. Ibid., table 3, page 41.

19. Pew Research Center, "Wal-Mart a Good Place to Shop."

20. See WakeUpWalMart.com, www.wakeupwalmart.com/facts, last accessed October 13, 2006.

21. Joe Hansen, "More Villian Than Victim," *USA Today*, April 18, 2005, available at http://blog.wakeupwalmarket.com/ufcw/2995/04/more_vilain_th.html, last accessed October 15, 2006.

22. Michael J. Hicks, "The Impact of Wal-Mart on Local Fiscal Health: Evidence from a Panel of Ohio Counties" (paper, Economic Impact Research Conference: An In-Depth Look at Wal-Mart and Society, Washington, D.C., November 4, 2005).

23. Sonya Carlson, "Is Wal-Mart's 'Efficiency' Based on a Government Subsidy? A Case Study of Oregon" (honors thesis, Lewis and Clark College, April 15, 2005). The Carlson study is a remarkably detailed (102-page) in-depth analysis of fiscal effects. While it does not provide an econometric analysis that controls for other determinants of fiscal effects, it is nonetheless a useful addition to Wal-Mart scholarship.

24. See Arindrajit Dube and Ken Jacobs, "Hidden Cost of Wal-Mart Jobs: Use of Safety Net Programs by Wal-Mart Workers in California" (Center for Labor Research and Education, University of California, Berkeley, October 4, 2004), http://laborcenter.berkeley.edu/lowwage/walmart.pdf (accessed August 11, 2006). Hicks's comment is found in his paper on "The Impact of Wal-Mart on Local Fiscal Health," 9.

Chapter 8: Wal-Mart and the Poor

1. Calculations were derived from analysis of data for twenty-five counties from U.S. Bureau of the Census "State and County QuickFacts," http://quickfacts.census.gov/qfd/index.html (accessed August 2, 2006).

2. Anita French, "Wal-Mart Caters to Hispanic Customers," *Morning News*, Springfield, Arkansas, May 14, 2006, www.nwaonline.net/articles/2006/05/14/business/9601wmhispanics.txt (accessed May 15, 2006).

3. Data are from the U.S. Bureau of the Census using the official poverty-rate definition. A five-year moving average is used to abstract from short-term cyclical

fluctuations in the poverty rate related to the business cycle. For the most recent poverty data, go to U.S. Census Bureau, *Income, Poverty and Health Insurance Coverage in the United States: 2005*, found at www.census.gov/hhes/www/poverty/poverty05.html, accessed on October 14, 2006.

4. U.S. Bureau of the Census, *Statistical Abstract of the United States, 2006*, 125th ed. (Washington, D.C.: Government Printing Office, 2005); and *Statistical Abstract of the United States, 1990*, 110th ed. (Washington, D.C.: Government Printing Office, 1990).

5. Ideally, we would have looked at poverty rates in Wal-Mart counties before and after Wal-Mart's entry into the market and compared those with rates in other parts of the same states, in much the same way as was done with employment in chapter 7. Unfortunately, reliable poverty-rate data at the county level are available only in census years.

Chapter 9: The Discount Revolution in Broader Economic Context

1. See Robert W. Fogel, *Railroads and Economic Growth* (Baltimore: Johns Hopkins University Press, 1964), chapter 6.

2. Productivity growth estimation before 1930 is a somewhat tricky business subject to considerable error. See, for example, Richard K. Vedder, *The American Economy in Historical Perspective* (Belmont, Calif.: Wadsworth Publishing Company, 1976) for extensive discussions of productivity growth before 1973. On modern-era productivity change, see the *Economic Report of the President* (Washington, D.C.: Government Printing Office, 2006), 341.

3. Data on total productivity come from the Bureau of Labor Statistics, while those for retail trade were obtained from that source as well as the Bureau of Economic Analysis. See, for example, the *Economic Report of the President* (Washington, D.C.: Government Printing Office, 2006), p. 340 for overall productivity data. For value added industry data, see www.bea.gov/bea/industry/gpotables/gpo_action.cfm?anon=246&table_id=1729&format_type.=0, last accessed October 15, 2006.

4. On this point, see U.S. Department of Labor, Bureau of Labor Statistics, "Productivity and Costs By Industry, 2003," August 26, 2005, ftp://ftp.bls.gov/pub/news.release/History/prin.08262005.news (accessed June 27, 2006). In over 50 percent of the eighty-six manufacturing industries examined, labor productivity rose more than 2.5 percent a year from 1987 to 2003, and in seven of those industries, the productivity advance exceeded 7 percent a year. See page 3 for more details.

5. For example, sales per employee at Home Depot actually fell in inflation-adjusted terms from 1990 to 2004, if the annual reports are to be believed, but we suspect changes in the method of counting employees account for most, if not all, of that. See Home Depot's 1990 and 2004 annual reports for details.

6. From 1947 to 1972, the average number of weekly working hours in retail trade fell from 40.3 to 33.6. See U.S. Department of Labor, *Manpower Report of the President* (Washington, D.C.: Government Printing Office, 1973), 190. By the 1990s, the decline had stopped at around 30.0 hours a week. In 2002, for example, hours worked actually slightly exceeded those in 1993. For hours of work for retail trade, see the monthly BLS Employment Situation press release, typically Table B-2. For example, in August 2006 the average retail trade employee worked 30.7 hours. See www.bls.gov/news.rlease/archives/empsit_09012006.pdf, last accessed on October 15, 2006. Complicating things in recent years is a change in the classification of industries that makes data comparison over time more difficult. Fortunately, however, by any measure, weekly hours worked have remained relatively constant in recent years.

7. Specifically, we assumed that the CPI-U overstated inflation by an average of 0.5 percentage points annually in the 1960s, by 1.2 percentage points in the highly inflationary 1970–82 period, by 0.8 points from 1983 to 1989, and by 0.6 points annually in the 1990s.

8. U.S. Department of Labor, Bureau of Labor Statistics, "Productivity and Costs By Industry: Wholesale Trade, Retail Trade, and Food Services and Drinking Places, 2004," September 27, 2005, 1, ftp://ftp.bls.gov/pub/news.release/History/prin.09272005.news (accessed June 27, 2006).

9. Fogel, *Railroads and Economic Growth*, chapter 6, especially p. 219.

Chapter 10: Wal-Mart and the World

1. Evan Ramstad, "Wal-Mart Leaves South Korea By Selling Stores to Local Rival," *Wall Street Journal*, June 23, 2006, A2.

2. Demographia, "High-Income World Metropolitan Areas: Core City & Suburban Population Trends," www.demographia.com/db-highmetro.htm (accessed June 27, 2006; author's calculations and analysis).

3. Competition Commission, *Supermarkets: A Report on the Supply of Groceries from Multiple Stores in the United Kingdom*, October 10, 2000, www.competition-commission.org.uk/rep_pub/reports/2000/446super.htm#full (accessed June 27, 2006).

4. Financial and operating data are from corporate annual reports, Hoover's (www.hoovers.com/) and Deloitte, *2005 Global Powers of Retailing*, and company 10-K reports.

5. Seon-Jin Cha, "Carrefour Korea Might Draw Bids Up to $1.84 Billion," *Wall Street Journal*, March 30, 2006, C4.

6. Clay Chandler, Susan M. Kaufman, Joan Levinstein, and Wang Ting, "The Great Wal-Mart of China," *Fortune*, July 25, 2005, www.foodmarket.com/sub/news.asp?Key=265425, last accessed June 27, 2006.

7. Peter S. Goodman and Philip P. Pan, "Chinese Workers Pay for Wal-Mart's Low Prices," *Washington Post*, February 8, 2004.

8. See Vedder, Gallaway, and Klingaman, "Discrimination and Exploitation," 217–62. See also Caroline Ware, *The Early New England Textile Manufacture* (Boston: Houghton Mifflin, 1931), or Robert Layer, *Earnings of Cotton Mill Operatives, 1825–1914* (Cambridge, Mass.: Harvard University Press, 1955).

9. Jagdish Bhagwati, *In Defense of Globalization* (New York: Oxford University Press, 2004).

10. Ibid., 71.

11. See, for example, Benjamin Powell and David Skarbek, "Don't Get into a Lather Over Sweatshops," *Christian Science Monitor*, August 2, 2005, available at www.csmonitor.com/2005/0802/p09s02-coop.html, last accessed October 16, 2006.

12. Derived from Maddison, *The World Economy*, 262, and authors' calculations.

13. Calculated from *Central Intelligence Agency Factbook* data. For 2005 data, see https://www.cia./gov/publications/rankorder/2004rank.html and for 1999 data, see https://www.cia.gov/cia/download2000.html. Charts entitled "exports" and "GDP Per Capita" were used. Data were accessed October 31, 2006. GDP was calculated using the purchasing power parity method. Data were converted to constant U.S. dollars using the Consumer Price Index. See 2006 *Economic Report of the President*, 351.

14. Bhagwati, *In Defense of Globalization*, 82.

Chapter 11: Critiquing the Critics

1. See Upton Sinclair, *The Jungle* (New York: The Jungle Publishing Co., 1906), H. C. Engelbracht and F. C. Hanighen, *Merchants of Death* (New York: Dodd, Mead and Co., 1934), and Ralph Nader, *Unsafe at Any Speed: The Designed-In Dangers of the American Automobile* (New York: Grossman, 1965).

2. On Standard Oil, see Ida M. Tarbell, *History of the Standard Oil Company*, 2 vols. (New York: McClure, Phillips, 1904).

3. These examples are merely illustrations, and we have not attempted an exhaustive review of the historical antibusiness literature. We have ignored some hugely important generic antibusiness polemics, such as Matthew Josephson, *The Robber Barons: The Great American Capitalists, 1861–1901* (New York: Harcourt, Brace and Co., 1934), and environmentally based critiques, such as Rachel Carson's *Silent Spring* (Boston: Houghton Mifflin, 1962).

4. On the railroads, see, for example, Paul MacAvoy, *The Economic Effects of Regulation* (Cambridge, Mass.: MIT Press, 1965); Gabriel Kolko, *Railroads and Regulations, 1877–1916* (Princeton, N.J.: Princeton University Press, 1965); and Douglass C. North, *Growth and Welfare in the American Past: A New Economic*

History (Englewood Cliffs, N.J.: Prentice-Hall, 1966). On Standard Oil, the classic attack on the allegation by Tarbell (and others) that Standard Oil successfully engaged in predatory pricing schemes to drive competitors out of business is John S. McGee, "Predatory Price Cutting: The Standard Oil (N.J.) Case," *Journal of Law and Economics* 1 (October 1958): 137–69. For more balanced accounts of the company and its founder, see Allan Nevins, *A Study of Power: John D. Rockefeller, Industrialist and Philanthropist*, 2 vols., revised edition of *John D. Rockefeller: The Heroic Age of American Enterprise* (New York: Scribners, 1953), or Chernow, *Titan*.

5. For more, see California Connection, "The Nader Affair," www.calconnect.com/cars/nader_affair/nader_affair.htm (accessed September 8, 2006).

6. Quinn, *How Wal-Mart Is Destroying America*, 4.

7. Fishman, *The Wal-Mart Effect*, 108.

8. Ibid.

9. Supporting the thesis that Wal-Mart is on net job-destroying is Neumark, Zhang, and Ciccarella, "The Effects of Wal-Mart on Local Labor Markets." Reaching a different conclusion, however, were the Global Insight study, "The Economic Impact of Wal-Mart," the Hicks study, "What Do Quarterly Workforce Dynamics Tell Us about Wal-Mart? Evidence from New Stores in Pennsylvania," and Basker, "Job Creation or Destruction?"

10. See Wakeupwalmart.com, "Six Demands for Change," www.wakeupwalmart.com/feature/benton (accessed June 27, 2006).

11. Joseph Stiglitz, *Economics* (New York: W. W. Norton, 1993), 71.

12. N. Gregory Mankiw, *Principles of Economics*, 2d ed. (Fort Worth, Tex.: Harcourt College Publishers, 2001), 193.

13. Export shares of GDP were calculated by taking the first, middle, and end years and averaging them for each period. Unemployment rates are based on all eleven years of data in each period.

14. Goods imports in 2004 were $1.473 trillion. Total Wal-Mart sales were about $280 billion in fiscal year 2005. If one subtracts foreign sales, profits, and expenses not related to goods, the total goods sales were well under $200 billion annually, and part of that was sales of domestically produced goods and services. See Wal-Mart, "Wal-Mart Annual Report 2005" for more details on sales.

15. Our source on Wal-Mart's turnover rate relative to industry standards is Wal-Mart executive Lee Culpepper, in a telephone interview with Richard Vedder, February 8, 2006. We would have preferred harder data to back up this assertion, but Wal-Mart did not meet our data requests in a timely fashion. As discussed in earlier chapters, researcher Michael Hicks has also argued that turnover rates tend to be lower at Wal-Mart than industry norms.

16. See Vedder and Gallaway, *Out of Work*, for considerable discussion and documentation of this assertion.

17. Cited in Theodore N. Beckman and Herman C. Nolen, *The Chain Store Problem: A Critical Analysis* (New York: McGraw-Hill, 1938), 50.

18. Quinn, *How Wal-Mart Is Destroying America*, 10.

19. Telephone conversation with Michael Hicks, February 3, 2006. Hicks informs us that his forthcoming book on Wal-Mart presents empirical evidence inconsistent with the hypothesis that Wal-Mart promotes urban sprawl.

20. Curt Woodward, "State Government Had Thousands of Workers Receiving Medicaid," *Seattle Times*, February 14, 2006.

21. Michael Barbaro, "Wal-Mart to Loosen Health Insurance Limits," *New York Times*, February 23, 2006.

22. Hicks, "The Impact of Wal-Mart on Local Fiscal Health."

23. See Vedder, Gallaway, and Klingaman, "Discrimination and Exploitation." For a more comprehensive account, see Ware, *The Early New England Cotton Textile Manufacture*.

24. As quoted in "Wal-Mart Watch," a column in *The Voice of Local 880*, United Food & Commercial Workers Union Local 880, July/August 2005, 6.

25. U.S. Department of Labor, Bureau of Labor Statistics, "Highlights of Women's Earnings in 2004," table 1, www.bls.gov/cps/cpswom2004.pdf (accessed August 13, 2006).

Chapter 12: What Should We Do About Wal-Mart?

1. If, as a matter of public policy, a local government were to give, say, tax abatements to all large new stores that opened, it would be wrong to deny that grant to Wal-Mart, since doing so would violate the desirable principle of neutrality and the goal of maintaining a level playing field among competitors. But we generally believe such subsidies to corporations are bad public policy, and would prefer a world where no such subsidies are given. Similarly, while we believe Wal-Mart should be treated identically with other firms with regard to tax and regulatory matters, we also believe that generally high rates of taxation and regulatory mandates can stifle the spirit of enterprise and have deleterious economic effects.

2. Despite our request, Wal-Mart did not provide us detailed data on the distribution of wage payments for its workers. Given the published data on average wages and some accounts stating that the starting wage in most states is at least $6.50 an hour, it is highly unlikely that more than 15 or 20 percent of workers would be affected by a $7.25 minimum wage, and very possibly less than that.

3. The literature on this point is voluminous. Nobel laureate in economics, George J. Stigler, pointed out the negative impact of minimum wage laws as early as 1946. See his "The Economics of Minimum Wage Legislation," *American Economic*

Review 36 (June 1946): 358–65. Academic work over the next several decades generally supported the view that minimum wages created unemployment and had other deleterious effects. See, for example, John M. Peterson, *Minimum Wages: Measures and Industry Effects* (Washington, D.C.: American Enterprise Institute, 1981), or Charles Brown, Curtis Gilroy, and Andrew Kohen, "The Effect of the Minimum Wage on Employment and Unemployment," *Journal of Economic Literature* 20 (September 1982): 487–528. The conventional view was challenged by David Card and Alan B. Krueger in the 1990s. See their "Minimum Wages and Employment: A Case Study of the Fast-Food Industry in New Jersey and Pennsylvania," *American Economic Review* 84 (September 1994): 772–93, or their *Myth and Measurement: The New Economics of the Minimum Wage* (Princeton, N.J.: Princeton University Press, 1995). The Card and Krueger findings have been very severely attacked, in our opinion with justification. For example, they relied on telephone interviews with fast-food restaurant employees for data that in fact contradicted information listed in payroll records considered more reliable. See David Neumark and William Wascher, "Minimum Wages and Employment: A Case Study of the Fast-Food Industry in New Jersey and Pennsylvania: Comment," *American Economic Review* 90 (December 2000): 1362–96. See also an earlier Neumark and Wascher study showing significant adverse employment effects of state minimum wage laws: "Employment Effects of Minimum and Subminimum Wages: Panel Data on State Minimum Wage Laws," *Industrial and Labor Relations Review* 47 (October 1992): 55–81.

4. David Neumark, Mark Schweitzer, and William Wascher, "The Effects of Minimum Wages on the Distribution of Family Incomes: A Nonparametric Analysis," *Journal of Human Resources* 40 (Fall 2005): 867–94. The quote is from the abstract of the article. See also Neumark and Wascher's paper, "Do Minimum Wages Fight Poverty?" *Economic Inquiry* 40 (July 2002): 315–33, or Richard Vedder and Lowell Gallaway, "The Minimum Wage and Poverty Among Full-Time Workers," *Journal of Labor Research* 23 (Winter 2002): 41–49.

5. Stiglitz, *Economics*, 133.

6. David Neumark and William Wascher, "Minimum Wages and Skill Acquisition: Another Look at Schooling Effects," *Economics of Education Review* 22 (February 2003): 1–10.

7. Aside from the Neumark and Wascher criticisms of the Card and Krueger results cited above, see Lowell Gallaway and Richard Vedder, "The Employment Effects of Social Security Tax Changes and Minimum Wage Regulations: A Case Study of the American Restaurant Industry," *Journal of Labor Research* 14 (Summer 1993): 367–74.

8. Michael Barbaro, "Maryland Sets a Health Cost for Wal-Mart," *New York Times,* January 13, 2006.

9. See *Wall Street Journal*, "Retail Rumble," February 16, 2006.

10. Ralph Thomas, "Safeway Urges Quick Action on Employee Health Benefits," *Seattle Times*, February 14, 2006.

11. See U.S. Bureau of the Census, *2006 Statistical Abstract of the United States*, table 1323, for some international comparisons of health expenditures as a proportion of total output for major industrialized nations. Earlier editions of the *Statistical Abstract* have data going back to the middle of the twentieth century.

12. Quoted in Joshua Green, "The New War Over Wal-Mart," *Atlantic* 297 (June 2006): 38.

13. The literature showing that higher tax rates have adverse economic effects is voluminous, too large to try to recount here. One survey of some of the literature is found in Richard Vedder, *Taxes and Economic Growth* (Cedarburg, Wisc.: Taxpayers Network Inc., September 2001).

14. Lebhar, *Chain Stores in America*, 103.

15. Ibid., 104.

16. It is possible to verify the claims here through various forms of empirical testing. For example, it would be interesting to look at the ratio of retail sales to personal income in nonmetropolitan counties in some year prior to the Wal-Mart era, like 1960 or 1970, and compare that to the ratio in metropolitan areas to see how that relationship has changed over time. Or one might examine population statistics for any indication that Wal-Mart is a cause, as opposed to a consequence, of increasing spatial concentrations of urban populations. Such analysis can be quite complex and goes beyond the scope of this work, but we understand Michael Hicks has done some exploration of the issue, reaching conclusions so far similar to ours.

17. CNNMoney.com, "Wal-Mart Calls for Minimum Wage Hike," October 25, 2005, http://money.cnn.com/2005/10/25/news/fortune500/walmart_wage (accessed June 27, 2006).

18. CNNMoney.com, "Leslie Dach Joins Wal-Mart as Executive Vice President of Corporate Affairs and Government Relations," press release, July 24, 2006, http://money.cnn.com/services/tickerheadlines/pm/200607241200PR-NEWS-USPR___DAm021.htm (accessed August 8, 2006).

19. Kim Hart, "A Bid to Get Religion? Wal-Mart Hires Ex-Nun," *Washington Post*, www.washingtonpost.com/wp-dyn/content/article/2006/07/17/AR2006071701270.html (accessed on August 8, 2006).

20. Greg Levine, "Scott Warns China Wal-Mart Suppliers Re 'Standards,'" *Forbes* on-line, October 20, 2005, www.forbes.com/10/20/wmt-environment-ceos-cx_gl_1020autofacescan08.html, last accessed March 11, 2006.

21. Wal-Mart, "Wal Mart Takes Lead On Supporting Sustainable Fisheries," press release, February 3, 2006, http://walmartstores.com?GlobalWMStoresWeb/navigate.do?catg=512&contId=6045.

22. "Wal-Mart CEO Calls for a 'New Commitment' between Government and Business Leaders," press release, February 27, 2006, http://walmartstores.com/GlobalWMStoresWeb/navigate.do?catg=512&contId=6068 (accessed June 27, 2006).

23. Anita French, "Wal-Mart Pushing Organics," *Springdale Morning News*, March 9, 2006.

24. Bloomberg.com, "Wal-Mart Stores to Increase Starting Pay," August 7, 2006, www.bloomberg.com/apps/news?pid=2-601087&sid=aRGQJ961Uw8s&refer=home (accessed August 8, 2006).

25. Available at www.forwalmart.com.

26. John Wanger and Ann E. Marimow, "Largess Preceded Md. Vote on Wal-Mart," *Washington Post,* February 10, 2006, B05.

27. Walton, *Made in America,* 233.

28. Ibid., 249.

Index

About the Authors

Richard Vedder is distinguished professor of economics at Ohio University and a visiting scholar at the American Enterprise Institute. He is also director of the Center for College Affordability and Productivity in Washington, D.C. Trained as an economic historian, much of his work has dealt with the history of American labor markets and issues such as immigration, internal migration, slavery, and unemployment. After serving as an economist with the Joint Economic Committee of Congress, Mr. Vedder focused on public policy issues dealing with labor markets and governmental budgetary policy. In the past decade he has worked on issues relating to education at both the primary/secondary and university levels.

Mr. Vedder's previous books include *The American Economy in Historical Perspective, Unemployment and Government in Twentieth-Century America* (with Lowell Gallaway), and *Going Broke by Degree: Why College Costs Too Much* (AEI Press, 2004). He has authored over two hundred scholarly papers, which have appeared in *The Journal of Economic History, Agricultural History, Explorations in Economic History*, and numerous other academic journals. His writing has appeared in the *Wall Street Journal, USA Today, Investor's Business Daily*, the *Christian Science Monitor*, and the *Washington Post*. The winner of numerous teaching awards, Mr. Vedder is a popular public speaker, having lectured on public policy issues across the country and in Europe and Asia. He has advised numerous political leaders on tax and fiscal policy or education issues. Mr. Vedder is a graduate of Northwestern University and the University of Illinois.

Wendell Cox is an international public policy consultant and principal of Wendell Cox Consultancy (Demographia), in the St. Louis area. He has consulted for government and private sector clients around the world on issues of public policy, urban planning, transport, and housing. He maintains three Internet web sites, including www.demographia.com, www.rentalcartours.net, and www.publicpurpose.com. He also serves as a visiting professor at the Conservatoire National des Arts et Métiers (a national university) in Paris. He served three terms on the Los Angeles County Transportation Commission (1977–1985), which supervised both highways and mass transit in the nation's largest county. He also served on the Amtrak Reform Council (1999–2002), and spent three years as director of public policy for the American Legislative Exchange Council, a Washington-based organization of state legislators.

Daily Book Scanning Log

Name: ShadiaOvalles   # of Scanners: 13

Date: 7/25/24

BIN #	BOOKS COMPLETED	# OF PAGES	NOTES / EXCEPTIONS
Bin 1	9	4775	
Bin 2	10	5946	
Bin 3	10	5899	
Bin 4			
Bin 5			
Bin 6			
Bin 7			
Bin 8			
Bin 9			
Bin 10			
Bin 11			
Bin 12			
Bin 13			
Bin 14			
Bin 15			
Bin 16			
Bin 17			
Bin 18			
Bin 19			
Bin 20			
Bin 21			
Bin 22			
Bin 23			
Bin 24			
Bin 25			
Bin 26			
Bin 27			
Bin 28			
Bin 29			
Bin 30			
Bin 31			
Bin 32			
Bin 33			
Bin 34			
Bin 35			
Bin 36			
Bin 37			
Bin 38			
Bin 39			
Bin 40			

(BOOKS/LIBROS) TOTAL: _____ / 600

(PAGES/PAGINAS) TOTAL: _____

2nd Shift   Station # 13